Making Peace

By the same author

Educational Strategy for Developing Societies
Planning for Education in Pakistan

Making Peace

ADAM CURLE

TAVISTOCK PUBLICATIONS

First published in Great Britain in 1971
by Tavistock Publications Limited
11 New Fetter Lane, London EC4
Printed in Great Britain in 12pt. Bembo
by Cox & Wyman Ltd, Fakenham, Norfolk

SBN 422 73640 6
© *Adam Curle* 1971

Distributed in the USA by Barnes & Noble Inc

To my incomparable companions
on many difficult journeys

Leslie Cross, Anne Curle, Joseph Elder,
Walter Martin, John and Joey Volkmar,
Kale Williams

and to
Ursula Vaughan Williams
for her matchless support in all these ventures

Contents

Acknowledgements

For the leisure and facilities needed to write this book I gladly and gratefully acknowledge my indebtedness to two institutions: the Carnegie Corporation of New York, and the Richardson Institute for Conflict and Peace Research of the Conflict Research Society, London. A generous grant from the former enabled me to spend my year of sabbatical leave from Harvard in reflection, writing, and travel without the financial worries that would have either distracted my mind from my work or tempted me to grub for money by consulting. In my proposal to the Carnegie Corporation I had asked for help in studying conflict and development, a preoccupation of mine for the last few years. When I got down to it, however, I found that the trail forked in a number of directions and I felt bound to follow as many as I could; some took me far from my original tentative ideas. I trust that Alan Pifer and Fritz Mosher, who kindly counselled me, will not feel that I have abused their confidence.

The Richardson Institute appointed me as research fellow and hospitably provided not only space, desk, and other essential services, but professional companionship, stimulus, and guidance in what was for me an alien field. Among many kind people, I must mention Michael Nicholson, the director of the Institute, and Gordon Hilton, its research administrator, who were unfailingly constructive and helpful. Indeed Gordon Hilton, whose room was next door to mine, was the model of what an academic adviser should be. I hope that, as a result of his careful coaching, I shall be a better one myself in future.

Several people have read the manuscript or earlier drafts of portions of it. Ursula Vaughan Williams gave it the benefit of her incomparable command of language and her informed concern for the issues with which it deals. Evey and David Riesman were exceedingly generous with time and encouragement over some of the material incorporated into this version; I hope they are not disappointed with it. To Phoebe and the late Thomas Wilson I am grateful for the affectionate and constructive frankness of their criticism. I must again thank my wife Anne, who is also one of those travelling companions to whom I dedicate the book. She cheerfully allowed herself to be uprooted for a year, she helped with the manuscript, and provided the background of warmth and order without which work – at least for me – is impossible. Finally I should say that I am grateful to my daughter Deborah, who gave me a fine notebook to write in.

I am most grateful to President Julius K. Nyerere of Tanzania, and to Oxford University Press (Eastern Africa), for permission to quote a passage from *Ujamaa: Essays on Socialism* (1968); to the Haselmere Declaration Group for permission to quote part of the programme set out in *The Haselmere Declaration* (1968); to the Director of the International Institute for Educational Planning in Paris for permission to reproduce an extract from my booklet *Educational Planning: The Adviser's Role* (Unesco/IEP, 1968); and to the Editor and Publisher of *Universities Quarterly* for permission to use material from my paper 'African Nationalism and Higher Education in Ghana' (1962).

Introduction:
Peaceful and Unpeaceful Relationships

Some relationships are inherently unpeaceful. They do damage to one or more of the parties concerned, through physical violence, or in economic, social, or psychological ways. Absence of peace, in my definition, is characteristic of many situations that do not present overt conflict. Unpeacefulness is a situation in which human beings are impeded from achieving full development either because of their own internal relations or because of the types of relation that exist between themselves (as individuals or group members) and other persons or groups. Thus the internal relations within an individual may be so discordant and conflicted that his enjoyment of life is destroyed and his capacity to act is paralysed: he does not, as we say, enjoy peace of mind. Again, an unharmonious marriage in which the capacities of either partner (or both partners) cannot flower is unpeaceful; so, on a much larger scale, is the relation between the colonizer and the colonized, and that between underprivileged minorities – racial, religious, or linguistic – and the majorities responsible for their lack of privilege; so also, in some senses, is that between the world's small number of wealthy nations and its many poor ones. War is such a relationship: it epitomizes all the evils of unpeacefulness.

Conversely, in my terms, peace is a condition from which the individuals or groups concerned gain more advantage than disadvantage. Ideally, it means something even more positive: the harmonious and constructive collaboration typified by a happy marriage, for example, or an effectively run common market.

In general, books dealing with peace or its opposite are concerned with hostilities between nations, groups, or individuals, and the ways in which they may be curbed or prevented. Lack of peace is usually associated with physical harm or obviously disturbed, unhappy, or potentially violent relationships. I, however, take the view of Galtung, who maintains that violence (though I would term it unpeacefulness) exists whenever an individual's potential development, mental or physical, is held back by the conditions of a relationship.[1] It may seem peculiar to suggest that emotional, social, or educational deprivation, or a low level of health, should be regarded as symptoms of 'unpeace' if conditions are otherwise 'peaceful' and if the people concerned are satisfied with their lot. An example may show, however, that in such cases – whatever one may think of the desirability of the relationship – there is a potentiality for overt, physical violence.

The American Negro ghetto communities in the 1950s were relatively peaceful in the sense that the blacks, though suffering violence, seldom responded in kind. The anger that flared in the 1960s on a large scale in many places was therefore not anticipated. But in the earlier, as in the later, decade, the black communities were underprivileged and subtly discriminated against: their educational level was lower than that of surrounding communities; their standard of nutrition was poorer; their life-expectancy was lower;[2] and many suffered from the psychological difficulties so well described by Grier and Cobbs (1968), two black psychiatrists. Yet one might go so far as to say that, despite their disadvantages, black people in the 1950s were 'satisfied': they were 'better off than their fathers', or 'knew their position', and were, therefore, at peace with the world. But it is clear that these were the conditions that led to the violence, the unpeace – which no one would objectively deny – of a few years later. Thus even if domination by one group produces the abject submission of another, the relationship (which is necessarily based on inequality) bears the seeds of rebellion. When the level of awareness rises in the dominated group, as we shall see later, the seeds germinate.

Before we are submerged in detail, I should perhaps attempt to identify my position in relation to various schools of thought on peace and conflict. Some writers, like Schelling (1960, 1966) and Etzioni (1967), are concerned with strategic studies which deal, essentially, with ways in which one unit (normally a state) can best improve its position. Others, such as Boulding (1962)[3] and Rapoport (1966), and many contributors to the *Journal of Conflict Resolution*, are largely involved with studies of conflict as a system of interaction in which, at whatever level it occurs, certain similarities can be observed. Yet again, the problems of peace and war may be approached through the study of international relations, and prominent writers in the field include Deutsch (1968)[4] and Kelman (1965). Lastly, there is the relatively new field of peace research, originating largely in Europe, and particularly associated with the name of Galtung. Although peace research is beset by controversy, it is perhaps fair to say that most workers in the area are particularly concerned with research whose results can be applied to the task of maintaining or restoring peaceful conditions. There is, naturally enough, a good deal of overlap among these branches of study and the dividing-lines are by no means well defined, but the broad differences of emphasis may be recognized. My own approach is related relatively less to strategic and conflict studies (though it is not entirely unconnected with them) than to international relations (though I also deal with interpersonal and intergroup relations) and peace research (though what I have to say results from experience and reflection rather than research and I am, in general, more practical than scholarly). But the general field is perhaps both new and broad enough for each explorer to tread out his own path. This I have tried to do.

Key Concepts
Conflict
In discussion of unpeaceful relationships it is convenient to use the idea of conflict. By conflict I mean, essentially, incompatibility. The cat, in the psychological experiment, that can reach its food only at the cost of suffering an electric shock experiences an inner conflict arising out of the incompatibility of wishing both to avoid pain and to gratify hunger. On the larger scale, conflict develops when one individual, community, nation, or even

3

supranational block, desires something that can be obtained only at the expense of what another individual or group also desires. This is a conflict of interest, which can all too easily lead to a conflict in the sense of war or strife.

My broad conception of unpeaceful relationships introduces, however, a controversial issue into the definition of conflict, on which I should state my position before proceeding further. My position constitutes, in effect, a value. If one holds that relationships that impede human development are unpeaceful, it follows that one holds an objectivist view of conflict. In this view, conflict is a question not of perception but of fact. Thus if, in a particular social system, one group gains what another loses, there is – even if the loser does not understand what is happening – a structural conflict, which is what Galtung means (see note 1) by his term 'structural violence'.

Readers who hold other values will inevitably disagree with much that I have to say. They might quote the example of the benevolent master and his devoted slave: the slave does not question the rightness of his role and sees no other part for himself; the two work together in perfect harmony. This, in the subjectivist view, does not constitute a state of conflict. In the objectivist view, however, there are certain privileges and possibilities that are not open to the slave. To the extent that he is unaware of them, ignorance may be bliss, but the fact remains that his existence is narrowed by social factors rather than by his own personal qualities. Moreover, although he is unaware of any incompatibility of interest, should he wish to change his role in the master–slave relationship (and if he does not, his son or his grandson probably will) the conflict would at once become apparent. For this reason, it would be hard to deny that, in situations where conflict is absent only because of low awareness, there is at least latent or potential conflict.

In such relationships there are usually, as I have indicated, quantifiable indices of inequality. Moreover, in my experience of many oppressed peoples, happy slaves are something of a myth. They may be politically unaware, but that is not to say that they are happy, and they normally live in circumstances conducive to misery. They are, in general, angry, resentful, and embittered; if they show a grinning face, it is for self-protection.

I maintain, therefore, that it is reasonable to treat the master–slave relationship (and, of course, all relationships represented by this term) as one of conflict, which should be changed. (These points are well argued by Herman Schmid, 1968.)

But what of the happy slave who doesn't want anything to be changed? *By what right do we interfere?* Is not our judgement of what *ought* to be done based on those very subjective values we claim to reject?

This is correct. Ultimately, any measurement of what is best for people is based on a judgement of value. My values emphasize life and health, the development of human potential, equality of opportunity. But these things cannot be empirically demonstrated to be better than their opposites. One has heard it argued that hunger is good because it promotes spirituality; that an early death is good because one ascends sooner to heaven, having – with luck – fewer sins to be purged of; or that a slow, painful death is better than a quick, painless one because one has more time to ponder on and expiate one's faults. One's views on these matters are based on values that are not amenable to proof.

I, then, hold the value that it is right to change the condition of the happy slave. If he does not want to change, it may well be that he does not know, in his present state of ignorance, that change is possible or what it might portend.

Balance and imbalance

The second concept I utilize is that of balanced and unbalanced relationships. The current convention is to refer to symmetrical and asymmetrical relationships,[5] but I find this unrealistic: symmetry implies a degree of similarity that is exceptional if not unknown. By a balanced relationship I mean one in which there is a more or less equal division of power. It need not necessarily be the same sort of power: for example, in the conflict between the government and the University of Ghana, the government obviously held all the conventional power, but the University could invoke many potent sanctions – international moral indignation, the alienation of educated Ghanaians, the loss of qualified foreign staff, and so on. The government made things most uncomfortable for the University, but in the last resort failed to impose demands that would have destroyed the central core of academic autonomy. The University, to put it another way, possessed strong deterrents. Clearly, in all other senses the government was the more powerful, having wealth, armed forces, and considerable coercive capacity, but these were of little use in this particular relationship. In assessing balance, therefore, we have to consider the extent to which, in a given setting, one party to a relationship is able to dominate another. Schelling (1966)[6] argues that power is the capacity to create uncertainty; but what matters is the degree of uncertainty and the means – economic, psychological, physical (including military) – by which it is created.

The situation in South Africa permits further exploration of the concept of balance. The white population there has great power over the non-white. Its police are well armed and ruthless; its armed forces well equipped and efficient. The seeds of rebellion have hardly germinated before they are uprooted. This is not to say, however, that the black population is entirely lacking in power: the evidence for this lies, paradoxically, in the strength that the whites, in their uncertainty, have felt impelled to build up. But the power of the non-white South Africans is potential rather than actual; at present, there is very little they can do to impose their views or wishes on the whites. By contrast, the whites, having rejected world opinion and being confident in the support of powerful vested interests, can do almost anything they please. However, if the 15 million non-whites were educated and organized to mount effective opposition to the apartheid policy of the 3·5 million whites, the balance of power would shift greatly. The essence of a revolutionary struggle in South Africa, as in any case of disadvantage and social injustice, would be to mobilize the underdogs to the point where they could rival the power of the rulers. Even so, the type of power wielded by the blacks might well be of a very different order – possibly

6

consisting of massive strikes and boycotts – from the military strength of the government.

A further instance of imbalance, subsequently discussed, is seen in relations between the rich and the poor countries. These seem to me to be, in general, unbalanced in the sense that the rich have the power (primarily economic, but backed by military power should the need arise) to impose economic and political conditions on the poor. That the latter have little redress is shown by the failure of the rest of the world to implement the policies advocated at meetings of the United Nations Conference on Trade and Development.

In the last two examples, the imbalance of power is used by the stronger partners in the relationships (South Africa, and the wealthy countries) to exploit the weaker. In fact, it may be taken as axiomatic that, since none would suffer it gladly, exploitation is in itself evidence of imbalance. But imbalance does not always entail exploitation. Although a parent may exploit a child emotionally (or, in fact, vice versa), the parent–child relation is ideally one that helps the child to mature and to grow stronger. The same might be said of relations between small-scale and large-scale organizations, such as local governments and national governments. In such cases, the power to impose self-seeking demands is subordinated to concern for nurturing the smaller unit.

It should be stressed that, just as not all unbalanced relationships are unpeaceful, so not all balanced ones are peaceful. Nations at war are often evenly matched at many stages of the conflict, as is shown by the long duration of some conflicts and the inconclusiveness of others. Indeed, sometimes the very fact that a state resorts to war instead of achieving its objectives by pressure – as did Hitler's Germany in Austria and Czechoslovakia – implies a greater degree of balance; the most powerful countries can sometimes frighten the weaker into submission. There are, of course, relatively clear cases of imbalance: Belgium, for instance, was ill-matched against Germany in 1914 – although there was a considerable degree of balance between the Allies as a whole and Germany. Then, again, there are confusing cases.

How does one assess the balance of Israel and the Arab states, the former so successful militarily, the latter so superior in manpower, and both perhaps equally well armed? Or the United States and its allies against North Vietnam and the NLF, the former strong in numbers and technology, the latter in morale and guerrilla skills? For the argument in this book, however, it is not necessary to attempt precision about the balance of power in conditions of war. If exploitative imbalance leads to an armed uprising on such a scale that it is characterized as civil war, the implication is that the imbalance has largely been corrected. In other wars, unless there is a swift victory, the implication is that neither side had a significant advantage at the outset of hostilities, though of course either may achieve one later. In every case, what each side is striving for is a superiority that will enable it to gain a more satisfactory settlement. These matters are discussed in Chapter 20, on 'Bargaining'.

In what follows, we shall be primarily considering exploitative imbalance as constituting a particularly prevalent form of unpeaceful relationship. The achievement of balance, in which the advantage no longer rests with the formerly more powerful party to the relationship, does not necessarily lead to peace. The struggle may be merely intensified, as it enters on a new phase.

Awareness of conflict

A third concept relates to the degree of perception, or awareness, of conflict. In many unpeaceful relationships, the parties are perfectly aware of the discordance of their aims. In others, however, the conflict is not clearly recognized. Thus, among colonial peoples before the independence movements, among many oppressed and ignorant people today (such as the Faqir Mishkin, who are discussed later), to some extent among students, among some segments of the black American population, and among many black South Africans, there has been little awareness of conflict. It has not been obvious to these people that their poverty, powerlessness, or subjection, or the injustices they suffered, related directly to the riches, power, and authority of the ruling group; that there was, in fact, a conflict of interests. Now that these interests have been made manifest, the conflict has become apparent to most of those concerned.

The dawning awareness of our age, an awareness affecting many of the issues discussed in this book, is described by Camus:

'What characterizes our times ... is the way the masses and their wretched condition have burst upon contemporary sensibilities. We now know that they exist, whereas we once had a tendency to forget them. And if we are now more aware, it is not because our aristocracy ... has become better – no, have no fear – it is because the masses have become stronger and keep people from forgetting them.'[7]

Types of Unpeaceful Relationship

The concepts discussed above enable us to suggest different types of unpeaceful relationship. There are those in which the power relation is approximately balanced and there is considerable awareness of conflict; those in which the power relation is unbalanced and there is considerable awareness of conflict; and those in which the power relationship is unbalanced but awareness of conflict is lower. There are also more ambiguous relationships in which there is something approaching the *appearance* of a power balance coupled with low awareness of conflict: for instance, in the South African Bantustan, the illusion of a certain degree of independence for the non-white blunts perception of the deep conflict of interest between black and white South Africans.

These relationships, together with a fifth category, are now described more fully.

1. Balanced relationship: considerable awareness of conflict

A fairly clear-cut example (though few issues are as clear-cut as the lessons we would like to draw from them) of this type of conflict was what, depending on one's point of view, one called the Nigerian civil war, the Ibo rebellion, or the Biafran struggle for independence. To oversimplify considerably, what the federal government of Nigeria was determined to do was to retain the whole of the former Eastern Region, which seceded in 1967 as Biafra, as an integral part of Nigeria, whereas the other side wanted to be independent. The essence of this conflict was, in effect, that what one side won the other lost. This all-or-nothing approach can lead to extremes of violence; consequently, one of the cardinal aims of conflict resolution is often to secure an arrangement by which both sides gain something, are satisfied with it, and so call off their hostilities. I consider the Nigerian war to have been balanced rather than unbalanced for the empirical reasons that it lasted two and a half years before the federal victory, that there were long periods of stalemate, and that the eventual losers had some significant military success. In war, one of the aims of the contestants is to build up their armed forces so that the relation between them becomes *unbalanced*.

The India–Pakistan war, with preceding and subsequent periods of non-violent conflict, provides a further illustration of this type of unpeaceful relationship. This example also demonstrates the point that such relationships need not necessarily be violent but are always in danger of becoming so.

2. Unbalanced relationship: considerable awareness of conflict

The essence of this type of relationship is the dominance of one party over the other, and the other's consciousness of that fact. It is the relation, for example, of the landlord to his tenant in semi-feudal West Pakistan; of the colonial ruler to the 'subject people'; of the national government to the tribe that prizes its autonomy; of many American whites to the black population; of some powerful nations to some dependent weak ones. These relationships differ from the unbalanced relationship that exists between the government and the citizens in a democratic state because there, although the citizen lacks the power and authority of the government, he has had a part in electing it and his individual rights are in many respects protected – even against the government. By contrast, the type of relationship under analysis here is one between a top dog and an underdog who has very little redress. The top dog is free to withhold his resources from the underdog and devote them to his own people: thus in South Africa a minuscule proportion of the money spent on education goes to schooling and social services for the Africans (see Chapter 4 below). The top dog makes decisions about the underdog that the latter should make for himself, and does things to or for him (including, in some cases, benevolent things) that invade his proper autonomy; for instance, again in South Africa, the servant of a white family is provided with quarters but may not bring his wife and children to live with him.

The undermining of an individual's autonomy by such means, sometimes harshly crude, sometimes subtle, does much to stunt the development of normal maturity. In particular, the individual's sense of identity is impaired and his self-respect eroded. Thus, in the Portuguese colonies, the educated African, by a kind of psychological capitulation, can come to enjoy many of the advantages of the rulers. He is termed an *assimilado*, one who is assimilated into Portuguese society as a reward for betraying his own heritage; but while ceasing in a sense to be an African, he never becomes European: who is he? In a similar way, whole communities, even whole nations, may be held back economically, socially, educationally; used and exploited; made to feel inferior; denied justice. These are conditions of unpeace as I have defined the term. Such relationships are unpeaceful for two reasons: first, they deny to many the opportunity to develop as they might in what we would like to think of as peaceful existence; second, they lead to, and sometimes cannot be changed except by, the eventual outbreak of physical violence in the form of insurrection, rebellion, civil war, and even international strife.

But these are extreme and obvious examples of unbalanced relationships. Elements of inappropriate domination may also occur in the most egalitarian and democratic societies and for reasons that are wholly well-meaning: the case of the Firm, discussed below (p. 126), is an example. Again, many of the ills of imbalance may occur when a government or other authority feels impelled, in the interest of the general good, temporarily to override the rights and ignore the feelings of a particular group: thus, in East Pakistan, the entire Chakma tribe was thrown into angry confusion and eventually displaced by a hydro-electric project that was designed to bring great advantage to the province as a whole. Moreover, time brings about changes, with the result that what seemed a reasonable relationship a generation ago no longer does so today: thus the events of the last few years show that the relationship between professor and student, at least in the eyes of many students, should be restructured. Yet again, many authorities – university administrations, governments, trustees, boards of management, etc. – and, on a personal level, spouses or parents, run the danger of cutting across the interests of others by doing what has – or what they believe has – to be done. The razor edge between constitutional and authoritarian behaviour is one on which many statesmen and many much more humble administrators, organizers, and private citizens have cut themselves, and full peace is more often jeopardized than we would like to think. In these less extreme and, in general, more benevolent circumstances, the unpeacefulness is not demonstrated by crass indices of ill health or injustice, and still less by violence. The symptoms are more subtle: lack of cooperation, self-damaging withdrawal, personal quarrels and vendettas, self-doubt, lack of trust, anxiety; and their effect may be to create circumstances in which many people fail to develop or to use their capacities to the full.

3. Unbalanced relationship: lower awareness of conflict

One example of this third type of relationship, discussed more fully below (p. 97), concerns the Faqir Mishkin of Chitral. They constitute one of the most depressed and oppressed groups in the world, but are so dominated, miserable, and ignorant that they are unaware of the abjectness of their position: they accept and endure it as a fact of nature like the bitter winters and the annual time of hunger.

Similarly, the peasant tribesmen among whom I lived thirty years ago in the Middle East were apathetic about their landlord. This does not mean that they were indifferent to him: they loathed and feared him for his selfish wealth, for his callousness and ruthlessness. When he rode by they cowered humbly at the side of the road, though when he had passed they followed him with hate-filled eyes. But they never considered turning him out of his fine house and taking his possessions for themselves. This was not so much because they feared the consequences of such a step as because they felt the difference in their conditions to be part of the order of things: they had always been poor, the rich had always been rich; it followed, as night follows day, that the rich oppressed the poor. By the same token, they could not change places. The peasants hated the landlord, but they did not envy him, because to envy someone is to imagine oneself in his place – and this was inconceivable.

4. Pseudo-balanced relationship: low awareness of conflict

These relationships are more common than one might suppose. They occur whenever a dominant group attempts to placate or assuage a less dominant group by creating a superficial appearance of balance. Thus the South African government, in establishing 'Bantustans', has attempted to give a sufficient impression of equality of power between black and white to resolve – at least in the minds of some Africans – the conflict of interest between the races. There is, in fact, an element of this kind of relationship in many attempts at conflict resolution where effort is devoted more to concealing conflict in the hope of avoiding disturbance than to peacemaking in the more positive sense of working towards relationships that are not conflicted. In the case of the Firm (see Chapter 10), the Amenities Committee was established at least partly with the aim of introducing democratic procedures that would satisfy the members of the community that their relationship with the directors was egalitarian, that is, balanced. But the directors did not see that this perception of them must inevitably be confused and ambiguous because they in fact exercised absolute power over key aspects of the community's life, such as the allocation of housing.

A considerable part of the work done on peace and conflict research has been devoted, in effect, to studying techniques for changing unbalanced high-awareness-of-conflict relationships into ones in which there is a pseudo-balance and a low awareness of conflict. This emphasis developed, not surprisingly, in the post-war period when interest in the expanded field was largely focused on the dangers of the Cold War. It was natural to concentrate attention on ways of controlling or cooling down tensions that might have led to nuclear war. At the same time, the other major trend of conflict research, dealing with industrial disputes and the negotiation or arbitration procedures through which they might be settled, was little concerned – naturally enough, considering the interests of industry – to effect radical changes in employer–employee relations. Most industrial disagreements were concluded by settlements which, some would maintain, did little more than paper over the cracks of an inherently unpeaceful relationship. As a result, researchers in these areas tended to act as though the absence of overt violence, or of disharmonies that might lead to violence, was an absolute value to be preserved at all costs.

5. Relationships of alienation

These constitute a fifth type of unpeaceful relationship, but one that does not fit into the pattern of the others. The salient feature here is not conflict in the sense of any objective incompatibility of interest, but the alienation of one group from another, often, but not necessarily, accompanied by a sense of grievance – even of conflict – which is completely unwarranted by the facts. In the single individual this is a condition approaching paranoia. It is illustrated at a more institutional level in the case study (p. 47 below) concerning the foreign adviser, whose plight stems from his failure to understand a situation he has come into and, to a lesser extent, from the failure of his local counterpart to appreciate what he has to offer. The relationship is unpeaceful because it involves a misuse of the adviser's talents and because it may easily result in tensions, and perhaps genuine conflicts. Thus I have known sorry instances where advisers and the local nationals with whom they should have been working in constructive harmony have been intriguing against each other and striving to undermine each other's position. The village of Thornley (see below, p. 140) provides an example of a community alienated from its surroundings for reasons that had little to do with the contemporary situation.

To conclude, relationships of alienation exist when one party to the relationship feels and acts as though he were the underdog in an unbalanced/higher-awareness relationship while the other feels and acts as though he were engaged in a peaceful relationship – or at least tries to do so. If, however, one is treated with suspicion and hostility one tends to react in kind, though probably not to the extent of changing the structure of the relationship completely.

Peaceful Relations
Peaceful relations can be defined negatively in terms of absence of conflict. Absence of conflict may, however, mean little more than absence of association: there are many people with whom one does not quarrel because one does not know them well and is never placed in a position where a clash of interests or personalities could arise. But I would term this negative peace. Another form of negative peace characterizes those relationships in which violence has been avoided or reduced, without the removal of the conflict of interest, or in which the conflict has been mystified, that is to say, concealed or disguised. The latter, as I have noted, is a not uncommon outcome of industrial disputes. The workers may have a genuine grievance which, if it were to be redressed, would be very costly to the employers; the employers therefore avoid both expense and disturbance by expressing sympathy with the workers, meeting with them cordially, and making some minor but ostentatious concession to them by which they hope the workers will be dazzled. In my terms, these forms of negative peace constitute unpeaceful relationships.

I prefer to define peace positively. By contrast with the absence of overt strife, a peaceful relationship would, on a personal scale, mean friendship and understanding sufficiently strong to overcome any differences that might occur. On a larger scale, peaceful relationships would imply active association, planned cooperation, an intelligent effort to forestall or resolve potential conflicts. This aspect of peace contains a large quotient of what I term development.

If development is to occur, that is to say, if a relationship is to grow in harmony and productiveness, it is axiomatic that there must be equality and reciprocity in large measure. The mutuality of a peaceful relationship differentiates it from an unpeaceful one: mutuality in which one partner assists the other to achieve his ends and so serves his own. In peaceful relationships there is neither domination nor imposition. Instead there is mutual assistance, mutual understanding, mutual concern, and collaboration founded on this mutuality. As I define it, the process of peacemaking consists in making changes in relationships so that they may be brought to a point where development can occur. As we shall see, some of these changes may not accord with other definitions of peace. Revolutionary upheavals may be necessary if, for example, the slave seeks equality with his master. But if he achieves it – and who can say what price should be paid or danger incurred for this end – the relationship changes into one of man to man. If two men can find common ground and live together without destroying each other (and this is the next task in the quest for peace), they may then begin to learn to work with and for each other; this is the quality of development that typifies positive peace.

Peaceful relationships may be balanced or unbalanced. Examples of unbalanced peaceful relationships would be those between parent and child, family and community, provincial and federal government, small state and large state, and so on. The essence of these relationships is that the smaller or weaker partner is helped to develop his potentialities and that, in the process, he contributes to the development of the stronger. It is equally easy to think of examples where such relationships have engendered an element of conflict: many Americans, for instance, are keenly aware of conflict between the rights of individual states and the demands of the federal administration; the relationship between parent and child may be agonizingly conflicted. In these cases the potential of the smaller or weaker partner is prevented from being realized.

I would emphasize these points relating to development and to the positive definition of peace because they dominate the arguments that follow. The kind of peace we want determines our approach to peacemaking and the methods we employ.

Figure 1 Peaceful and unpeaceful relationships

| | UNPEACEFUL RELATIONS | | PEACEFUL RELATIONS |
	Lower awareness of conflict	Higher awareness of conflict	No conflict
Balanced		Approximately evenly matched conflict; e.g. India/Pakistan.	Development; e.g. the European Common Market and other peaceful and constructive associations.
Unbalanced	Ignorantly passive groups; negative peace; e.g. the Faqir Mishkin.	Revolution of the underdog; confrontation, violent or non-violent; the essential effort is to achieve a more equal relationship; e.g. the Black Americans.	Development; harmonious relationship of unequal partners; e.g. parent/child, state/federal government, France/Monaco.

Figure 2 A pseudo-balanced relationship

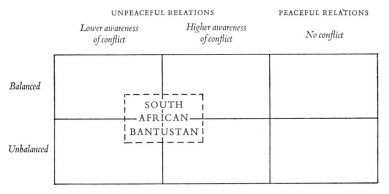

Note: No one could assert that all South African blacks have a low perception of conflict in their society, but in many of them awareness is low and this has prevented the development of an effective resistance movement. The creation of Bantustans gives some impression of a balanced relationship and serves to maintain in many their low perception of conflict. In effect, of course, the conflict persists.

These types of peaceful and unpeaceful relationships – except alienation, which is in a somewhat different category – are set out in *Figure 1*. Note that no example is given of an unpeaceful relationship in a balanced/lower-awareness-of-conflict situation, since this combination is probably never as clear cut as the others, though there is an element of ambiguity in many. The nearest to it is a pseudo-balanced relationship coupled with a low awareness of conflict, as shown in *Figure* 2.

The Case Studies

The case studies presented in Part I of this volume illustrate the five types of unpeaceful relationship outlined above and cover a very varied field. I have drawn my examples from different countries and on different scales: they include the alienation of individuals and of nations at war; small-scale group relations; relations between the wealthier nations and the poorer; and very violent and completely non-violent relationships.

The choice of these case studies itself indicates the book's purpose and nature. I have gone far beyond what might be considered the conventional topics of peace and conflict studies because I believe that unpeaceful relations are to be found at all levels of human interaction and that, since they possess common features, they should be described as a totality. A large number of my instances derive from the poorer areas of the world. This reflects a dominant concern as well as much of my relevant experience. I should stress, however, that an extremely high proportion of the world's unpeaceful relationships are in what is often termed the Third World. This is largely a result, in my opinion, of its relationship with the affluent world, whether communist or capitalist, which has made its own demands and attempted to impose its own standards and values upon it.

I should also observe that both in the case studies and in Part II I draw upon my own experience where it seems suitable. I did this in an earlier work (Curle, 1966) and was accused by some critic of writing a gossipy travelogue rather than a serious textbook. But the purpose, then and now, is highly serious. In the 1966 study I wished to illustrate the problems and limitations of the foreign adviser (some of whose experiences are included in one of the case studies below), and felt I could most cogently do so through personal examples. In this book I am discussing relationships, that is, systems of interaction between two or more people or groups. Anyone, such as a conciliator, who tries to influence

18

a relationship becomes, in some degree, part of that system. To pretend that he is an impersonal outside observer is dishonest. It is better to say as openly as possible what he did and how he felt.

Despite their diversity, most of the cases can be categorized fairly readily according to the framework of *Figures 1* and *2*. That is to say, they describe unpeaceful relationships which are either balanced or unbalanced, and in which there is either a relatively high or a relatively low awareness of the conflict of interest; or relationships in which there is some ambiguity concerning balance and awareness, as exemplified in *Figure 2*. Some of the cases illustrate relationships of alienation, in which the perception of conflict is one-sided and not justifiable objectively. (*Table 1*, pp. 32–3, shows how the cases are divided between the different categories.)

The art of peacemaking is to move the relationship out of one of the unpeaceful categories into a peaceful one. I shall not, however, deal with the transformation of unbalanced unpeaceful relationships into unbalanced peaceful ones. This is, of course, perfectly possible. In certain circumstances, as for example between parents and children or between national and local governments, unpeaceful unbalanced relations can become peaceful unbalanced relations, and very often the same processes are involved as when peaceful balance is achieved. In particular there is likely to be some element of confrontation involving a certain redistribution of power and the acceptance, after bargaining, of safeguards that render the imbalance advantageous to both parties, or at least not harmful to either. In many circumstances, however, such a resolution more closely approximates the pseudo-balanced/ low-awareness relationship of the South African Bantustan shown in *Figure 2*. For this reason we shall be mainly concerned with what may be done to change the various types of unpeaceful relationship, including relationships of alienation, into ones that are more balanced and in which there is no conflict of interest.

In some of the vignettes of unpeaceful relationships that comprise Part I there are accounts of peacemaking approaches. For example, in 'Returned Prisoners of War and their Society'

I have described the therapeutic role of the Civil Resettlement Units; in 'Employers and Employees: the Firm' I have outlined my work as an intermediary; in 'Pakistani Villages and the Government' I have written about the essentially conciliatory part of the Village AID organization. However, in 'Colonialism and Neo-colonialism', 'Two Wars', and 'Adamzadas and Faqir Mishkin: Chitral', no specific peacemaking activity is advocated. These may simply be taken as descriptions of different types of conflict and the reader may divert himself with speculation as to how they might be rendered more peaceful.

In Part I peacemaking is related specifically to individual cases and is not discussed theoretically. In Part II, 'The Practice of Peacemaking', there is an attempt to generalize. Six components of peacemaking are identified, and in the context of these there is wider discussion of the work described in Part I. The six components are:

Research, through which the would-be peacemaker acquires enough knowledge of the situation to work effectively.

Conciliation, through which he lays the psychological foundation – the changed perceptions, the heightened awareness, the reduced tension – necessary for rational discussion and negotiation.

Bargaining, in which the two parties to a quarrel try to reach agreement without making excessive concessions.

Development, in which a formerly unpeaceful relationship is restructured along peaceful lines.

Education, through which the weaker party in a low-awareness/ unbalanced relationship gains awareness of its situation and so attempts to change it.

Confrontation, through which the weaker party to an unbalanced relationship asserts itself in the hope of gaining a position of parity, and hence the possibility of reaching a settlement that will lead to a restructuring of the relationship. Confrontation may have many forms, ranging from revolution to non-violent protest.

In the case studies, most of the peacemaking described is in the form of conciliation or, to a lesser extent, of development, as in the example of the Pakistani villages. Research, though referred to only a couple of times, is to some extent a component of most cases. There is an element of confrontation in 'Employers and Employees: the Firm', and of bargaining in 'The University and the Government: Ghana'. Suggestions are made, however, concerning other peacemaking techniques – education, for example – which might have been applied in these and comparable cases.

Finally, I should apologize for the completely non-quantitative nature of the case studies and their discussion. The small size of the sample precludes statistical treatment. However, wider experience and a greater refinement of method may make it possible to test the validity of some of the ideas and approaches put forward by 'harder' techniques than I have been able to apply. In the meantime, I hope that the case method, which has proved its usefulness at the beginning stages of many studies that have subsequently become more empirical and more quantifiable, may illustrate the themes I am interested in, promote argument, and encourage further – and more precise – inquiries.

Revolution

It will have become obvious from what has been said above that I consider it essential, in many cases, for relationships to undergo radical change if they are to be made peaceful. I have referred to the awkward case of the happy slave and to confrontation as a peacemaking technique. But what is involved is close to, and may become, revolution – a prospect that poses a fearful dilemma for a student of conflict who may have been drawn to the subject out of sincerely pacifist idealism. The following brief discussion of revolution does not attempt to resolve the basic problem but to present some of the issues that will be expanded in the chapter on 'Confrontation' (p. 196).

In all revolutions there must, at some stage, have been a movement from lower to higher awareness of the situation, followed by a striving for greater balance. The resultant rebellions have been either put down, in which case there may have been another uprising later, or successful, when they have led to a greater degree of balance between the parties. Most colonial wars of liberation have resulted in the independence of the colonies and, despite the impositions of neo-colonialism, in a much greater balance in their relationship with the former rulers. Likewise, in many European countries, political evolution (as in France), through which oligarchies have in general given way to democracies, has reduced or blurred differences of class or birth: the conflict of interest, though perhaps in places never entirely resolved, has usually shifted its focus from hereditary to achieved position and has become much less sharp. It is tenable (though I would not fully agree) that, with some qualifications and exceptions, the various social and economic groups that comprise a modern democratic state (or, for that matter, one of the Eastern socialist states) are not in conflict with each other and may jointly contribute to the good of the nation in what I term the stage of development.

There are other revolutions, however, that do not stop at the point of balance. They continue until the power structure is entirely reversed and the former rulers are annihilated or rendered completely impotent. Such were the revolutions of Russia, China, and Cuba. Such, there is little doubt, will be the revolutions in any nation where the entrenched ruling group is located within the country and stands to lose all if the underdogs attain power. It is hard, for example, to imagine any compromise, any agreement to share equal power, between black and white in South Africa, or between the guerrilla bands of Latin America and the oligarchies they oppose.

There can certainly be no peaceful relationships while such oligarchies remain in power, and if the power cannot be held in common one may argue that peace can be achieved only by eliminating them. But the idea jars. If peace can be won only by turning the top dogs into underdogs (or perhaps dead dogs), can it be said to be peace? There has simply been a reversal of the power position. Although the oligarchy may have been small in number and its rule odious, it was composed of human beings who should be fitted equitably into the new system. If they are brutalized, or continue to exist as a resentful or disadvantaged minority, peaceful relationships can hardly be said to have been fully established.

For this reason, revolution must be accompanied by conversion (this, as we shall see, is part of the purpose of confrontation). The revolutionaries must win not only the power but also the minds of their opponents. Rather than just defeat them, they must change them to a point where they reject their own past and are prepared to take an equal part in the future.

Oligarchies, admittedly, are not easy to convert. Unless revolutionary tactics are used against them with intelligence, consistency, and courage, their self-assurance is unlikely to waver. But the smaller the amount of violence employed, the greater the eventual likelihood of harmony. Once the killing begins, bitterness and anger burn deeply into the human spirit, often precluding real accord for generations.

The problem, moreover, is not only what to do with the top dogs but what to do with the roles of the top dogs. In those cases where the top dogs are evicted, as from a former colony that acquires independence, the general tendency has been to retain an administrative structure very similar to that of the colonial power, though, of course, with the jobs filled by natives of the country. The latter, then, have all too often begun to behave towards their subordinates in the same way as did their colonial predecessors; this, indeed, is a form of unconscious concealed neo-colonialism. Only in countries such as Tanzania, and in the revolutionary movements in Portuguese Guinea and Vietnam, has this danger been appreciated. Revolutions are not achieved merely by putting new people into old positions; the social system must also be changed. It is not enough to kill our opponents and to retain the social system that they – and with frightening frequency we also – support. It is more important to change the structure of society, and in order to do this we may first have to change ourselves. In the wisdom we may acquire in so doing we may learn also how to carry our enemies with us – as friends.

23

Sequences of Peacemaking

In the extensive discussion of peacemaking in Part II it will become apparent that some techniques are more appropriate than others to particular forms of conflict, or rather, to particular stages in the transformation of unpeaceful into peaceful relationships, and an appropriate sequence of peacemaking methods related to stages of conflict is described. The implied corollary is that techniques in themselves valid are useless or harmful when applied at the wrong juncture. There is little point, for example, in attempting to conciliate the top dog in an unbalanced relationship. The structure of the relationship will not thereby be changed and he may well be confirmed in his sense of power and authority by our approaches; at best he will, at his pleasure, treat us with condescending indulgence; at worst he will be convinced that he can go to any lengths without reprisal. Such, perhaps, was the mistake of Neville Chamberlain at Munich.

Conciliation and bargaining are of very little use in revolutionary situations, or in situations that cannot be changed without a revolutionary adjustment of relationships. These methods will lead only to a false solution in which the conflict is obscured and the underdogs are fobbed off with some illusion of improvement or concession. Yet much peace research has been devoted to techniques for applying them more efficiently. In fact, one purpose of this book is to show that, although the methods of conciliation and bargaining are vital at the right juncture, there are more limitations on their effective use than is generally believed. By the same token, I hope to present an extended range and variety of activities relevant to the complex process of peacemaking. This may perhaps help those involved in unpeaceful relationships to analyse their circumstances more constructively.

Conclusion

Finally, I should stress that there is nothing sacred – or, for that matter, diabolical – about relationships except in so far as they affect human beings. It is arid to talk of peace and peaceful relations only in terms of structures and organizations. They are only means to human ends, and if we forget this our quest for peace may be corrupted, becoming an empty search for ideal forms which cannot of themselves confer warmth or creativity. Peaceful relationships constitute a desirable, perhaps a necessary, but certainly not a sufficient, condition for human developments that could advance and complete the developmental work we have already considered.

For these human developments to flower in the context of peaceful relationships we need a new, or perhaps rediscovered, understanding of man's nature and potentialities. For too long the Christian and later the Freudian view of man's nature, in an unnatural alliance, have persuaded us of our wickedness and our limitations; and to the extent that we have believed them, we have been emotionally, intellectually, and morally stunted. However, if we derive our norm not from the failures, as has been common in a psychology based on the psychopathological, but from the successes, our view of man's potential is much more encouraging. He may even have the capacity to build and preserve a world of truly peaceful relationships. There is evidence – much of it, paradoxically, from both Christian and psychiatric sources – which suggests that man's nature is richer, his capacity for joy, creativity, intellectual effort, altruistic service, spontaneity, courage, and love far greater, than we commonly suppose; that he is more complete, more consistent, gayer, and stronger.[8] Alas, we have a long way to go before our potentialities are widely realized. Our political, social, economic, and educational institutions have evolved very largely in accordance with a drab philosophy of human nature. The traces of this philosophy are all around us. Indeed it would have been unnecessary to write much of this book but for the existence of degrading and dehumanizing institutions such as colonialism and the imperialism of race or class. No one can give conscious support to such systems, and many do, without tacitly accepting the indignity of man – both oppressor and oppressed. And, by a sad irony, those who are oppressed the more easily accept the oppressors' evaluation of them. In general, suffering is not good for people.

I am not suggesting that we have first to make peaceful relationships and then engage in the more delicate task of raising the human condition. On the contrary, it may be impossible to make peace unless we all become more fully human. Indeed, the two tasks are interdependent, and must always remain interwoven. If I have written about peacemaking in the sense, ultimately, of restructuring relationships it is because I have been largely involved with this approach, not because I give it priority.

Because the extension of development in the peacemaking sense merges with development in the sense of individual growth, it is vital to avoid a contradiction between what we do in the name of peacemaking and what we do in the name of human beings. As the reader has seen, I have become convinced of the necessity for revolutionary change. Unfortunately, much of this is likely to come through a dehumanizing violence. One of mankind's most urgent challenges is, then, to find ways of eliminating unpeaceful relationships without eliminating people, to help people to change their perceptions and enlarge their understanding, not to destroy them.

1. Thus Johan Galtung (1969a), in speaking of peace and violence, says: 'Violence is present when human beings are being influenced so that their actual somatic and mental realizations are below their potential realizations', and violence is defined as 'the cause of the difference between the potential and the actual' (p. 3). Galtung divides violence into personal violence, physical and psychological; and structural violence, by which he means uneven distribution of resources and uneven distribution of power over resources (p. 11). The absence of the former he calls negative peace and of the latter he calls positive peace or social justice. The two together constitute peace in the full sense. Thus, although he employs different terms, his concept of violence is close to mine of the unpeaceful relationship in which, while there may be no overt conflict behaviour, damage is done to human potential and the seeds of future open conflict or personal violence are sown.

2. In 1940 infant mortality among non-white Americans was 12·5 per cent higher than among white Americans. In 1965 it was 9·3 per cent higher, but the maternal mortality rate, four times as high for non-whites as for whites, was relatively higher than it was in 1940. In 1965 life-expectancy for whites was 6·9 years higher than for non-whites; and, at the age of 25, life-expectancy for non-whites is 11 years shorter than that for whites (National Advisory Commission on Civil Disorders, 1968, pp. 270–2). There is no suggestion that the greater mortality is due to genetic weakness (this possibility is examined and dismissed by Myrdal, 1944, pp. 140–4). Myrdal records that in the late 1930s registered infant mortality for Negroes was 96 per cent higher than for whites, and that this was probably an underestimation.

   One way in which the socio-economic handicaps of black Americans are demonstrated is in evidence that, for blacks, a relatively high level of occupation attained by the father is not often reflected in the son's employment. A government document shows that whereas a majority of the sons of white white-collar workers are employed at the same level as their fathers, this applies to only 10 per cent of the sons of black white-collar workers (US Department of Health, Education and Welfare, 1969, p. 24).

3. It should be added that Boulding's versatile genius has played over most aspects of conflict and peace studies.

4. It might also be noted that in his publication of 1967 Deutsch deals with large-scale issues of strategy.

5. At least among those concerned with peace research. See, for example, Schmid (1968) and Galtung (1969b). Schmid (1970) rejects the concept, however, as likely to lead to pacification.

6. There is also a valuable discussion of power in Dahl (1963).
7. Albert Camus in 'Create Dangerously' (December 1957); quoted by Fulbright (1970, p. 71).
8. The most systematic exponent of this approach in psychology is Maslow (1968); see also Chiang and Maslow (1969).

PART I

Case Studies of Unpeaceful Relationships

.

Introduction

I have already remarked on the very great diversity of these cases and can only hope that the differences will prove stimulating rather than confusing. If common features are observable, however, the differences may serve to emphasize principles.

The diversity of the case studies makes it difficult to compare and classify them with precision on the basis of type of conflict. Nevertheless, it seems to me that they mostly tend to fall fairly readily into one or other of the five categories. Admittedly, the distinctions are not always clear cut (as in the case of South Africa), but conflict, particularly when on a large scale, is not clear cut either: those engaged have complex and contradictory motives embracing patriotism, self-interest, fear, inertia, desire for revenge, and the like; the different parties to the struggle are themselves composed of groups whose perceptions of the issues and awareness of the conflict differ greatly. Thus few conflicts may fit in every respect into a particular category. Given these limitations, *Table 1* (overleaf), which attempts to classify the cases and to suggest comparable conflicts not considered here, may prove helpful to the reader.

Table 1 Examples of categories of conflict

	Balanced/ Aware	Balanced/ Less Aware	Unbalanced/ Aware	Unbalanced/ Less Aware	Alienated
THE CASES	Two wars: India/Pakistan and Nigeria	(The blacks and the whites: S. Africa)*	Colonialism and neo-colonialism	Adamzadas and Faqir Mishkin: Chitral	Foreign advisers and their local counterparts
			The university and the govt: Ghana	Francis and Hilary: a marriage	Returned prisoners of war and their society
			Governments and people	Employers and employees: the firm†	Some English villages and the local govt
			Pakistani villages and the govt	Employers and employees: the factories	
			The Chakmas and the common good		
			The blacks and the whites: USA		

		The students and the professors: Eng. and USA		
OTHER EXAMPLES	Most wars or violent quarrels between states: World War I; Malaya/Indonesia confrontation; Arab/Israeli conflict.	Any dispute in which the conflict has been glossed over or concealed to give an impression of peace; concessions made to students, strikers, or disaffected colonial people, which do not radically change their position, produce this category of conflict.	Most colonial struggles for freedom, violent and non-violent; insurrections against oppressive régimes; class struggles; much industrial conflict, especially in the past in Europe.	The 'ignorant slave' situation, periodically prevalent, until recently, among US Negroes and in many colonial territories; still existing in backward areas under autocratic landlords and other rulers.	Paranoia or less serious maladaptation at the individual level; I know of no example of one-sided alienation at the international level, though, of course, unreasonable beliefs become prevalent in times of conflict.

* The parentheses are to indicate that this categorization is not clear cut.
† This case is hard to classify; in some respects it belongs to all five categories.

A. THE POOR COUNTRIES

1. Colonialism and Neo-colonialism

Note on Terminology

I should explain why I employ the term 'poor countries' rather than the phrases by which, over a period of time, it has been customary to describe these countries. First came the epithet 'backward', which has been generally discarded for its blanco-centricity. A little later we spoke of 'underdeveloped' countries. This was not entirely unsuitable for, in fact, the resources of most poor countries are underdeveloped, but it ignores the point that they may have reached a high state of cultural and artistic development: how would we categorize ancient Egypt, the Peru of the Incas, or the empire of Kubla Khan? Moreover, it ignores the underdevelopment of many rich countries – the slums, the ghettos, the corruption, and the crime. The stupid phrase, 'developing' nations, was next in vogue, succeeding 'underdeveloped' because it seemed less insulting and more encouraging. But actually it retained the insult by implying that the poor countries were not yet developed, and it is inaccurate to boot: the trouble with the poor nations is precisely that they are not (economically at any rate) developing. Next came the euphemistic 'emerging' nations: emerging, presumably, from the darkness of ignorance and poverty into the light of informed affluence. This has all the faults of 'developing' coupled with an unpleasantly patronizing flavour. Lastly, we came to speak of the 'modernizing' nations, a particularly offensive term in its implication that these nations should simply become like us, having previously been medieval. I rarely refer to the poor nations as the Third World, because this is a political categorization of those countries allied to neither the communist nor the rich capitalist countries: I am more concerned with growth and change than with political alignment.

34

I have enlarged on this terminological confusion because it reflects a widespread ambivalence, uncertainty, and self-deception about the poor countries. And these feelings are, in turn, not unconnected with the unpeaceful relationships of the poor countries with the rich ones.

A great revolution of awareness has taken place in the poor countries. This revolution has swept more than fifty colonial territories into independence as sovereign nations since the end of World War II. The awareness was not simply of colonialism as something monstrous that could – and therefore must – be opposed. It was an awareness that tyranny and oppression, domestic as well as alien, must be swept away. The revolutions in China, Egypt, and Cuba, as well as guerrilla movements in, for example, Bolivia and Guatemala, are as much revolutions of awareness as those that occurred in the newly independent countries. More so, in fact, since some of the latter achieved freedom in circumstances of great geniality from colonial powers that had nothing to gain but trouble by hanging on to them.

This has been one of the most dramatic revolutions of history. It began with a surge of nationalist and anti-imperialist feelings which swept through much of the world (China and India for example, Morocco, Egypt, and Turkey, where the enemy was both external control and inner corruption), though much was also left untouched, at the end of World War I. The revolution was completed by World War II, which affected so many other areas of the world. These areas emerged from a cataclysm brought upon them by the white peoples with a firm determination to reject their rule. As Emerson (1960, p. 30) puts it: 'The sins of imperialism had been broadcast to the world, the prestige of the white man had been wiped out, and colonialism was dead.'[1] In general, the convulsions of a war fought to 'preserve democracy and freedom', the growing influence of the USSR, and the great improvement in communications opened eyes everywhere to the evils of alien rule and of oppression and exploitation in some colonial and non-colonial territories.

In some parts, awareness came with amazing speed. The servile peasants whom I mentioned in the introduction are now militant revolutionaries, but when I first knew them they had no dreams of freedom. Throughout most of sub-Saharan Africa, too, although there was resentment and bitterness against the colonial rulers, there was no awareness of the possibility of change: it is significant that virtually all African political parties were founded after World War II. Yet within twenty years all African countries were either free – the great majority – or struggling for freedom. I recall travelling in the Congo eighteen months before its independence was granted in 1960. At that time there were a few faint rumblings of unrest, but in Orientale Province there was complete political apathy. This does not mean to say that there was no hatred. As we drove along the road, the repair gangs would resentfully straighten up, doffing their hats. The combination of servile gesture and sullen expression was a bitter condemnation of us, the whites. At about this time a high Belgian official had to resign because he wrote in a report that Belgium must consider the eventual freedom of her rich colony within, he suggested, twenty-five years. But the infection spread with enormous speed, often encouraged, it must be admitted, by the colonial powers themselves. Britain in particular launched some rather reluctant small nations, such as Gambia, on to the choppy seas of political independence.

The awareness had a dual character. Perhaps, indeed, awareness of injustice must always have two components if it is to grow into an awareness that leads to change. One must be aware of one's subjugation and one must also be aware that one can break the bonds of servitude. In the early stages this awareness did not come easily. In the first place, those who were sufficiently educated to perceive the falseness of their position and who, because of their status, could have wrought a change, were immobilized by their relations with the colonial power. The great native rulers of India, the rajas and maharajas, the emirs of Northern Nigeria, owed much to the British. The colonial power paid them honour, supported them, protected them; they had never been so secure before. In return, they had to maintain law and order. They had no reason to want change and, indeed, when the independence of Nigeria was being considered, many powerful Northerners were opposed to it.

This system of indirect rule was not applied everywhere by the colonial powers, but, even where it was not, the local people were frequently bought off, as it were, by the largesse of colonialism. They were educated, and they obtained positions of affluence and influence (although, of course, on a much lower level than their masters) through serving the white régime. If an alien power takes over, the average man can rarely achieve a measure of potency except through alliance with it. Thus government service became a popular career in almost all colonies and a great deal of education was thought of primarily as a means of preparation for that service. In the colonies of France and Portugal, the educated native became a sort of honorary Frenchman or Portuguese. He abandoned his identity as an African and focused all his social libido on the metropolitan country. It was strange and somewhat frightening to hear a group of Senegalese or Cameroonians, discussing, in French, the crudities of their less-educated fellow-countrymen. It is an often voiced truism that education has done more than anything else to divide the poor countries. This is not just that some of the native people became literate while others did not. It is that in becoming literate they became slaves to an alien culture, to aspirations and a way of life that removed them from their own people.

This can be seen in the strange ambivalence with which some peoples come to view their traditions and their art. In Iran in the 1930s painful efforts were made to give the country a veneer of the West. The wearing of national dress was forbidden, electric signs were prescribed for all stores in certain parts of Tehran, and camels were prevented from entering the city. A friend of mine was walking through Tehran with an Iranian diplomat when a camel which had somehow evaded the regulation stalked by. The Iranian, much embarrassed, remarked: 'I suppose you haven't seen camels in the streets of London for many years.' A Pakistani acquaintance has written mordantly of what he calls the 'Pakistani whiteys' (Masihuzzaman, 1964).[2] They favour Western dress; their children call them mummy and daddy, and go to school where they learn about Robin Hood and Humpty Dumpty; though Muslim, they sing Christmas carols; they copy for their homes styles of architecture quite inappropriate to heat and glare; they congregate in clubs where only the servants wear 'native dress', shunning intellectual discussions and playing darts and games of chance. The effect of colonialism in Pakistan, according to my friend, has been to create a segregated class which despises its own culture. The difference between Pakistan and the United States is, he concludes, that in Pakistan it is a minority that discriminates against a majority. The most pernicious imperialism was one that enslaved men's minds. Moreover, it is one that still exists. Pakistan became independent twenty years before this analysis of whiteys was made.

The revolution of awareness in poor countries may, then, have two facets: political and cultural. Of the two, the former is the easier to consummate, even though it may be the more dramatic. It is easier because, for the very reason that men serve a colonial government – to gain a measure of power – they may crave the greater power that political independence brings. The cultural revolution is complicated in that many men's ambitions have been ensnared by the West and they have adopted many of its techniques and values. Even the toughest anti-colonial leaders have used political methods learnt in the West to fight for freedom and so – their enemies say – they have been contaminated by the West. Sometimes the pull between the new and the old, the colonial and the native, the luxurious vices of the oligarchy and the penurious virtues of the peasantry, is felt keenly by the unhappy individual who is caught – as many are – in the middle. A Liberian friend who came from the minority ruling group known until recently as the Americo-Liberians, but who sympathized with the masses who were not of American origin, was particularly torn. He was a young man who loved the large American cars that the élite, if they accepted certain practices, could easily afford. At the same time he hated the system. 'But whenever I see those cars', he used to say, 'I think I'll just have to join them.' It is significant that Ghandi, the first and greatest of the independence leaders of the century, emphasized so strongly the return to a traditional craft and culture. The weaving of cloth and the panning of salt, in themselves relatively trivial activities, were potent symbols of return to the ancient values of India.

The question of identity is closely interwoven with the poor nation's revolution of awareness. If one is a subject of an alien power, how does one identify oneself? If one's only way forward is by rejection of one's roots and acceptance of an alien culture, who is one? Who, for all his affluence and position, is the poor Pakistani whitey? He has to struggle with the inheritance of over a hundred years of policy laid down by Lord Macaulay, who aimed to form 'a class of persons Indian in blood and colour but English in taste, in opinions, in morals and in intellect'.[3] The revolutions of awareness that have led to political independence have also struggled to achieve the cultural independence that would make identity, the sense of belonging, more clear. Emphasis is given to national arts and crafts (even though the responsible authorities may feel ambivalent about them). School curricula are built up to foster national awareness. The language is reformed: in India and Pakistan the almost indistinguishable languages of Urdu and Hindi have become, in twenty years, greatly different through accretions of Sanskrit to the one and Persian and Arabic to the other. Altogether, many different kinds of effort are made to build up pride in the national heritage.

This type of development has been condemned as chauvinism. Indeed, so it might become, though there is little evidence of this in most places. It is perhaps better to think of it as a necessary part of the process by which a group of people begin to feel kinship. Whether or not that sense of kinship is transformed into aggressive nationalism depends upon other circumstances, both internal and external. Indeed, I would maintain that warlike policies often derive less from inner unity than from disunity, and that strong national feeling may be contrived in order to conceal deep rifts within a group.

Many new countries are artificial creations of the colonial powers, who put together a number of peoples for administrative or commercial convenience rather than because of the affinities or inclinations of the peoples themselves. Countries so formed have particularly difficult problems of identity, having little to unite them except the unhappy accident of joint colonialization. This situation predominates and is especially serious in Africa, where most of today's nations are composed of congeries of tribes. To most Africans, the tribe is the fatherland, the people, and claims a preponderance of loyalty. It supplies, often, the language, the social system, the moral values, the religion, the political structure, and the law. The African leader, while still – as virtually all of them have been – an identifiable member of his tribe, must think in wider terms. It demands a great imaginative strength to envisage a new national union which transcends the centrifugal forces of regional or ethnic groups. It is not surprising that there have been problems of unity; it is remarkable that so much has been achieved. Nevertheless it should be borne in mind that these countries do have a dual difficulty. First, their citizens have to contend with the general confusion of identity caused by colonial rule; they have to restore their sense of belonging to their own group and to value that belonging. Second, they have to cope with their new national identity as Ghanaians, Nigerians, or Tanzanians.

Revolutions of awareness have already taken place in virtually all the colonial territories. In all but a handful – the Portuguese colonies in particular – they have been successful in the sense that the former dependencies are now independent. The countries of Latin America fall into a different though related category. With a few exceptions these are ex-colonies in the same sense as is the United States, but in some ways they have merely internalized their colonial problems. The Spanish colonial rulers rejected the dominion of Spain just as the Americans rejected Britain, but this did nothing to ensure that the Indians or other groups low on the social scale would not be treated as subject people. At the present moment, revolutions of awareness characterized by guerrilla warfare are going on in about half of the nations of Latin America. In some, for example, the Dominican Republic and Guatemala, they have failed only because of external intervention. The Latin American revolutions of awareness have brought their crop of heroes – Regis Debray, Fidel Castro, Che Guevara – who are an inspiration to the students of the world, thus linking two levels of the revolution.

We are not solely concerned with the feelings that developed within the poor nations towards the rich ones as a result of past colonial experience. We must note also the present behaviour of the rich ones. There was some indignation among the latter, in the early 1960s, when the term neo-colonialism began to be applied pejoratively to much that was done by the former colonial powers and, indeed, by whites in general. Had these countries not generously been accorded political independence: what more could they want? Why were they being so ungrateful?

What they want can best be defined by a brief glance at contemporary political and economic relations between the two blocs. The wealthier countries of the world (those of Western Europe, North America, Japan, Australia, and New Zealand) are growing proportionately wealthier and wealthier. *Per capita* income is increasing in some of the poor nations, in others it is static, and in yet others it is decreasing, but in no single instance is the gap narrowing between rich and poor; in fact, the rich are streaking away from the poor like the galaxies of the expanding universe. The rich countries could be said to constitute something like an economic system which has relatively little need of the poor countries save as a source of raw materials. However, because of the degree of economic control exercised by the rich countries, the poor countries by no means always make adequate profits out of the deals made. For example, whereas, during Nkrumah's rule in Ghana, cocoa production in that country almost doubled, the drop in the price paid on the world market meant that between 1958 and 1963 the increase in revenue for Ghana amounted to only 7 per cent. During a comparable period Brazil's coffee exports increased by 9 per cent, but revenue decreased by 35 per cent.[4] At the same time, the prices the poor countries have to pay for manufactured goods – ironically, often made from their own exported materials – continue to rise. It has, in general, been the policy of the rich countries to give loans and other forms of aid to the poor countries that will promote the interests of the rich – and these include preserving the poor as markets. Thus much more assistance has been available for extract-ive than for manufacturing industries. The results have led to tragic absurdities. For example, at the time of their independence, the Ghanaians exported bauxite, but had to import costly alu-minium goods; they exported cocoa – their main product – but imported chocolate and even sacks in which to export the cocoa beans; they exported palm oil, but imported soap; they exported hides but imported leather goods; they exported timber but imported furniture made from it (Nkrumah, 1965, p. 27).

Such anomalies have steadily worsened the economic situation of the poor countries relative to that of the rich: whereas the poor countries' share of the world's exports stood in the early 1950s at one-third, by 1962 it had shrunk to one-fifth. Thus, as Worsley sums it up:

'Present trends, unchecked, mean an increasing gap between the rich and poor nations, not a narrowing one. Falls in raw material prices outweigh aid given by foreign powers and international agencies; expanding production is soaked up by worsening terms of trade; capital is flowing increasingly to the rich. And much of the aid given is predominantly military-political in purpose; it frequently goes to the most loathsome regimes rather than to 'democratic' countries; it rarely reaches the peasant; and it distorts the economy of the recipient in the interests of the donor. Nor does it help modernize agrarian economies' (1967, p. 257).

This economic situation might appear to be brought about by the impersonally callous self-interest of most rich nations who, while doling out slivers of aid to salve their consciences,[5] adopt general policies inimical to the poor nations. (I know, for in-stance, that one of the major aid-giving nations cut from its aid programme the one element that would have been of greatest value to the recipient nation because, had the latter developed in this respect, one of the donor's markets would have been damaged.)

To be fair, however, I must admit that not all the dealings of the rich countries lack altruism; and there are smaller states, and private organizations, that have contributed greatly to the relief of suffering. There are also many citizens of wealthy countries who, serving both governments and private or international agencies, have selflessly poured their life's energy into service of the poor ones. Alongside the old exploitation in its modern guise there is a new spirit abroad in the world, and the motives of nations, like those of men, are mixed. But what is done out of a genuinely compassionate concern is counterbalanced, all too often, by policies dictated by unfeeling self-interest.

Occasionally, nevertheless, the naked selfishness of the rich nations becomes apparent and they go to extreme lengths to protect their economic interests. The sordid military and political manipulations in the Congo in the early 1960s afford a frightening example of neo-colonialism and, indeed, the whole of Africa learnt a grim lesson: namely, that whether the African nations were or were not politically free, the wealthy nations would not hesitate to intervene with their enormous power if they considered that their concerns were jeopardized. Guinea learnt another type of lesson when, on achieving independence, it refused to join the French community: not only was all financial assistance withdrawn, but, when the French civil servants and technicians left, they stripped the place like vindictive locusts, even going to the length of taking typewriters and telephones. And many of those former French colonies who maintained ties with the metropolitan countries and who therefore continued to receive aid and technical assistance learnt yet another sort of lesson: they paid for loans, grants, and equipment in the currency of political subservience and economic obedience. A different lesson again was learnt in Guatemala when the left-wing government of Arbenz, having offered perfectly adequate compensation, was in the process of nationalizing the (American) United Fruit Company holdings: Arbenz was overthrown in an uprising in which the CIA played a definitive part, an authoritarian régime – which in one form or another has persisted – was installed, and the United Fruit Company got back its land.

The political aspects of neo-colonialism are related to the

economic ones, for it is obviously the military and economic power of the rich nations that enables them to impose upon the poor ones either, as we have just seen, for gain, or for ideological and strategic reasons, such as defence against Communism. The newly independent nations began with the highest hopes of bringing about economic development, social reform, and land reform; of increasing their education, health, and welfare services; of developing their own culture and sense of identity; and of maintaining friendly and reciprocal relationships in trade and diplomacy with the former colonial power and with any other nation they might choose, regardless of its political complexion. For many, these hopes have failed. Kathleen Aberle (1967a)[6] claims that, since they obtained independence, some fifty of the world's new nations have returned to a client relationship with one or other of the world's great powers, especially the United States. Only such nations as Cuba, Tanzania, Guinea, and Cambodia can be thought of as being fully non-aligned, in the sense that their policies are not to any significant extent dictated by an external agency. Several of these, as is all too well known, have paid a heavy price for their self-sufficiency. When Tanzania broke off relations with Britain over Rhodesia, Britain cancelled a £7 million loan. Cuba suffered economic and then military attack from the United States. Other nations tried, but failed, to break away from servile relationships to the rich nations: Lebanon, the Dominican Republic under Juan Bosch, Honduras, Thailand, Venezuela, and others. Egypt suffered invasion by France and Britain in 1956. The United States sent its planes into the Congo with complete disregard of that country's sovereignty.

Apart from economic and political domination over the poor countries, the rich nations exercise what I might term psycho-technological supremacy. Their technical experts are everywhere – in the fields of economics, agriculture, health, education, communications, planning. The people of the poor nations, being ambivalent about their own culture and abilities, accept the expertise of the rich ones with a mixture of eagerness and resentment. Some knowledge, of course, is universal. There is no such thing as 'African science', for example, just as there was no such thing as the 'German science' vaunted by the Nazis. But knowledge may be applied more, or less, appropriately. Even in so empirical a field as medicine, for instance, the training for physicians must be related to the conditions in which it is to be practised. An African or Asian country needs, primarily, men skilled in public health, nutrition, sanitation, family planning, and health education, but in many medical schools a disproportionate amount of time is spent on such things as neuro-physiology and sophisticated surgical techniques, and, in general, on curative rather than preventive medicine.

The poor countries are extremely various. They range in size from the colossi of China and India to the island pygmies of Barbados, Numea, and Samoa. Some have extremely ancient civilizations; others are only a generation from pre-literacy. Some are Communist; others are traditional monarchies such as Ethopia, Afghanistan, and Morocco. Some are or have been at war with each other. But they have in common their poverty, which is heightened rather than reduced by the intervention of the rich countries, and they share an awareness of the unpeacefulness of their relationship with the rich nations. This awareness was first made manifest at the Bandung Conference in 1955 when the Afro-Asian states signed a declaration in which they undertook to withdraw from great-power defence agreements, not to interfere in each other's affairs, and to refrain from acts of aggression. Bandung stood for the neutralism of the poor countries, their suspicion of and their refusal to become involved with the rich nations of either great political bloc. At the 1964 and 1968 meetings of the United Nations Conference on Trade and Development, set up to attack the economic disadvantages of the poor countries, it became even more clear that the eighty poor nations, however divergent politically, culturally, and ideologically, were increasingly agreed in their view of their relationship with the rich nations – this much is obvious from the voting.

The relationship is unpeaceful because it inhibits the growth and maturing of the poor nations. It is unpeaceful because in at least twenty nations today there are bloody struggles being waged against colonial régimes (principally Portugal) and against the governments of clients of the great powers. The latter wars are being fought because the powers, to serve their own ends, support obnoxious and repressive régimes. These events may seem remote from the affluent world: the internal squabbles of far-away nations which, even if their governments were to change, are too small to hurt us. But it is as well to recall that China, with its vast and militant population and its nuclear potential, is one of the poor nations, and one that, since the opium war of 1841, has been brutally exploited by the West.

It is difficult to see how relations between the rich and the poor nations of the world can be made more peaceful without the most convulsive changes. The interests of the rich countries, and those of the élites of the poor nations who serve those interests to their own great advantage, are so widespread and so interwoven that local uprisings will have little effect (even if they are not crushed) upon the exploitative system. Yet the alternative, a worldwide abdication of capitalist interests coupled with an equally worldwide commitment to a more positive form of aid, is hard to imagine. All we can hope for, perhaps, is a gradual awakening of awareness, an increasing number of increasingly rigorous confrontations leading eventually to a more balanced relationship between the rich and the poor. This process may be agonizing and protracted and, to be successful, will almost certainly necessitate some erosion of conventional nationhood. The poor countries, as single units, will seldom be able to confront the rich ones effectively. If, however, they are prepared to surrender certain aspects of sovereignty in order to act in concert, their chances will be greatly improved. The way will certainly not be easy, but the only other possibility is for the situation I have described to get steadily worse.

1 Foreign Advisers and their Local Counterparts⁷

Since the end of World War II a new type of professional person has appeared on the world scene. He is the technical adviser who possesses (or is thought to possess) some skill needed by a foreign country. Until recently, most of the nations of the world exported diplomats and businessmen to one another. To these must now be added some 100,000 technical assistance experts, a developmentally oriented group which has now almost replaced the virtually extinct colonial administrator and which provides us with an interesting example of some of the key problems relating to alienation.

These advisers come from a variety of sources: from international agencies, multilateral and unilateral aid programmes (United States AID, for example, and the Colombo Plan), foundations, churches, and business organizations. Some are direct employees of the government they are serving; some are professionals who are making a career with, for example, the World Bank; others are on leave from universities or ministries in their own countries. Some are engaged on assignments lasting two or three years; others have only a few weeks in which to do their jobs. The tasks they have to carry out are almost as varied as the range of human knowledge. There are advisers on economic planning, poultry-raising, population control, preventive medicine, irrigation, agriculture, barrage construction, fiscal policy, communications, fertilizers, flood control, administrative reorganization, the construction of bore-hole latrines, city planning, the extraction of minerals, and foreign trade.

What all advisers encounter, whatever their expertise and whatever their assignment, is the attitude of nationals of the host

47

country. This may be one of hostility, or distrust, or hopeful ambivalence – or perhaps, in exceptional cases, of pleasure. Initially, however, the response to a new adviser is usually negative, though I hasten to add that this by no means precludes the adviser from being accepted eventually, and even becoming popular. The early negative reaction is very understandable.

In the first place, the very role of adviser is a kind of veiled insult. It presupposes that the persons for whom the adviser's services are intended are, at best, inadequately trained to do their own jobs properly and, at worst, stupid and incompetent. It is, of course, true that most high officials have advisers to guide them on technical matters, which they can hardly be expected to understand, but these advisers are, so to speak, their servants. The adviser who comes into a technical assistance programme is in a much more elevated position in relation to the people with whom he works. He has often, for example, a more advanced degree than they have, he is usually paid much more, and he lives in a style far beyond what is possible for his local counterparts. This does not make for his easy acceptance, and the difficulty is increased because the adviser, at least on his initial tour, usually knows little of the country he is supposed to advise. He may make what often appear to be ignorant and foolish comments. 'What', think his local counterparts, who receive him politely and listen to his irrelevant comments based on erroneous ideas about their country, 'has he to contribute? What has he done to justify his high status as adviser and the affluence in which he lives?' These feelings may be heightened if the adviser, unaware of social amenities or nervously anxious to make a good first impression, or both, plunges rashly into problems he cannot yet understand.

One of the barriers between the adviser and those with whom he must learn to work can be the reason behind his appointment. An adviser may be appointed because of a fad of a Minister who wants an expert on such and such a subject; but his selection and appointment may take months. What if by then the Minister has gone out of office? His successor, who might have quite different interests, will be saddled with an adviser he doesn't want. Cases are not unknown of advisers being appointed by a Minister in the hope that they may discredit, or at least weaken the influence of, some official hostile to him. Needless to say, circumstances such as these hardly make for harmonious working relations. Some advisers are appointed because a forceful representative of an agency or foundation has put pressure on the government. Others are appointed because the giving of desired material or financial assistance is made conditional upon the acceptance of an adviser. Others again are appointed because they enhance the status of the Ministry to which they are attached, even though it does not need or want them. I have known advisers who have been appointed because of mistakes or misunderstandings; or on the ground of vague agreements, long forgotten, which have neverthless set in motion an inexorable bureaucratic process which has culminated in the depositing of an unwanted and unexpected adviser on an alien shore.

These, perhaps, are extreme and depressing examples. The commonest adviser–advised situation is one in which the advised resents the idea that he needs advice, or at least has mixed feelings about it – he may want the help but not the helper. This is perhaps particularly true when the recipient country is a former colony and the adviser comes from a rich nation. In this case, those to be advised are often highly sensitive, feeling that the white adviser is somehow perpetuating the colonial tradition. If he is affable, he is being condescending; if not, he is arrogant. But the relationship is basically difficult in any case. No one, unless he has taken the initiative in the matter himself, likes the idea that someone has been sent to show him how to do his job. This, of course, is far from being the whole story, but it feels like that.

What is thought about advisers partly results from what they think about themselves. The tyro adviser, it is perhaps safe to generalize, approaches his new task with a combination of pride and trepidation. He is proud of his skill and intelligence, which have led to his being chosen as a kind of technical ambassador. He would be less than human if he did not feel that his selectors had shown discriminating judgement. His anxiety stems from the fact that he is going to face an unknown situation. How a man responds to this combination of feelings is a matter of temperament. One will be cautious and quiet; another will be assertive and even truculent, attempting to persuade others – and perhaps primarily himself – that he really can do the job. The latter response naturally tends to intensify local hostility. But, irrespective of how he reacts in this regard, the average new adviser usually expects to be rather more important than he actually finds himself to be. He envisages himself, as his plane speeds him to his destination, being greeted enthusiastically by a high officer of the government, being listened to with deference, having immediate access to the minister, and being interviewed by the press. When things turn out very differently, as they almost always do, he may feel a twinge of disappointment or even resentment that his abilities are not properly appreciated. The suggestion here is that the false expectations of the new adviser may to some extent impede the development of his relations with his local counterparts. But we should not be so cynical as to suppose that advisers' presuppositions lead only to ruffled feelings of affronted *amour-propre*. Many technical assistants are drawn to the vocation because they see it as an opportunity to contribute to one of the world's most urgent problems. If for any reason the altruistic adviser is not really accepted, he feels that his gift of goodwill is being spurned. The experienced adviser will usually, it is to be hoped, have worked his way through these emotional and intellectual entanglements. If he has not, however, his mood may have hardened into cantankerous disillusionment in which he exemplifies all the qualities originally, and perhaps falsely, imputed to him. He may have become aloof and superior, laying down the law, and convinced of both the correctness of his counsel and the unworthiness of its recipients. He will have come, in fact, to approximate to the image of him seen by the local people.

It is not surprising that a number of advisers fail to develop sufficiently good relationships with their local counterparts to make full use of the skills they have at their disposal. However well an adviser may have been trained in his own country and however wide his experience may have been there, it is axiomatic that, when he comes to ply his trade in another country, it is not his old trade but a new one. Obviously, certain elements remain similar, otherwise there would be no point in having advisers. But the difference in context creates a major difference in content. There is an almost philosophical point here. The adviser on some aspect of education or social development (such as I have been) has to learn that activities in these fields are, of necessity, different in, say, sub-Saharan Africa and Western Europe. The whole social, political, historical, and economic matrix ensures that what will succeed in a rich country in one continent may not work in the same way in a poor country in another one. But the unfortunate adviser naturally feels that, having been chosen for his skill, he must market it: thus if country B cannot do the same as country A, then it is his task to ensure that it learns to do so. It is hard for him to realize that B must do something quite different from A and that it is his task to adapt, and even radically change, the techniques and theories of his own country for use in a new environment. It is particularly difficult for him to do this because he is thereby discarding his own intellectual base. The assumptions that have served him well for years must be jettisoned, and this, for a professional man, is like appearing in public without his clothes.

But it is not only the subject-matter of the job that is different; the structure of the job itself usually has little in common with what the adviser did before. In the first place, he is an adviser – a complex, dubious, and untidy role in which it is easy to stumble over exposed emotions. In the second place, he usually has to act at least partly as an administrator – which he may never have done before – and, what is more, operate through an alien administrative structure. The dual impact of intellectual confusion and operational difficulty usually strikes a new adviser within a few weeks of his arrival in the new country. When the initial excitement of interest has died down, he becomes shatteringly aware of his problems and of his underdeveloped relationships with local counterparts. Most people respond to these circumstances with depression. They feel useless and unwanted, surrounded by problems they cannot solve, and disappointed in themselves. They are, in fact, in a situation not unlike that which occurs at the end of the period of honeymoon rejoicing following the prisoner of war's return home (discussed in Chapter 9).

The most constructive attitude to adopt is one of reappraisal. This is not easy, for the adviser is compelled to question the fundamentals of his professional life. He may have considered himself to be, for example, an expert in educational testing, but as it becomes apparent that his expertise cannot be exported intact, he is forced to speculate on the relativity of his knowledge. Doing this impels him to re-evaluate his local counterparts, to try to understand the relevance of their knowledge, and eventually to establish with them relations as between colleagues rather than relations reflecting the polarity of adviser and advised. Persons going through this painful process of readjustment customarily go, as it were, into retreat. Their self-assurance wanes, they are more reluctant to express opinions, they feel worried and guilty because they recognize that they cannot contribute to the situation they came to deal with. Above all, they try to learn, particularly from their hosts.

There can be, however, a completely opposite reaction. This is to reject the threat to self-esteem and intellectual security by going over to the offensive. The adviser who takes this course utterly rejects the idea that the value of theories and practices depends on the context in which they are applied. If something has worked in his own country, which is (he affirms) highly developed, it must be best for this one, which is not. In his opinion his country has the best system of vocational training or educational administration or whatever. Very well, the greatest benefit he can confer on his temporary home is to introduce this system as completely as possible. If it does not work, there can be nothing wrong with the system, for has it not been effective in Bonn or Milan or Chicago; in Valparaiso or Tokyo or Delhi; in London or Nairobi? Any failure must be caused by the obstinacy, corruption, sloth, and stupidity of the people to whom he has brought it. A man who defends himself against assault of doubt by projecting his failures on to others cannot easily develop normal give-and-take working relations. The more threatened he feels, the more hostile he will become to the environment that is menacing him, and the more he will characterize it as bad, backward, or degenerate: a classic example of mirage-formation by a man who is losing all awareness (see Chapter 19, p. 209).

Faced with the very common difficulties I have tried to describe, what does the adviser do? If he does not cut himself off emotionally from his environment, he tries to understand it. His first enlightenment comes when he realizes that the people he has come to advise know much more about the situation than he does – not just about the social and political context, but about the professional details and possibilities. At this period of depressed humility he may well ask himself why he has been brought out at all. However, since he is there, he might as well make the best of a bad job and try to be quietly useful. In reassessing his own competence he may find that there are some minor tasks to which he can make a contribution. No longer formulating grandiose and irrelevant proposals, he will buckle down to these unglamorous tasks and, in so doing, almost imperceptibly develop a working relationship with his counterpart. When the telephone rings and his counterpart says, 'Can I come and see you? There is something I would like to ask you about', he can feel very happy. The breakthrough has taken place. In fact, the adviser's skills are not useless; they merely need to be adjusted to the tasks in hand.

Viewed in this light, the relationship of the foreign adviser to the country he has come to advise, and specifically to his local counterparts, illustrates several principles. Clearly, if the adviser is to do his work, he must draw close to his counterpart, but the institutional relationship is such that difficulties are almost inevitable. If things do not go well at the outset, the resentment of the one and the disappointment of the other may keep the two so widely separated that their relationship is one of mutual debilitation interspersed with feuds and quarrels. I have borrowed from psychoanalytic terminology to call the two extreme positions the adviser can adopt depressive and schizoid. If he faces reality – his failures, and the need both to reject his past and to reconstruct his techniques for the future – he has indeed cause for depression. (It was a most painful experience for me to recognize that I must abandon many of the intellectual, and to a certain extent emotional, props that had served me well for many years.) If, however, he adopts the schizoid position he shields himself, at the expense of his ability to help, from the recognition of his ineffectuality. He builds up his mask of omniscience and through it he perceives an image of a feckless, sly, and worthless people who are resisting his efforts to raise them from the depths of their ignorance. It need hardly be added that this position can be maintained only by cutting off awareness.

I have discussed this theme from the point of view of the adviser, which is the way in which I have experienced it. However, by a fairly easy reversal it could be shown that the advised goes through similar strains and difficulties, ending up either masked in prejudice or more tolerantly aware. He, for his part, has to recognize that an outsider may have something to offer and that his own preparation may be inadequate for the job he is doing. The extent to which he is capable of recognizing this will obviously affect the capacity of the adviser to come to terms with his own situation. Here, as in all human situations, the end-product is the result of constant interaction between human beings helping or hindering each other, bringing each other light or darkness, awareness or rejection.

To conclude, the relation of foreign advisers to their local counterparts is essentially one of alienation. If it persists as such – as indeed it has done in the case of some unhappy individuals – the resultant growing hostility can inflate differences of opinion and perception into genuine conflicts of interest in which adviser and advised vie with each other for influence and position.

2 The University and the Government: Ghana[8]

This case study describes the deteriorating relationship between the government of Ghana and the University College (later the University) of Ghana, its premier institution of higher education. We shall be mainly concerned with the period between January 1959 and June 1961, when I was a senior member of the faculty of the university, because this is the period I know most about. The difficult situation, however, continued for several years thereafter.

The University College of the Gold Coast, as it then was, was founded in 1948 as a result of the recommendations of the Asquith Commission's Report, published in 1945. The terms of the Report make it quite clear that the establishment of the College was intended as a measure to promote the eventual independence of the Gold Coast, and as such the College could not be stigmatized, as many West African schools have been, as an institution geared to the production of subordinate officials to maintain the British rule. The Report, mindful of the sorry standards of Indian higher education, was insistent that the standards of this new College (and of other similar ones in different territories) should be as high as possible. To this end it was recommended that it should possess the same measure of autonomy as similar institutions in the United Kingdom, which would prevent political interference. Proper academic standards were to be maintained by a period of tutelage to an English university. London University, in fact, agreed to establish a system known as a 'special relationship' with the College, by means of which this tutelage was operated. This meant, in effect, that the standard of entry was determined by the requirements of London, that syllabuses were developed jointly, and that examinations were set and corrected in the same way. Representatives of London University paid periodical visits to the College to study and advise on the courses being offered, and nominees of London sat on all appointment committees for faculty posts. Considerable initiative was left with the College so that it could develop in its own way, with London exercising from time to time what might be called an elder brotherly restraint. As far as the students were concerned, the end-product was a London University degree. This arrangement was universally welcomed by the Africans as demonstrating that they were being offered an excellent qualification which would be accepted throughout the world.

The University College actually opened with ninety students in 1949. By the summer of 1961 the number of students had risen to over 700, and faculties of social studies and agriculture, together with several other significant departments such as law and education, had been added to the original faculties of arts and science. But the once cordial relations between the College and the government had been seriously impaired. It is interesting to inquire at this point how the very measures that had initially been decided upon to ensure that the College made the best possible contribution to the development of the future Ghana now caused suspicion and resentment in many of the leaders of the country.

(a) The constitution of the College made it difficult for the government to impose its policies on the College without causing an embarrassing amount of commotion. In fact, until the very end of the period we are considering, the government contented itself with exercising an influence that was oblique rather than direct. In the early years of its existence, the autonomy of the College had been intended to protect the educational freedom of the Ghanaians from interference by the British administration. It was said at this stage that some of the British civil servants were resentful of what seemed unduly generous terms of appointments for expatriate academics and were eager to exercise some control over the institution. Later, however, the freedom of the College came to be interpreted somewhat differently by Ghanaian politicians: it was thought to be a ruse on the part of a group of selfish neo-colonialists to maintain themselves in affluence at the expense of the Ghanaian taxpayer.

(*b*) The College was located some eight miles from the centre of Accra, partly for reasons of health, space, and quiet, and partly because the site had been considered sufficiently far from the seat of government to prevent the students from becoming embroiled in politics. Later, it was claimed that the College deliberately isolated itself from the life and needs of the country. The phrase 'ivory tower' was much used in this connection.

(*c*) The buildings and grounds were laid out with extreme lavishness and considerable expense. There was much talk of ill-spent resources, of complete failure to recognize the realities of a poor nation's economy, of teaching Ghana's youth false standards. But fifteen years before, on the rising tide of excitement and hope, it had been repeatedly stressed that only the best was good enough.

(*d*) The London degree, welcomed initially as a qualification of high repute, was later said to be inappropriate to the needs of the country. Some maintained that the entry standard was too high and excluded many students who should have university education; others talked of the 'academic imperialism' of London, and asserted that the syllabuses were not sufficiently geared to the African scene.

(*e*) It was pointed out that more students followed 'useless' courses (particularly in some of the arts subjects) than 'useful' ones in physics, chemistry, agriculture, etc. An 'unrealistic and inappropriate humanism' in certain prominent members of the faculty was blamed for this. However, it is equally true to say that the tendency of Ghanaian students had been to follow the types of arts courses through which most of their own leaders had passed and which, in earlier days, formed the educational background of the British rulers. (It is also a fact that it had been more difficult to provide adequately for science than for arts teaching in the schools – as it is in most parts of the world – and that a number of potential scientists were in any case sent abroad to study medicine and other subjects not taught at the College.)

The shift in government opinion on these policies and characteristics of the College led to an increasing gap – filled, as so often in such circumstances, by suspicion and rumour – between the academics and the administration. The angry comments of officials in Accra that the College, while eating up the country's resources, was indifferent to its needs, were countered by resentment on the part of the College faculty that important contributions in a number of fields – agriculture, economics, sociology, zoology, etc. – were consistently ignored, and that the high intellectual standard of the College graduates was discounted.

It is not possible, however, to consider the position of the College outside the context of changing national politics. Ghana became independent in 1957 in a mood of national, and even international, euphoria. The immediate postwar tensions had largely been forgotten during the years in which British and Africans worked together harmoniously and enthusiastically for the firmly based freedom of the colony. When Ghana became independent it had the world's goodwill, its treasury was well stocked, and its administration was strengthened because a number of British officials, genuinely dedicated to the country's service, remained in important positions. But the achievement of freedom from a colonial power inevitably leads to considerable changes in the internal politics of the new nation. Almost all countries of tropical Africa are artificial congeries of tribes. They owe their geographical unity to the historical accidents associated with annexation by the colonial power, and their national solidarity has largely derived from the effort to break away from that power. Once freedom is achieved, however, tribal and regional loyalties begin to reassert themselves, exerting a centrifugal pull upon national unity. If an opposition emerges, it is more likely to be one based upon tribal ambitions than upon alternative policies. Local autonomy or secession, even at the expense of civil war, is often the main goal of African opposition groups. It is this that has led many national governments to act toughly and 'undemocratically' against them, and to build up the party (in the case of Ghana, the Convention People's Party) as the chief organ of national cohesion. Thus in Ghana, the labour unions and a number of sporting organizations and women's organizations were all welded onto the party structure.

The sorry example of the Congo disunity certainly reinforced anxiety among the Ghanaian leadership about the explosive forces of tribalism and the dangers of external intervention by imperialist powers. This combined with other outcomes of the crisis to increase hostility to the College. For one thing, the sinister hand of the 'neo-imperialist' came to be seen everywhere; for another, Ghana, when speaking strongly of the line that African states should take in relation to the Congo, suffered taunts from other countries for employing so many highly placed expatriates. It was also significant that at this period the establishment of Ghana as a republic finally severed the links with England.

It would, of course, be untrue to suggest that the more revolutionary elements were non-existent during the diarchy, or that there was no friction between Nkrumah's government and the College before the attainment of national independence. There were indeed clashes, but many of these appeared to concern personality as much as policy. There is no indication that the government was in any fundamental sense opposed to the College. Certainly, at the time of independence and for perhaps two years after, the relationship was on the whole calm and cordial. There was applause for the statement by the College that it would soon be competent to grant its own degrees and would therefore terminate the special relationship with London and become a full university.

As the political situation I have described began to develop, increasing dissatisfaction with the College became apparent. The attacks took two forms. First, there were hostile speeches by Ministers, including Nkrumah. Second, there were directives from the Prime Minister's office stating that the College should alter its policy on, for example, leave passages to England, and appointments. More than once these directives touched on genuine anomalies in College administration and policy, but the College authorities feared that to accede to government pressure in relation to matters of internal regulation would be to invite an increasing measure of interference in quite inappropriate spheres. On the other hand, outright rejection of official directives or requests would have courted another form of disaster. The government, after all, supplied the College's finances and could not be expected to tolerate defiance. The problem was, as it so often is in much larger contexts, to find a compromise solution that could be accepted without damage to the pride or integrity of either side. The College was both helped and hindered by its affiliation with London University. The fact that it was not entirely a free agent academically accounted for its legitimate inability to yield on certain points, but attention was drawn at the same time to the pervasive influence of an institution in the very centre of imperialism.

It must be admitted that the attitude of the majority of the faculty of the College (of whom, by the summer of 1960, there were over 170, five-sixths being expatriates, mostly from the United Kingdom) did not facilitate the negotiations of the Principal with the government on these difficult issues. An academic in a country where there is no university tradition is constantly on the alert for infringements of academic freedom. Moreover, his inevitable sense of insecurity tends to induce a somewhat intransigent attitude. Anything likely to affect his life is rejected as an attack on academic freedom; and this damages the concept of such freedom. The Ghanaians, quick to notice 'colonial hypocrisy', bitterly attacked the expatriates for sheltering behind an abused idea. They considered that the Europeans invoked this principle most grandiloquently when their own comfort and prosperity were at stake, and believed that their concern for genuine academic freedom was secondary. (By 'genuine academic freedom' is meant the freedom of a university institution to teach, to undertake research, to appoint staff, and to admit and examine students.)

These government attacks, however, were not pressed home. They were more like the skirmishes of a reconnaissance party testing its defensive strength, than actual assaults. It is likely, of course, that any yielding on vital matters by the College would have been taken advantage of, but the government was not ready at this stage to risk a head-on collision by enforcing its mandates. Instead, it planned to assemble an international commission on higher education in Ghana. This, it was hoped, would remove from the government the odium of responsibility for reorganizing the College, and particularly for determining its character as a university.

However, as might have been expected, relations deteriorated steadily. In the first place, the ingenuity of the College in dodging government attacks caused increasing annoyance. Second, and more importantly, as political tension developed in the country as a whole, so the College appeared as a growing threat to national unity. This was probably responsible more than any other factor for hardening government opinion against it. The main object of resentment was the political attitude of the students. Few students were government supporters. They tended to be politically in-active, being exceedingly keen on their studies, but they had be-come too deeply imbued with attitudes of scholarly objectivity to be able to accept much of the propaganda put out by the Convention People's Party; they were too liberal in outlook to tolerate the gradual erosion of civil liberty to which its anxieties had driven the government; and, like most students throughout the world, they were against the 'establishment'. But it was understandably distasteful for the government to get no return from its heavy investment in higher education except a 'bunch of disaffected intellectuals'. The rulers of any country without a tradition of university education might in these circumstances have been resentful; resentment was turned to bitter anger in one passing through the growing pains of freedom. What made things much worse was that the situation looked to the naïve, but perhaps influential, party member like a subtle imperialist plot. In Accra, nearly all expatriates in key positions had been weeded out, but they were still in strength in the College. They were said to live in luxury, to do no work that was of the slightest use to Ghana, and, worst of all, to pervert the flower of the country's youth, filling their minds with pernicious non-African rubbish. By these means, it was said, the colonialists maintained control in the most obnoxious way. These fears were no doubt exaggerated, but they grew not unnaturally in the soil of contemporary African politics, and could not be airily dismissed.

All these attitudes, as has already been observed, were heightened by the troubles in the Congo in the summer of 1960. People who had left Ghana in June for three months' vacation noticed immediately upon their return a change of atmosphere. The Ghanaians are the most friendly and easy-going people, but the overwhelming tenseness and anxiety could not be hidden. The senior officers of the College who were concerned directly in relations with the government soon realized that exceptional difficulties lay ahead.

The evolution of the University crisis was slowed down because for some weeks over Christmas and the early new year the government's commission on higher education held its deliberations. However, by May 1961, it became clear that President Nkrumah had at last decided to intervene in the affairs of the College to get rid of persons who were, for one reason or another, undesirable and to arrange for closer government (or party) control of the institution. In fact, a long siege was beginning. The first step was the dismissal of six faculty members, which led to the resignation of various others, including myself. (I did not leave in angry lack of sympathy. I feared, however, that if such actions continued, what had, for all its shortcomings, been a good institution, would be destroyed: it seemed at the time that to resign was the most effective way in which I could draw attention to the danger.) During the next five years, until Nkrumah's fall, there were sporadic crises. For the most part the new Vice-Chancellor, Conor Cruise O'Brien, whom no one could suspect of colonialism, fended off the attacks successfully with skill, wit, and integrity, but there were more dismissals, more imposed appointments, more party demonstrations. In spite of these, however, the University retained a core of autonomy.

After the fall of Nkrumah early in 1966, six or so years of conflict between the University and the government came to an end. By this time the University was certainly better adapted to the needs of Ghana. And it had not suffered the decline of scholarly standards which the pessimists had predicted would follow any adjustment to the contemporary scene. At the same time, the differences between the government and the University, which had largely resulted from the ideology of the Convention People's Party, disappeared with the advent of a new régime having a new political philosophy.

I cannot leave this topic without a final clarification. It has not been my intention to laud the eventual triumph of academic reasonableness, or to decry Kwame Nkrumah. I simply cite the case of the government and the University of Ghana as an interesting example of an unpeaceful relationship that was sufficiently balanced to prevent victory by either side, and in which the conflict was too acute for full resolution. It is one of those awkward cases in which one can see both sides of the question: I think Nkrumah's complaints were largely justified; I think the University was right not to yield to demands that would have destroyed it. I think both sides played their cards badly – and I am prepared to take part of the blame for this.

As for Nkrumah himself, I believe him to have been a very great African leader to whom the whole continent is indebted. He has been much execrated in the pro-Western press and undoubtedly things went very wrong during his last years, but the full story remains to be told. In the meantime his work for African unity and his exposure of neo-colonialism constitute an unshakable memorial to him.

3 Two Wars:
India/Pakistan and Nigeria[9]

In many cases, the legacy of colonial rule has compounded the dangers of development, adding an element that has turned bad to worse, and worse to terror and death. This is exemplified by the continued tension between India and Pakistan, which has burst into violent conflict more than once. The Nigerian civil war is a further example.

The India–Pakistan quarrel was, of course, based on the conditions in which the Indian subcontinent was partitioned in 1947 into the sovereign states of India and Pakistan. This is a division founded on the insistence of the Muslim population that a separate homeland be provided for them. The boundaries of the new countries depended on the concentration of Hindus and Muslims, but the former Indian Empire also included over 500 princely states with a considerable degree of internal autonomy, which were given the right to accede to India or to Pakistan or – theoretically – to remain independent. By the time of independence, the affiliation of only three states was uncertain and two of these, which had Hindu majorities though Muslim rulers, were shortly thereafter joined to India. The third was Kashmir. This state had a Muslim majority but a Hindu ruler. The ruler, Hari Singh, probably wished to retain his independence from both countries. Two months after independence, however, Kashmir was invaded from Pakistan by a force composed largely of Pathan tribesmen, and Hari Singh acceded to India in order to get military help in repelling them. For over a year, until January 1949, there was fighting in Kashmir. Then, after acceptance of a cease-fire arranged by the United Nations Commission for India and Pakistan, both sides withdrew behind cease-fire lines. The terms of the cease-fire gave Pakistan occupancy of much of the largely mountainous and sparsely inhabited north of Kashmir and a strip along the western border. India retained the famous Vale of Kashmir, a beautiful resort area, with the bulk of the population.

And now, after twenty years, innumerable minor engagements and one sharp war, the situation remains the same. For some years it seemed, off and on, that there might be a solution to the problem through some such device as an internationally controlled referendum, but whenever hopes were raised something happened to postpone or change the arrangement. Now India claims that Kashmir is an integral part of the Indian union and cannot be separated from it. Pakistan, for its part, insists that India should stand by the earlier decision to settle the issue by plebiscite, and the 'liberation' of Kashmir has at times taken on the quality of a *jehad*, a holy war. On both sides there are complex legalistic arguments; each accuses the other of the same sort of insincerity, deception, and treachery. Some observers would maintain, however, that tensions over Kashmir only symbolize the much more deep-seated hatred between Muslim and Hindu based on the strength of their religions and the ancient resentments of dominant and subservient races. Certainly the ghastly and pointless killings in which, at the time of partition, over a million died demonstrate the existence of an explosive and unreasoned violence. But whatever its essential cause the situation is still with us and is perhaps further from solution than it was fifteen years ago.

The war in Nigeria can be viewed, in one sense, as stemming from a power struggle between the three main linguistic or ethnic groups – the Hausa-Fulani of the North, the Ibos of the East, and the Yorubas of the West. These, when British rule was withdrawn in 1960, constituted the dominant groups in the three administrative regions of the country.

It very soon became clear that collaboration between them in the national interest was not going to be easy. The Northerners established a considerable political influence over the government of the Western Region, and this led to a period of political instability which had deteriorated by late 1965 into a state of near anarchy. This came to an end with the first military coup in January 1966. In this coup several prominent Northern politicians and a number of Northern soldiers were killed, mainly by Ibo members of the army. A military government, led by the Ibo commander-in-chief of the army, was then established, but there was a Northern counter-coup six months later in which the Ibo commander and a number of Eastern soldiers were slain. Shortly thereafter there was a series of massacres of Ibos in the North, ending with a bloodbath in September 1967. The Ibos withdrew into the Eastern Region and for several months increasingly futile efforts were made to find some constitutional arrangement which would satisfy both Eastern Nigeria and the federal government. The Easterners demanded a degree of autonomy which they claimed would be necessary to guarantee their safety and give them assurance that no single part of the country could ever again be menaced by another. The federal government insisted on maintaining the integrity of the country and protecting the minority groups in the East who might not wish to be dominated by the Ibos. Eventually, at the end of May 1967, the Easterners became convinced that they could no longer hope for the type of settlement they wanted, and declared their independence, proclaiming the Republic of Biafra. This led quickly to the start of the war in which the aim of the federal government was to prevent the secession of that part of the country.

I have given this brief background to two unhappy struggles to provide a setting for defining the colonial legacy that has been responsible for so many unpeaceful relationships. In both these cases the prime cause of the trouble was the manner in which people had been put together and then separated. The partition of India was an act of terrifying implications and, in fact, of horrible consequences. Whether because of Kashmir or ancient hatreds, or both, the world has had to sustain yet another armed rivalry. Both India and Pakistan, moreover, are caught in a spiral of fear and suspicion which diverts resources from development to defence and prevents the cooperation that would be so beneficial to them, as the following example shows. Under British rule the jute grown in what is now East Pakistan used to be processed in the great factories around Calcutta. Since partition, because Calcutta is in India, the jute has been sent to Scotland, and the Indian mills have remained largely idle; lately, however, India has begun to grow its own jute and the factories have begun to work again. But the land now used to grow jute in India was formerly employed for the rice crop, and this change of land-use contributed to the severity of the recent famine.

The arrangement that made it possible for Kashmir to hesitate and then, under pressure, to choose India, is not entirely dissimilar to that which led to the Nigerian war. In both cases, semi-autonomous groups having some sense of identity were left in an ambiguous position *vis-à-vis* larger groups. The African situation is more clear-cut, however. Nigeria, like most African countries, is divided into tribes, which are, in many respects, nations. (Indeed, I use the word tribe under protest only because there is no easy synonym; but it is a dirty word with its connotation of something barbaric that decent, civilized people can do nothing about – giving them an excuse for both apathy and contempt.) The British arrangement in Nigeria was comparable to joining three European nations together and telling them to get on with the job of running a single country. Since the North was larger than the East and West put together, it was like joining, say, France or Germany with Belgium and Holland.

An alternative plan would have been to divide Nigeria into a larger number of regions on the assumption that none would then be strong enough to dominate the rest. This would also have meant that a number of the smaller tribes would have been detached from the large ones which control the main regions, and given a measure of independence. It is interesting to note that this is what has now been done: Nigeria is divided into twelve states. A second possibility would have been for Britain to grant separate independence to three or more regions of the country. This, in effect, was what the French did in respect of their colonies. However, if Dahomey, Togo, and other small states have been spared the convulsions of Nigeria, they are also small enough to permit the French to continue some degree of economic, and by the same token political, control. That, perhaps, is an equally obnoxious legacy.

But in Nigeria the rivalry of, particularly, the North and the East led inexorably down the path to war. It is not necessary, of course, for different tribes, or nations, to fight each other just because they are different. However, if they are joined together in a way that makes it possible and advantageous for one group to dominate another, disturbances become very probable. The likelihood of strife will, moreover, be increased by certain types of differences that separate people to a point where they cannot communicate with each other. The Hausa-Fulani of Northern Nigeria are Muslims and their somewhat feudal society is ruled by great princes, the emirs. The latter were given support and considerable freedom by the British in return for maintaining law and order. The emirs asked, and the British agreed, that missionaries should be excluded; especially, they did not want Christian schools which would convey false values to their children. In consequence, the Muslim North today is relatively uneducated and the social fabric is largely traditional (though it might be added that in some of the minority areas things are different). In the south of Nigeria (i.e. the Eastern and Western Regions), which was more directly ruled, Christianity and education were accepted much more widely. First the Yoruba, and later, with greater enthusiasm, the Ibos and Ibibio of the East, accepted Christianity, and with it Western education. In 1965 there were 1·20 million children in primary school in the Eastern Region as compared with ·74 in the West, which is about the same size, and ·26 in the North, which is larger than the other two put together (Education and World Affairs, 1966).

Thus the Easterners, in particular the Ibos, became a highly educated group. In addition, they possessed a vigorous entrepreneurial spirit. They spread as traders, technicians, and teachers all over the country, especially in the North where the lower level of education provided many openings for their talents. They made money, they had the best jobs, they were successful, and – the Northerners said – they were overbearing in consequence. Their religion added to their unpopularity. So separate were the two groups that their images of each other were dangerously deceitful: the Northerners were primitive, fanatical, bloodthirsty, and stupid; the Easterners were cunning, arrogant, rapacious, and unscrupulous. It is not surprising that, when the evolution of the power struggle brought the quarrel into the open, ghastly violence ensued. In this respect also, the British, by their different policies towards various regions of the country, had perilously heightened the differences between peoples whom they yet expected to live harmoniously together.

While I am not trying to establish exact parallels between the conflicts in India and Nigeria, it is certainly true that religion and education played their part in both. British educational policy in India was to promote 'European literature and science among the natives of India'.[10] This form of education was in general accepted by the Hindus but rejected by the Muslims of the subcontinent. The Muslims up to this time had had their own educational institutions just as the Northern Nigerians had had their Koranic schools. Many of these, descended from the proud heritage of Muslim scholarship, were of high quality, but under the threat of Western education they went, so to speak, into opposition. But there was little they could do except cling doggedly to the old ideas, becoming increasingly isolated, rigid, and out of touch with modern learning. The British had come to India when the Mogul rule was decaying, but for 1000 years a succession of Muslim invaders – the Arabs, the Muslim dynasties in Persia, Afghanistan, and Turkistan, and finally the Moguls – had ruled or ravaged much of India. Although their power had waned by the eighteenth century, they were still feared by many, and European education offered protection and influence to the Hindus. At the time of independence 100 years later, however, the Hindus, more numerous, and holding the important posts that can be gained by education, were much more powerful, though many still felt the resentments deriving from centuries of subjection. The more traditional Muslims spoke with the same bitterness about the educated Hindus as did the Hausa about the Ibos. Unlike the Hausa, however, but like the Ibos, the Muslims of India were a minority group and so sought their safety in separation. Once they became independent, the Pakistanis found that the shortage of trained and educated people in their country was one of the most severe handicaps they had to overcome. The great majority of the civil servants, being Hindus, were left in India. There were very few scholars or professional men. Here again, the differences of education and religion, the former resulting largely from British colonial policy, served to intensify disparities and differences between two former colonial groups.

Until recently, neither Pakistani nor Ibo (or Biafran) nationalism was a factor in Indian or Nigerian politics. Pakistani nationalism developed as a widespread phenomenon only on the creation by the British of Pakistan. This, it is true, followed several years of protest by the Muslim League, demanding an independent homeland for the Muslims of the subcontinent, but until 1947 there was no geographical entity of Pakistan – it is hard to be chauvinistic about an abstraction. The Eastern Nigerians, though all living in the same region, likewise had very little sense of political identity. The political system of the Ibos was highly decentralized: the basic social unit among them and the Ibibio, one of the two major subgroups in the region, was the extended family, and the largest political group was the village. It was only with the establishment by the British of an administrative unit in which all the Ibos were actively involved, and through which, as a result, they felt both threats and opportunities, that a powerful sense of identity, of nascent nationalism, began to emerge.

These circumstances aggravated the conflicts and confusions inherent in change and the achievement of political independence. It is not surprising that the groups in each situation became increasingly separate, unable to talk to each other, unable to perceive each other, drifting to a point where one additional element introduced into the dangerous mixture detonated the whole.

4 The Blacks and the Whites: South Africa[11]

In South Africa there are some 16 million non-whites, of whom 13·3 million are Africans, dominated by 3·7 million whites. The average income of a white family is about twenty times that of a black family. In proportion to non-whites, six times as many whites receive post-primary education and, whereas the state spends £65 a year per white student, it spends only £6·4 a year per African student. The infant mortality rate for the African population is 3·5 times as high as for that for the white. These figures demonstrate a formidable material inequality, but the political and psychological inequalities that promote and maintain the material inequality are even more searing.

The basis of government policy is social separation, apartheid, which is the supreme example of racism carried to its logical conclusion. Until the end of World War II there had been a snail's-paced policy of liberalization, but when the Nationalist Party came into power in 1949 this policy was sharply reversed. The party doctrine has developed a philosophical, even a theological, mystique. (Sermons are preached on such texts as 'Those whom God hath set apart let no man put together'.) We need not bother with that. Essentially, the doctrine is a hard, coldly reasoned method of preserving the supremacy – and affluent comfort – of the white minority. To that end the black Africans (as opposed to the white Afrikaners of Dutch descent) are kept as a subject people. They are permitted to live in white areas only as registered servants; otherwise those who work in such cities as Johannesburg must inhabit ghettos known as African townships. Racial segregation operates in respect of numerous facilities: post offices, bathing beaches, park benches, public transport, taxis, toilets, hotels, restaurants, cemeteries, public buildings, hospitals, cinemas, and schools. The facilities provided for the blacks are inferior to those for the whites. The Immorality Act bans sexual relations between the races. The cynically named Extension of Bantu Education Act of 1959 forbids non-white students to attend English-speaking universities (they had not, in any case, been permitted in Afrikaans-speaking institutions).

The older generation of African leaders, men like Albert Luthuli and Z. K. Matthews, asked only for full citizenship for their people. Like Martin Luther King, they were integrationists rather than radicals. They were Ghandian in their openness and non-violence. But the apartheid theorists have another view of citizenship. They argue that Africans are different from whites; that their strength is the strength of traditional society and the whites would be doing them a great disservice by assimilating them: therefore they must be allowed to 'develop separately'. This separate development is to take place on Native Reserves, commonly known as Bantustans – areas of the country set aside for Africans where, under careful surveillance and strong in-direct control, they have limited autonomy. But the Bantustans, mostly poor agricultural areas, comprise – for 75 per cent of the population – only 13 per cent of the land. These, nevertheless, constitute in theory the 'native homeland'. If people choose to live outside the Bantustans, as many must for economic reasons (over 30 per cent of the Africans live in the large cities), they must accept the implication that, like foreigners in many countries, they cannot enjoy the privileges of full citizenship. In no recent case except Nazi Germany, however, has denial of full citizenship entailed so comprehensive and insulting a forfeiture of what we regard as natural human rights.

The South African government has been extremely systematic. Less intelligent oligarchies have made the mistake of educating their people into awareness. The South Africans, by contrast, have not only kept school enrolments at a low level but, in addi-tion, have taken over all the mission schools; thus they can ap-point and dismiss teachers, and control a curriculum which has the avowed aim of 'keeping the Bantu child a Bantu child'.

Indeed, in an ingenious endeavour to prevent the formation of national movements, education aims to keep not only the Bantu Bantu, but the Zulu Zulu and the Xhosa Xhosa. Even at the tertiary level, the colleges established to compensate for the closing of the universities to Africans are split on linguistic lines. If education and general experience in the ways of the world are the criteria of a people's capacity to govern themselves, then the black people of South Africa should have ruled their land before the Ghanaians, the first sub-Saharan African people to be freed from colonial rule. Yet now, year by year, they are slipping behind their brothers.

In 1960 and 1961 there were some optimists who believed that, if not revolution, at least change was around the corner. South Africa had been forced to resign from the Commonwealth. Many countries had placed an embargo on South African exports. There had been serious riots in Pondoland. It was believed that many of the more moderate members of the Nationalist Party felt that Verwoerd, then prime minister, had gone too far and too fast. The Liberal Party, with both white and non-white members, was vigorous and humane under the leadership of the incomparable Alan Paton. A group of resolute idealists considered that it would not take much to topple the government. They held that a programme of clandestine propaganda and some tactical acts of sabotage directed towards such targets as power stations and dams would encourage dissatisfied politicians to change the government, or at least to force it to modify its policies.

Of particular concern to my friends in education was the exclusion of the Africans from the universities. This had been a grievous blow, for if there were ever to be a change of régime there must be educated Africans to step into positions of responsibility. But now South Africa, which had once boasted the most highly educated group of Africans, was dropping behind in the race to achieve a literate population. Ghana, Nigeria, and other countries were surging ahead. Moreover, such education as was offered in substitution for attendance at genuine institutions is meted out at what are usually termed Bantu colleges. These are controlled by the department responsible for Bantu affairs rather

73

than by the Ministry of Education. The curriculum is antiseptic and the structure of the system – different colleges have been established for the several tribal and ethnic groups – promotes disunity among the Africans, and between the Africans, the Asians, and the Coloureds. Thus the educational arrangement reinforces the principles of apartheid: indeed, in a sense it extends them into the relationships of the non-whites with each other.

A further fear, a false one as events up to the present have proved, was that the hopeless bitterness created by this final humiliation would lead to equally hopeless violence: the Africans would rise in futile desperation only to be butchered in great numbers after taking – thus, ironically, things often fall out – a few innocent lives.

At one period there was a scheme for remedying this situation, or at least for providing a more suitable experience of higher education for the deprived Africans. This was to set up in one of the neighbouring territories – Swaziland, for example – some form of college. Here the students, African and other, would receive an education worthy of free men. Even if, their legal re-entry to South Africa presented difficulties, they could wait in the wings – serving, perhaps, some other African country – until the time was ripe for them to assume responsibilities as administrators, teachers, legislators, professional people, in their homeland.

But, like so many other hopeful schemes of this period, this one came to nothing. Not enough people were ready and involved, the planning was amateurish and inadequate, the authorities were too suspicious. Now, ten years later, the young activists, once so high-spirited and debonair, are all dispersed, many exiled, some in prison. The exclusively African liberation movements, Poqo, the Spear of the Nation, and the National Liberation Committee, have been smashed. Their leaders, more militant than the old generation of resisters, are imprisoned or underground. A specious calm, a tasteless and complacent affluence, have spread over the white community like a slick of oil. Protected by the ruthless efficiency of the police, by the *cordon sanitaire* of their sordid allies in Mozambique, Rhodesia, and Angola, and by their shame-faced wealthy supporters, they are living through a period of prosperity in what might be termed peace with misery.

Yet if ever there was a country that should be torn by rebellion, it is South Africa. Why has there been no revolution? Confrontations tend not to take place because of absolute misery. Oppressed and ignorant masses do not rise up in anger: they are too weak and unaware. Especially they do not rise against strong governments that control the police and the army. There may be sporadic outbreaks of violence, but not the sustained and purposeful effort needed to conduct a revolution. Revolutions are much more apt to take place when the people are taught, organized, and led by vigorous activists, when fairly prosperous and successful people are constrained by bounds of class or privilege, and when the government is weak. In South Africa, the Africans are weak and the government is strong. The Africans have not reached the point of affluence where they feel that white power is inhibiting their further progress.[12] On the other hand, they need white help in achieving what is for Africans a high standard of living. There is a long way to go, both socially and economically, before they are within striking distance, as it were, of the whites and so can strike them. Just as rewards for good Africans are considerable, so punishment for bad ones is swift, implacable, and harsh. Any potential African revolutionary leader is harassed and imprisoned, his followers are threatened and dispersed. The white revolutionary, by the same token, feels sadly discouraged. Few care or dare to rebel. The dangers of dissent are too great, the prize for compliance is too beguiling. Above all, the black South Africans are too divided, too under-educated, too frightened, and – in a few cases – too comfortable, to rebel. Their level of awareness and of hope is too low.

For the last dozen years people have been speculating as to when the South African revolution of awareness will take place. Some estimates have always placed it in the very near future, but the prophets of such views are perhaps being more moralistic than realistic. Now, barring outside intervention, we have to expect that many years will pass. There is, however, one circumstance that may bring revolution closer – or may retard it. Even the limited self-government accorded to the Africans in the Transkei may sow a germ of awareness, a consciousness of the meaning of power, in enough hearts to create a popular movement of liberation. On the other hand, as I have already suggested, it may create an illusion of equality, of a more balanced relationship, and so serve as a soporific rather than a stimulant.

II. Governments and People

During the last twenty-five years the poor countries have been torn by strife. There have been over fifty disturbances large enough to be characterized as wars, about the same number of military coups, and a host of guerrilla actions and bloody incidents of one sort or another. Some political scientists, noting the political instability of many of these countries, have argued that poverty, instability, and a tendency to violence go together and that only a higher level of development can bring a better chance of concord.

I argue somewhat differently. In the first place, many of these wars have been colonial wars of independence, such as those fought in Indonesia, Algeria, Kenya, and Vietnam (under the French), and those still being waged in Angola and Portuguese Guinea. Other struggles also can be thought of as wars of liberation, but wars waged against oppressive internal rather than external régimes, such as those in Bolivia, Guatemala, Yemen, and Thailand. Others again, though occurring in independent countries, have been closely associated with the former colonial status of those countries. In these cases, either incompatible peoples had been put together, as in Nigeria, in a fashion that made conflict almost inevitable; or independent nations had been set up though areas of dispute remained between them, as in Somalia and Kenya, India and Pakistan, Malaysia and Indonesia. The even more dramatic cases of the two Vietnams and of Israel and the Arab countries are clearly, to a large extent, consequences of colonialism or of manipulation by wealthy countries.

We must also take account of the malign influence that the great powers frequently exert through their support of obnoxious régimes. They combine with these régimes to spoliate their peasant peoples. In fact, there exists what can be considered as a worldwide exploitative network composed of capitalist interests in the rich countries, which derive wealth and advantage from extracting resources from the poor countries, and of their agents in these poor countries, who profit from such association at the expense of separation from their own society and its needs. These agents comprise many of the élite of the wealthy countries' poor client states. And when, eventually, the rural populations arise in desperation, they are put down as 'communists' or 'criminal elements' with the assistance of napalm and other products of civilization supplied by the foreign benefactors of the élite. In such situations the governments, lacking any popular support, are, in general, highly unstable. Their members are drawn from a particular privileged class whose other members are eager to unseat them and enjoy the perquisites of power – especially when there are fat pickings from concessions, foreign loans, and the like. Hence the constant palace revolutions that characterize many Latin American states. But these revolutions have nothing in common with confrontation (as discussed in Chapter 18); they merely exchange one tyranny for another equally indifferent to the needs of the people.

Thus the relationship of the governments of the rich countries to those of the poor ones, far from being a stabilizing influence, is one that makes for constant flux and frequent violence. More-over, it is my purpose here to demonstrate that the actual efforts made to achieve development, which is supposed by some to reduce violence, can themselves be a source of violence. These efforts need not be corrupt or exploitative or ill-intentioned (though possibly they are ill-conceived) to have their disruptive impact.

A supporting, if inconclusive, argument for the dangers of development may be the negative one that the most backward human societies tend to be the least warlike. An analysis of 652 primitive societies (defined as self-determining peoples who do, or did, not use writing) shows that only one-third engage in anything approximating warfare (Broch and Galtung, 1966). Moreover, the greater the growth of civilization (civilization meaning the degree of formal political and economic organization) among these societies, the greater the prevalence of war. This analysis does not actually prove anything, of course, for poor societies are not primitive ones. It is thought-provoking, nevertheless, since many of the inhabitants of poor societies belong to groups – tribes, clans, and so on – that are closer to primitive than to modern society.

The state as we know it today is, with very few exceptions, a modern structure. It may not work efficiently, it may be corrupt and autocratic, but the apparatuses of almost all governments have a great deal in common. The forms of political or economic life they represent are far more like each other than are those of the primitive societies just referred to or, for that matter, those of the tribes that comprise so many modern states. There is no doubt that the exigencies of living in the contemporary world, with its international agencies, diplomatic exchanges, network of communications, economic interdependency, worldwide news media, alliances, and so on, produce a tendency towards a measure of conformity. Most nations proclaim similar aspirations regarding the welfare of their people, their education, their emancipation from the ignorance and prejudices of the past, and the like. It is quite clear that these objectives are not always in he tinterests of the ruling oligarchy – no dictator of intelligence would educate his people if he could help it – but it is hard for any nation not to pay lip service – and indeed more – to the prevailing trends of world opinion.

In most poor nations, the modern structure of the state contains a number of what might be termed particularist groups. The members of these groups owe their loyalty and concern to the extended family or the tribe, to the regional or ethnic group, rather than to the nation. In Africa the division tends to be vertical, separating relatively self-contained tribal groups. In Latin America and Asia there is greater likelihood (though of course in neither case are these tendencies mutually exclusive) that the division will be horizontal between class or caste, and based on religion or race. The strength of a nation's particularist groups is a measure of the weakness of its national institutions, which, almost by definition, are likely to cut across the interests

79

of the particularist groups. These groups may or may not contribute vigorously to national development, but if they do so it is usually because they are serving their own interests thereby rather than because they are concerned with the wellbeing of the country as a whole. For these reasons, the government machinery of a nation attempting to develop is bound to impose itself upon its tribal or other groups: compelling them to pay taxes and maintain law and order; involving them in large-scale irrigation projects or other development works that may not necessarily be in their immediate interests (for an example, see the chapter on the Chakmas, p. 102 below); inducing them to practise more efficient methods of agriculture; educating them; administering them; disciplining them with its police; preventing them from pursuing what it considers wasteful or immoral practices; attempting to wean the young people away from their traditional 'primitive' and non-developmental way of life; endeavouring to bring the groups into the mainstream of national existence; making them conform to a national legal code that may be entirely different from their customary law; seeking to break the centrifugal power of the tribe – trying, by all these means, to create a nation. And of course, where the government does not have the interest of the people at heart, these things may be done in a peculiarly callous way, with no attempt made to soften the pains of change and deprivation by the provision of hospitals, clinics, and other welfare services.

Most tribes and peasant communities in the world prize their autonomy, or at least a relative freedom from interference, and value their traditions. The more they do so, the more will they resent and resist the encroachment of this alien government force, which means so little to them, blundering blindly and destructively into their known life, bringing much that is strange, unknown, and damaging. Its administrators tax them and put them into jail for offences they do not understand, its police harass them, and its army menaces them if they protest. They may, like the Nagas or Karens, actively oppose this alien domination for years. More probably they will sullenly give in, their self-confidence and peace of mind whittled away, feeling insecure and out of place, no longer quite knowing where they stand, a prey to the alienation that attacks those who have lost one world without gaining another, easy victims for political or religious agitators who would exploit their unhappiness or confusion. This is the raw stuff of conflict. It should be emphasized, however, that particularist groups do not always react in negative ways in the face of national development. By no means are all such groups too ingrown to participate in national life; many are both strong enough and flexible enough to do so and to profit therefrom without loss of their essential qualities. But the dangers are considerable; most African countries have potential Katangas and Biafras.

Apart from the general tensions produced by change, some more specific strains are likely to arise in the process of development. The expansion of education and of the mass media (in this respect the transistor radio has been an important revolutionary tool) has increased political awareness in most countries throughout the world. A generation ago, in most poor nations only a few educated citizens were concerned with the political process. Now, some degree of political mobilization is widespread nearly everywhere. It is also true, however, that there has not been a corresponding growth of political institutions through which this new-found awareness can be expressed in action. Indeed, in many countries the succession of coups, the swings between radical and reactionary administrations, the constitutions that prove unworkable, the experiments that fail, exemplify a sort of political decay rather than growth (Huntington, 1965).[13] It is very hard for a politically awakened population, encompassed by this state of decay, to take pride or have hope; all they can do is overthrow the current government – and replace it with an equally inept régime. In this sort of anarchic situation conflicts are the more probable because corruption and exploitation become prevalent. This is especially likely to be the case if opportunities are opened to some individuals or groups (as tends to happen with the infusion of development funds) and there is no effective institutional control over their abuse.

The mass media, coupled with education, also contribute to other types of potential conflict. The expansion of education, which has been particularly rapid in the post-colonial period as a means of establishing national identity, has aroused expectations that have not been fulfilled because the growth of the economy has been less rapid – sometimes, ironically, because the cost of education has been so high. In a number of countries the chief virtue of education is seen to be that it is the means of entry to employment in government service or at least in the modern sector of the economy – that it is a means of escape, in short, from rural and agricultural life, which most students learn to think of as backward. But if the economy has not grown enough to provide enough new jobs, there is resentment and confusion. In Nigeria in 1966, for example, there were approximately 750,000 school-leavers and only 150,000 new jobs in the modern sector of the economy (Education and World Affairs, 1966, pp. 20–2). In average circumstances the school-leavers are loath to return to agriculture. They are more apt to congregate in the towns, picking up a dubious living on the fringe of society, becoming a group comparable to plastic explosives: both malleable and easily detonated.

Through education, as well as through the mass media, people become more readily aware of grievances and differences in privilege. They become less prepared to accept their fate with resignation or apathy. Again, the lack of political machinery may make it very hard for them to do anything constructive about it. Where a measure of development has been achieved, however, people may be emboldened to resort to revolution to change intolerable conditions.

Another factor is that the gap between the relatively richer and the relatively poorer areas of a country sometimes appears to widen as the country begins the slow ascent towards affluence. In describing this and comparable pressures, Gunnar Myrdal (1957) quotes the New Testament: 'To him that hath shall it be given, from him that hath not shall be taken away even that little that he hath.'[14] If scant resources are available, a preponderance of them is invested in areas that appear to have some economic potential, while individuals, business, and agencies with energy and enterprise also flock there. Thus the less fortunate regions are denied the advantages of the others: they get fewer good schools, their hospitals are poorly equipped and staffed, commerce declines, their best young people drift away. Being left behind in the general move forward, they tend to become isolated, reactionary, and hostile to the national government.

The towns are often the most prosperous places: industries are centred where there is a large labour force; commercial interests concentrate in them; there is a great influx of diplomats, technicians, and foreign advisers, especially in the capitals. To the average citizen, the streets of a city are paved with, at least, silver gilt and he goes there hoping to satisfy the ambitions aroused by hearsay and newly gained awareness of the world. Thither goes also the school-leaver, hoping for the type of employment he feels to be his due after five years or so of elementary education. Apart from the fact that, prosperous though they may be, the bloated cities cannot offer work to all who flock to them, they create another hazard to harmony. The majority of their newly arrived inhabitants are losing touch with their roots, are abandoned and confused, and ready to seek alternatives to the culture they have lost.[15] The alternatives they find may often be anarchic or rebellious.

These are all influences making for unpeaceful relations of different kinds, manifested in a variety of ways: from apathetic withdrawal to violence, from the military coup to the tribal war of independence, from the angry demonstration to the horrors of the Nigerian civil war. Moreover, to the extent that they are at least partly brought about by development policies and practices, they reflect certain approaches to development.

As I noted earlier (p. 44), the poor countries have to a considerable extent adapted the rich nations' technology and nowhere more completely than in the field of development. Their former white mentors in planning tended to be classical purists:[16] economic development meant a sufficient increase of capital, and once this was achieved all other good things would follow – but the latter were not really the economist's business; he left the details to the various specialists such as doctors, engineers, educationists, and so on. When I was first involved in this work as a humble adviser on social affairs to a planning agency run by economists, all the areas with which I was concerned – education, health, welfare, housing, labour, community development – were officially known as 'non-productive sectors'. One of my local colleagues once bitterly observed: 'A field, or a cow, or a machine is productive; but the man who tills the field, milks the cow, or tends the machine is not.'

There has been a failure to appreciate the non-economic consequences of measures taken to produce economic development (such as the cancerous growth of urban slums that often follows industrialization, a favourite tool of the economic developers), and a failure to recognize that such side-effects often impede the economic effectiveness of the measures taken.

The policies of economic development have seldom been related to any general philosophy of total national development (but then, who usually makes the plans, and to whose advantage?). To be sure, most plans have a preamble signed by some high dignitary who, whether he is African, Asian, or Latin American, predictably talks of alleviating the miseries of the poor, promoting justice and prosperity for all, serving the people, building a strong and united nation, etc. This having been said, the plan unfolds as a pure piece of developmental technology. In general, capital accumulation has been thought to be enough and has been considered outside the context of such irrelevancies as the prevailing culture, ideology, and general growth potential of the country concerned. The irony lies in the fact that although much disequilibrium has been caused by the attempt to build up capital, the success of these efforts has been relatively small.

Most planners now acknowledge that they must give attention in their projects to the welfare of society in general. They admit that individual human beings do play a part in development and that provision should therefore be made for them in development plans. Even so, the use of such phrases as 'human resources development' (the planners' synonym for education) shows that the individual is still thought of primarily as an adjunct to economic growth.

It is now common to talk of modernization rather than of

84

economic development. The first implication of this term is that to achieve development we must think beyond economics and consider the restructuring of society – its bureaucracy, political system, data-collecting processes, research organizations, communications, and so on. This is clearly sensible. The second implication is, however, that the country concerned should become as similar as possible to the 'modern' nations: it is not without reason that most citizens of poor countries equate 'modernize' with 'Americanize'. Here again there seems to be little regard for the totality of the system that is to be affected by the 'modern' approaches.

The application of development policies to a country's economy, and still more to its institutions, without a clear realization of the probable effects such policies will have on the national life as a whole, has been responsible for much unpeacefulness. It takes a man both bold and wise to steer away from the conventional wisdom of the developers and to chart a new course, no less progressive, but more appropriate for his people. Such a man is Julius Nyerere, President of Tanzania, who wrote of the Arusha Declaration[17] in which the policy of his country's development was defined:

'This growth must come out of our own roots, not through the grafting on to those roots of something which is alien to our society. This is very important, for it means that we cannot adopt any political "holy book" and try to implement its rulings – with or without revision.

It means that our social change will be determined by our own needs as we see them, and in the direction that we feel to be appropriate for us at any particular time. We shall draw sustenance from universal human ideas and from the practical experiences of other peoples; but we start from a full acceptance of our African-ness and a belief that in our own past there is very much which is useful for our future.

The Arusha Declaration is also a commitment to a particular quality of life. It is based on the assumption of human equality, on the belief that it is wrong for one man to dominate or to

85

exploit another, and on the knowledge that every individual hopes to live in society as a free man able to lead a decent life in conditions of peace with his neighbours. The document is, in other words, man-centred.

Inherent in the Arusha Declaration, therefore, is a rejection of the concept of national grandeur as distinct from the well-being of its citizens, and a rejection too of material wealth for its own sake. It is a commitment to the belief that there are more important things in life than the amassing of riches, and that if the pursuit of wealth clashes with things like human dignity and social equality, then the latter will be given priority.

For in a Tanzania which is implementing the Arusha Declaration, the purpose of all social, economic and political activity must be man – the citizens, and all the citizens of this country. The creation of wealth is a good thing and something which we shall have to increase. But it will cease to be good the moment wealth ceases to serve man and begins to be served by man.

With our present level of economic activity, and our present poverty, this may seem to be an academic point; but in reality it is very fundamental. For it means that there are certain things which we shall refuse to do or to accept, either as individuals or as a nation, even if the result of them would be a surge forward in our economic development' (Nyerere, 1968a, pp. 92–3).

5 Pakistani Villages and the Government[18]

In Pakistan, as in most poor countries, there is little rapport between the government and the people of the country areas – the peasants and tribesmen, the nomads and the hill people who like to keep to themselves. To most of them the government has been the victimizer, whether it was controlled by the colonialists or by their own people. It put them in prison for mysterious offences which had nothing to do with their own system of morality. It levied taxes from which they saw no return. It billetted its armies on them so that their food was consumed and their women were raped without redress. It took their young men to fight its meaningless wars. It fined them, registered them, and interfered with them. A Pakistani friend of mine, a wise and humane administrator, was driving through a village when a little girl ran suddenly in front of his car. He rushed the badly hurt child to the nearest hospital, but she died on the way, and he took her back, grieving. He fully expected to be mobbed by the angry villagers, but was so distressed that he did not mind. However, the girl's grandfather simply said: 'God has taken our child; that cannot be undone. We ask nothing of you except that you should not tell the police. If you do they will come here to make an investigation. They will stay for weeks; they will eat all our chickens. They will find out all about us and blackmail us; if anyone protests, he will be beaten and taken to jail.' The average official, for his part, has had an attitude of disdain for the villagers, considering them ignorant, backward, sly, and uncooperative.

Since the early 1950s there have been various attempts to bring the government and the people closer in these areas, to dissolve the mutually hostile images, so that the villages could contribute

87

more effectively to the economy of the nation, and in so doing help themselves.

The first of these was a community development organization known as Village Agricultural and Industrial Development (Village AID). Essentially, community development aims to improve the social and economic conditions of the community by involving it as much as possible in work for its own welfare and by stimulating its initiative. It is a method of helping communities to manage their own affairs constructively, an operational training-ground for democracy that has real and cogent meaning for people since the decisions they have to make do not concern remote ideological issues, but practical matters of immediate importance to themselves. As in the wider democracy, it is based on the twin principles of participation and responsibility; but these are nurtured by common concern for what is of manifest significance to all. From the exercise of these two principles empirically applied, grows – and I use the word advisedly to express a phenomenon so universal as to appear natural – the appropriate form of organization for the administration and expansion of community services.

It is an important aspect of community development that it depends on participation and responsibility not only within the community, but also between the community and the authorities stimulating the development. In this way a bridge is built over which – in both directions – pass knowledge and understanding. This has many advantages. Here I will mention only that the effect of linking the smaller and the larger community eradicates one of the most dangerous side-effects of social change. When the small group acquires the sense of functional belonging to the wider society it loses the feeling of being at the mercy of implacable outside forces – a feeling that induces a range of sad reactions including subservience, resentment, apathy, and disorder. On the contrary, people are taking part in – indeed initiating – processes of change that most closely affect themselves; processes that are developing in response to needs that they themselves are best qualified to express. In consequence, in any community development area one will find a nucleus of enterprises in agriculture, irrigation, animal husbandry, cooperative buying and selling, and so on, based on scientific rather than traditional procedures. Thus community development provides an introduction to technological situations in which proto-technical conventions are dissolved as new skills are learnt. In so doing it also contributes directly, as well as indirectly, to material development.

In Pakistan, the Village AID organization had built up a number of development areas, each of which covered as many as 150 villages. In each development area was a development officer and two superintendents, and some thirty village workers each of whom was in charge of about five villages. Although these people were government servants, their role was very different from that of most government administrators. The latter were proconsuls, men responsible for collecting taxes (in some areas they are still actually called collectors), for administering justice, for maintaining law and order, and in general for representing the government. Whether the administrator was a commissioner in charge of a vast area or a *tehsildar* in charge of a small one, the all-inclusive nature of his power was the same. He did things for the villagers or to them, but not with them. In general, he was more interested in maintaining the peaceful *status quo* than in development or change. And although many an administrator would have a special fad about irrigation, or improving the strain of livestock, or training hawks, this was a personal matter and not part of a general programme of betterment. The Village AID approach was entirely different. The first duty of the development officer and his men was to promote change. They were to do this, moreover, by working with the people, encouraging them to express their needs, and then collaborating with them to find ways of meeting those needs. For example, if it was important to build a bridge so that the village produce could be taken more easily to market, it could be arranged that the government would supply the engineering skills and the special equipment and materials, while the village community would provide local materials – wood, stone, and so on – and unskilled manpower. The Village AID worker did not come to sit in an office, collect taxes, and receive tribute from villagers hoping to keep on the right side of him; he came to work with the villagers, and could do nothing unless they for their part were prepared to help themselves.

During the three years in which I was adviser on social affairs to the government of Pakistan, I saw some remarkably successful ventures in community development among people as widely different as Tibetan-speaking Baltis, Pathans, Punjabis, and Bengalis. These are people as unlike in temperament, language, and general social background as, in Europe, are, say, the Italians, the Danes, the Russians, and the Lapps. Yet approximately the same philosophy and approach have achieved the same type of liberating effect.

I would cite as an example one particular village in the Punjab in which there was prevalent not only the traditional hostility to authority, but also a series of internecine feuds so violent that they seemed to preclude any chance of the villagers' collaborating on anything. There were four mutually hostile segments in the community, each associated with a particular mosque, which effectively destroyed the group life of the village. The village council, the *panchayat*, with its very limited responsibilities, was quite incapable of achieving common action. In time it became almost impossible to walk through the narrow village streets, for everyone dumped his rubbish outside his own doorway and never bothered about clearing the street because it was also used by his detested neighbours. The water supply became infected, and the feeling of general resentment grew so violent that one might say that the whole life of the community was also infected. The village worker was a young man, inexperienced, but intelligent and honest. He attempted to tell the villagers that he had come to work with them, and that they should try to define the ways in which they wanted the government to help them to do what they wanted to do. He was met, as were village workers elsewhere, with profound suspicion from the villagers. What could this be but a sinisterly ingenious trick on the part of the government to cheat them? But, as had happened elsewhere, so in this village: the consistency and integrity of the village worker persuaded the villagers to test him on a simple project concerning a single well. If it did not become apparent that the government was out for their money or their goods, then they would try something more elaborate. The worker passed the test: the well was reconstructed and the villagers were not imposed upon. This incident began a period of slow acceptance and of increasing activity. At the end of eighteen months an enormous amount had been done. Some irrigation channels had been built, benefiting the whole village; the streets had been cleared and paved (the rubbish from them was piled several feet high on an open space the size of a football field just outside the village); new classrooms had been built for the school, and paid for by a tax which had been levied on itinerant tradesmen; a bull and a stock of seeds had been cooperatively purchased for the use of the whole village; the water supply had been purified.

In this example, four things are of great significance. First, as the possibilities for new developments became apparent, the villagers were able to subdue their mutual antipathies and to work together. There may be a tendency (it seems to be illustrated in the English villages referred to in Chapter 12) for splits within a community to be related in some circumstances to cleavages between that community and the larger outside world. It would also seem likely that in more hopeful and prosperous conditions internal tensions subside. Second, and related to the first point, these changed attitudes were brought about by a committee, bridging all sections of the community, which was created by the villagers in response to their new situation of widening opportunity. It was, in fact, a new form of local government in embryo, and far more effective than that which existed already. Third, much of what was achieved seems to have been done solely on village initiative; communities, like people, appear to become more vigorous and constructive when released from enmities and suspicion. Fourth, relations with the authorities, since they had shown themselves to possess a more reasonable and friendly side, had become more realistic. I would not go so far as to say that there had been a growth of national sentiment, but the basis for such growth had been formed. In the future it would be easier both for the government to enlist the support and understanding of the village in its development plan, and for the villagers to resist the wrong sort of pressure; as their community grew stronger and wealthier, the old debilitating impositions could not be so easily made.

To the regret of many, the Village AID programme was abandoned in 1959, shortly after President Ayub came to power. Some said it was because of excessive waste and corruption – and certainly there had been notorious failures as well as the successes I have mentioned. Others, including high officials in the Village AID organization, said that the old-style administrators felt that this parallel and more liberal approach to communities with which they also dealt would undermine the regular hierarchical pattern of authority.

To fill the gap, a new socio-political function was given to the villages and equivalent urban areas, which, in the exercise of this function, were termed Basic Democracies (BDs). These did more than occupy the vacancies caused by the removal of Village AID. At the time of the coup, Ayub had suspended political parties, claiming that they had been ineffectual and corrupt and that the pretence of democracy had merely masked tyranny (this was often true: the rural elector knew perfectly well what would happen if he did not support his landlord). The BDs now also filled the hiatus occasioned by the end of political activity. Each was to choose a representative who would serve on the union council of ten or a dozen villages and would also cast a vote at the times when the president or certain other high officials of the state were elected. The BDs, through their union council and the higher bodies with which it was linked, were also authorized to work towards the development of their areas. The development aspects of the Basic Democracies have been described as follows:

'1, to give the villager representation at the level of government closest to him, the Union Council, which would know his problems and respond to his needs. This body was given broad taxing powers and development responsibility.

2, to give the villager's elected representative a role, though at diminishing proportions, at all the higher tiers of the Basic

Democracies, and thus to bring the needs and problems of the village to all levels of the structure.

3, to blend the viewpoints and experience of the representatives of the people and of the trained civil servants, officers of the provincial departments, who are intermingled at all levels above the Union Councils.

4, to decentralize and, at the same time, coordinate the work of the departmental officers under the guidance of the chairmen of the Councils.

5, to produce an integrated structure, the chairmen of each tier serving as members of the Council at the next level, with integrated policy-making power and responsibility.

6, to orient the structure toward development' (Gilbert, 1963, p. 6).

However, although the BDs had an important developmental role which was expected to strengthen their political function, just as their political function was intended to give purpose to their work in development, progress was slow. The main reason for this was lack of resources. It is true that the BDs had taxing authority at low administrative levels, but the communities were too poor for this authority to be used vigorously. At the same time, the sum that the provincial governments were able to contribute was too small to be used effectively for development. In addition, most villages had had little practice in the exercise of civic responsibility. In consequence, although the institution of BDs had some psychological import in that the people came to recognize their elective powers, it had little practical value.

In 1962, however, a programme was initiated in East Pakistan (and spread to West Pakistan) which exploited the psychological readiness of the people and gave to the BDs the developmental capacity needed to make them fully functional. This was the rural Works Programme. In Pakistan, as in all poor countries, there is much unemployment and under-employment. The main purpose of the Works Programme was to put inadequately used manpower to work on programmes that would be of value to the nation and would, in turn, create more employment. Irrigation schemes were to be established; feeder canals were to be built, which would enable more rice crops to be grown; low-cost housing estates were to be established; schools were to be constructed; clean water supplies and drainage were to be installed; and land was to be reclaimed. The launching of the project was made possible by the liberal provision of United States Commodity Aid, without which much of the potential value of the BDs would have been lost. A significant point about this programme for the BDs was that they were given a say in choosing the projects and, of course, in working on them. All available reports show that, from the beginning, the Works Programme, particularly in East Pakistan, aroused great popular enthusiasm. For the first time, 'the man in the rice field' was part of the organization set up to identify his problems and help him to plan constructively to meet them through the exercise of his legitimate political rights. Previously, many great development works had been carried out, but these had all been remote from the individual. He had had no say in their planning, and at best only a menial part in their execution, and often he derived no obvious benefit from them. But now, since much was done at the lower levels, the humblest cultivator was directly involved. Thus the combination of the Basic Democracies and the Works Programme, which used as its planning and executive agency the various councils of the BD structure, has brought about something of a revolution in awareness of what can be achieved and of the value of cooperation. This undoubtedly has played some part in the great advances made by the Pakistan economy in the last few years. It is particularly significant that rice production has reached new record levels. This could not have happened (unlike, for example, an increase in the GNP due to a sudden discovery of mineral wealth) unless the skill, energy, and hope of millions of individuals had been cultivated and engaged.

It may be useful to consider the relationship between these villages and their government in terms of our model of peaceful and unpeaceful relationships. Initially it was without question a most unbalanced relationship, in which there was in general (though not in some remote areas) a fairly high awareness of conflict, for the government extorted taxes and in various ways imposed itself upon the people without, in their eyes, making any return. But with very few exceptions there was no conflict behaviour; the villagers had neither the nerve nor the strength to rebel.

With the establishment of Village AID, things began to happen in a rather unusual fashion. Instead of the people having to try to increase their power, the government was trying to give power to them (in the sense of greater control over their destiny). And for a long time, in most communities, this was rejected suspiciously as a trick. Eventually, however, the communities that accepted the government's offer achieved a greater measure of equality than they had ever experienced before. Admittedly, the power of the government and the power of the village cannot be balanced. But whereas in the past the authorities could ride roughshod over the interests of the peasant farmers, now they were seeking to promote those interests. A peaceful relationship is one in which, irrespective of balance, the potential of both parties is more easily realized because of the quality of that relationship. This sort of relationship began to develop sporadically and fragmentarily through the work of Village AID.

It was taken a step further by the Basic Democracies. Pakistan was still, of course, far from being democratic, but the BD structure did give the local communities a small measure of political as well as developmental power. Perhaps more importantly, it educated them to understand what they had not got. In any case, if power is the capacity to make trouble, they had gained a fair amount of it, and contributed to the fall of Ayub in 1969. It is ironical that he was perhaps a victim of the measures he had himself taken to involve the people in the processes of government. His fault was that he did not give them enough to satisfy their whetted appetites. Their mistake was that they did not bring about a radical change of the system.

Now, as this book goes to press, a year or so after the preceding pages were drafted, there is bitter conflict between East and West Pakistan. Much that had been achieved will undoubtedly be lost, and what can be recovered will depend on a long and difficult cycle of peacemaking, the nature and outcome of which are unpredictable.

6 Adamzadas and Faqir Mishkin: Chitral[19]

Chitral is a small state, autonomous in its internal affairs, but part of Pakistan in terms of such things as currency and foreign relations. It is embedded in vast mountains, the Pamirs, the Karakoram, and the Hindu Kush. In fact the highest peak of the Hindu Kush is in Chitral: Tirich Mir, over 25,000 feet. (The name of this range, incidentally, means 'killer of the Hindus', and if one has seen it one can understand why it is so named.) Chitral is about 100 miles long, a narrow finger touching China at its uttermost point, separated from Russia by the narrow Wakhan. Chitral consists of the valley (and surrounding mountains) of the river known in its various stretches as the Kunar, Chitral, Mastuj, or Yarkhun, and its tributaries. When I was there, Chitral had about 120,000 inhabitants. The origin of these people is obscure, but the evidence suggests that the original Chitralis were the same as the Kafirs who survive in a few valleys in the southern part of the country. (Kafir is the Arabic word for heathen, a name given to these people because they are not Muslim. There are two groups – the Black Kafirs or Kalash, and the Red Kafirs or Kati. The latter were mostly slaughtered by the Afghans at the end of the last century. Ironically, Kafiristan was renamed Nuristan – 'the place of light' – to indicate the conversion of the survivors to Islam, and the butchery of those who resisted.)

The modern history of Chitral might be said to have begun with the incursion of Mirza Ayub into the country sometime in the sixteenth century. Mirza Ayub was the great-grandson of an exiled king of Herat and a seventh-generation descendant of Timur. He himself was a *pir*, a holy man, who settled in Chitral with his devotees; subsequently his grandson, Sanghir Ali,

97

married a daughter of the ruling house. He died in 1570, one of the few firm dates in Chitrali history. His descendants composed the clan of Adamzada, or at least its top stratum. The Adamzadas are not permitted to work. Nominally their function is to follow their ruler into battle, but there are no battles now. They live off the labour of the peasant lower caste, the Faqir Mishkin, large numbers of whom are virtually their slaves. The most aristocratic Adamzadas pay few taxes, and the higher the grade of nobility, the less they pay; the top level are spared *ashimat*, a potentially crippling tax levied to support the ruler and his family. Directly or indirectly the Adamzadas are maintained by taxes amounting to approximately a tithe of all produce, and by virtual slave labour from the Faqir Mishkin. This unhappy caste is also impressed for what amounts to *corvée*, forced labour on the roads and bridges.

The Adamzadas have a gay and airy charm. They are excellent companions and lavish hosts. They also have an unmatched reputation for treacherous and lighthearted cruelty. Their history is a dreary succession of intricate feuds and struggles for petty advantages in which the closest kin – fathers, sons, brothers – have slain each other on the smallest pretext and without remorse. Many of the killings have been slow and bestial, showing an insensate love of cruelty. The great Chitrali families inhabit vast castles, perched like eagles' aeries on the crags. Here they live in uncouth magnificence. They rejoice in delicate Chinese silks, in falconry, and labyrinthine plots. Their minds are replete with fairy tales, memories of bloodshed, and complex resentments.

The Faqir Mishkin are grey and hungry; many have pendulous goitres, stretching almost down to their chests. The commonest cause of death among them is stomach blockage caused by eating grass, for there is a lean period before the harvest when the previous year's crop has been mostly consumed. If one lives in a bitter region of rock and moraine, at an altitude, as many do, of 10,000 feet, one cannot grow very much; and if, in addition, one is taxed in kind, the result is chronic famine.

Perhaps I may illustrate the character of life in Chitral from personal experience. My wife and I entered this state after a journey lasting several days from Hunza by way of Gilgit and the tiny princedoms of Ishkomen, Yasin, Punial, and Koh i Gizar. It was a strange and beautiful journey. Much of the way lay through deep ravines, huge mountains soared implacably above, angry torrents flowed hundreds of feet below. We rode along tracks which had been carved into the cliff's face. Sometimes they actually consisted of brushwood resting on a precarious foundation of stone slivers stuck into rock crevices. As we walked, the whole track would quiver. Sometimes the trails were no more than two feet wide and usually, if one was riding, one's outside knee hung over space. It was discouragingly evident that horses were not always surefooted. After several miles of this sort of journey the valley would widen and there would be a patch of more or less level land, sometimes extending for many acres, sometimes no more than a football pitch in size. There we would rest under the pleasant shade of trees – apricot, apple, or walnut. People lived there in low stone houses (in Chitral, where almost the only fuel is a sort of dried dock, houses were often so low, in order to preserve the heat, that we could not stand upright). These tiny settlements were real oases in a desert of granite and ice. They had a tender charm contrasting strangely with the desolate austerity of the rest of the journey – the landslide to be dodged, the rope bridges to be crossed, the torrents to be forded.

The last stage before Chitral was rather different. It led over a high, windy plateau – the Shandur Pass. The way up to the plateau was decked with alpine flowers; roses and irises grew by the side of streams. The plateau was jewelled with lakes. Yaks were playing there, cavorting like gay mythical creatures in the dawn of time. At the far side, however, the scene was at once more ugly. The Laspur valley into which we had to descend was overhung with dirty glaciers flowing down the flanks of Buni Zom, a moderately sized mountain of 21,000 feet.

The way down to Laspur was long and steep. When we reached the village, which from high above looked pleasant and welcoming, it turned out to be bleak and poverty stricken. The tiny houses were separated by rushing streams under the grey glacier, which cast an early shadow upon them. The three men who had come with us from Koh i Gizar unloaded the horses as quickly as they could and started up towards the pass, saying that the Chitralis were bad men. And so indeed it seemed. My wife and I sat uncertainly on our luggage as an obviously hostile group of villagers approached. They gesticulated angrily and shouted, but I was able to understand that their anger came from humiliation. We were visitors, but they had nothing to give us; they were hungry themselves. We told them not to worry, we would appreciate warmth, but did not need to eat. So a fire was lit in a tiny house and we all passed a friendly evening together – the first of three supperless evenings we spent in Chitral.

They arranged for horses to take us on the next day's journey to Mastuj and we were up and away before dawn, but already men with blankets wound around them were wandering like ghosts through the tiny fields and beside the rushing streams.

That evening we reached the great castle, vast mud walls enclosing orchards and courtyards, of one of the powerful families. The princeling who welcomed us had all the charm, cruelty, and madness of his caste. Courteous and helpful at first, as he fed us with fried chupatties under his apple trees, he became dangerous and threatening as the evening wore on. He regaled us with atrocious stories of poisonings, hangings upside down over slow fires, gradual and delicate cuttings up with sharp knives, dashings out of babies' brains, torturings of aunts, violations of grandmothers, butchery of trusting guests like ourselves. After each recital he laughed wildly, commenting with seeming approbation on the bloodiness, as he put it, of his people. The next morning he would not let us go. His mood had changed from expansive and excitable to sombre and laconic. No, he told us, he could not give us horses, there was no means of transportation. We wandered disconsolately outside the castle walls and he followed, smirking to himself. In the outer yard there was a polo band, consisting of a drummer and a pair playing instruments that looked like something between a clarinet and an oboe. Polo is said to have originated in this area (*polo* is the Tibetan for ball) and whenever it is played a band comments through its music on the state of the game – indicating that the home team has attacked strongly, the opposing captain has missed a pass, etc. As we came out the band played vigorously, though what it portended I do not know. However, our insane young host had by this time gathered a wild group of retainers. They wore sheepskin cloaks and carried short swords, and, as the youth giggled, grimaced, and pointed at us, they advanced steadily but, I felt, reluctantly.

My wife whispered that we were about to be killed and that the only way out was for me to behave like a colonel (the prince's father, like many of the hill nobles, had done his stint in the Indian army). I barked at him angrily and haughtily, and told him we had had enough of this tomfoolery; he had better get us horses straight away or it would be the worse for him. The effect was immediate. He almost shrivelled physically, and dismissed his men; and within a quarter of an hour we left. We rode fast for three days in case he recovered a vengeful nerve.

If ever there was an obnoxious system, based on a profound conflict of interest, that needed a revolution, it was Chitral in 1958. (I understand that things have changed somewhat since then.) But there was no awareness. No one – Adamzada, Faqir Mishkin, Yuft (the tiny middle class) – conceived that things could change. The life of Chitral was conducted in terms of what was understood and valued there. One could slightly improve one's personal position: if one was very fortunate, one could ease oneself upward from the top of the Yuft to the bottom of the Adamzada clan. One could have a somewhat better house or a little more to eat. But there were no political parties, no revolutionary *Zeitgeist*, to encourage ideas of change, let alone rebellion. There was no awareness of injustice, no hope of amelioration, no view of a wider world in which things were done differently. There was only hunger, oppression, misery, and the bleak aspirations of those who can hope for nothing more than enough to eat tomorrow.

7 The Chakmas and
the Common Good

In the most easterly region of the province of East Pakistan, abutting Assam and Burma, is an area known as the Chittagong Hill Tracts.[20] It is a remote and beautiful part, hard of access, and populated by tribal peoples very different from the Bengalis who inhabit almost all the rest of East Pakistan. While serving with the Pakistan Planning Commission, I heard rumours that some of these people would be affected by a dam being built on the Karnafuli River at Kaptai, on the edge of the Hill Tracts. The dam was being constructed with international help, technical and financial, and was supposedly going to confer great benefits on large numbers of people: it would supply electric power which would assist the development of industry; it would control the flooding of the river and facilitate navigation; and it would help irrigation projects. It appeared, however, that there was one disadvantage: the waters backed up by the dam would flood some of the valleys inhabited by the tribal people. But nobody in Karachi, where the Planning Commission was then located, knew much about it.

Admittedly Karachi, in West Pakistan, was 1,500 miles away. But in the capital of East Pakistan, Dacca, no one knew much about it either. In consequence, some colleagues and I decided to look into the matter on the spot.

We flew to Chittagong and drove thence by jeep to Rangamati, the capital of the Hill Tracts, where at length we began to discover a little more. So far as anyone was aware (and even the technicians were relatively ignorant, for much of the country was little known), the waters would back up almost to the border, flooding the steep narrow valleys for over fifty miles to the north-east. The people who would be affected were mostly the Buddhist tribe of the Chakmas and probably nearly 100,000 of them, virtually the whole nation (for so they considered themselves), would be dispossessed. At this time (although it was subsequently postponed) the catastrophe was a mere eighteen months away, yet nothing was being done except that an elderly civil servant of low rank was assessing the compensation to be paid to evicted families.

For several days we travelled, accompanied by the uncle of the young head of the nation, the Chakma Rai, in these doomed valleys. For the most part we went by jeep, but we crossed the rivers by country boat and once went several miles by elephant. We were at once saddened and captivated. The Chakmas were gay and welcoming. When our jeep got stuck they would push it out of the mud with much laughter and gusto. Whenever we arrived at a village we were besieged with invitations to drink rice wine in different houses. Most of the houses were built on stilts and on one occasion so many people came to see us that the house began to sway and finally collapsed gently to the ground. I was worried, but our host laughed and said that the house was getting old anyway and would soon have had to be rebuilt. Children played in the bright water of innumerable streams. Old men pottered around with hoes. Beautiful girls wove the cloths with which they sometimes covered their breasts. The people were not rich, but they were certainly not very poor or in great want. The valleys were extremely fertile and the people grew additional crops on the hillsides by the wasteful method of *jhuming*, that is, burning the forest and then cultivating. They were perfectly happy with their life. Only a handful had left the area to work in the great paper mill down the river, and of those who had gone away for education almost all had come eagerly home. The people were virtually all farmers, the markets being run by traders from the coast. My delight in Chakma society is not a defence of poverty and backwardness: I have spent much of my life trying to combat these things. I am simply saying that, when I met them, the Chakmas had been living a peaceful and happy life. All they wanted, they said, was food and freedom.

And that, until the dam was under construction, was what they had had. But by the time of our visit their happiness was undermined by anxiety. Nobody had actually told them anything, but they all knew that something, which was all the more awful for the uncertainty, was going to happen. Men had been going round making marks on trees and the Chakmas had watched, wondering and worrying.

We told them what we could, because they had a right to know and because, unless we could gauge their possible reactions, it was hard for us to make plans. One old man said that when the river flooded the ants climed the house posts and, when they could go no further, they were washed away: 'and so it will happen to us'. Others, more positive, said they would move across the frontier to Assam. A few intended to fight. The majority, however, shook their heads in bewildered despair. One thing was sure: if they were forced to abandon the valleys and take to the less fertile hills they would suffer not only physically from hunger and discomfort, but also socially, because their system of close-knit communities linked by kinship could not be maintained in the more scattered settlements that hill-farming would necessitate. It would mean the end of the nation as they knew it. We were witnessing almost the death of a people and, because of our official position, we felt like murderers by association.

Ironically, the official policy of the British, and subsequently of the Pakistanis, had been to keep the Hill Tracts isolated, 'unspoilt'. The administrators, like ourselves, had found the gaiety and innocence of these people most appealing, and had tried to keep them from the 'corrupting' influence of the coastal towns. Permission to enter the Hill Tracts was not lightly given and the hill tribesmen were not encouraged to leave the area. This was fine as long as it lasted, but when the modern world, in the shape of the dam, burst in on them – as it was bound to sooner or later in one form or another – they had few skills of mind or hand to forge an alternative existence.

On the way back to Dacca we spent a night at the dam site. Here, huge machines cut deep wounds in the red earth and labourers in their thousands carried away the debris in baskets on their heads. We were entertained in an antiseptic mess hall – it might have been anywhere in the world – on hamburgers and ketchup, while the engineers verified the Chakmas' approaching disaster.

This story illustrates a moral problem. How much suffering for how many can be justified by how much good for how many? In this case, how does one match the long-term economic gain from the dam for East Pakistan as a whole (and hence perhaps also for the Chakmas) against the immediate loss, disruption, and despair for 100,000 human beings? The difficulty of the problem was compounded by the fact that the advantages of the dam, until actualized, were conjectural. How could we be sure that the additional wealth (if indeed it came) would not go mainly into the pockets of foreign investors or already wealthy merchants and industrialists? If it did so, we might assume that it would enable them to undertake fresh enterprises providing employment and greater riches for increasing numbers, but it was all rather tenuous. On the other hand, the damage to the Chakmas was all too concrete and immediate. In the last resort, I suppose, we try to assess an issue of this sort by two entirely different kinds of criteria. The value of the dam can be estimated in terms of the predominantly Western standards of economic development. But the disruption of the Chakma people is a question of human suffering and of the right to a particular way of life. These two sets of 'measurements' are on different scales, which cannot be compared. In any event, whatever the advantages of the dam, the callous laxity of the authorities in taking no measures to reduce the extent of the disaster they were causing could not be excused.

There was little that could be done to make the relationship more peaceful. Clearly the construction of the dam would continue: millions had already been spent and enormous contracts signed. All we could do was to stir up concern about the fate of the Chakmas in the hope that steps would be taken to minimize the effects of the catastrophe. We wrote a document for the Planning Commission and ensured that it had wide circulation among influential people. In this report we emphasized that not only the Chakmas' livelihood, but their traditional existence as a people was in jeopardy. We then outlined various measures that might help them to survive.

We said that the country must be surveyed (much of it was virtually unexplored) to locate new sites for Chakma settlements; that these sites must be made accessible by new roads, and that they must also be prepared by earth-moving equipment, since many would be in rough and forested terrain. The sites would have to be both large enough and sufficiently close to each other to preserve the social structure.

Since the fertile valleys would no longer be available for farming, alternative means of livelihood would have to be found. The lakes formed by the dam should be stocked with fish (but the Chakmas, when we suggested this, said they would be too afraid of crocodiles to fish; there are no crocodiles). Lake-shore cultivation should be undertaken in the dry season when the water was low. Cash crops should be grown and marketed on the coast, which would now be much more accessible by water. Suitable cottage industries should be promoted. Terrace cultivation of the hillsides to which the Chakmas would have to retreat should be substituted for the prodigal and destructive *jhuming*. A difficulty here was that there was practically no stone (throughout East Pakistan roads are made of bricks which are first baked and then broken for the purpose), and so experts would have to be brought over from Indonesia and other places with similar problems to advise on appropriate methods. And so on.

We advocated training the Chakmas in community development, to assist them in making all these changes. We also recommended a general expansion of education in the hope that a more lettered population would be better able to cope with the adjustments it would have to make in order to survive. Previously, living in a benevolent environment, the people had been well served by the old ways. Now they would need the skills of the twentieth century.

Finally, and most importantly, we advocated the establishment of a specific agency responsible for the resettlement of the Chakmas.

A committee was in fact set up by the government of East Pakistan and I attended some of its meetings, but as I write, thirteen years after my visit and eight years after the commissioning of the dam, it seems that our fears were largely justified and our efforts largely wasted. This I gather from my friends Barbara and John Thomas, to whom I am greatly indebted. They visited the area early in 1970 and sent me the information on which the following paragraphs are based. It may be of interest that I wrote the preceding part of this chapter before hearing from them.

Serious efforts were indeed made to resettle the Chakmas physically in newly developed areas. The first of these was a place called Marisha. The jungle was cleared, and the people were evacuated to it; they built houses and began to settle in. But the waters rose higher than the engineers had anticipated, flooding the new town and necessitating a further evacuation. There is now a model town of about 30,000 inhabitants at Kasalong, and there are several lakeside villages perched on the hillsides as well as other settlements deeper inland.

To further economic rehabilitation the government has promoted and provided loans for a number of agricultural developments, particularly the growing of pineapples, bananas, and cashew nuts, but these affect a relatively small number of people. Fishing in the lake has been encouraged and assisted by the provision of equipment, but the Chakmas have not taken to it very readily. In addition, the government has set up schools for weaving (a traditional skill of the Chakmas) and carpentry. Finally, there has been cash compensation for the loss of land and property, but it is said that since these people had very little experience of a cash economy they failed to make good use of the money; they were more apt to squander it on such attractive items as portable radios than to invest it for their future wellbeing. All in all, the compensation and the craft and agricultural projects have simply not made up for the loss of 54,000 acres of paddy land now under water. There is a general impression (no statistics are available) that the Chakmas are poorer than they were. This is emphatically asserted by educated Chakmas.

The Chakma social system seems to have suffered just as much as we feared it would. As Barbara Thomas puts it: 'The once close-knit society has been fragmented. Kinship clusters formerly in adjacent villages have been dispersed throughout the hills. The immense lake makes it more difficult to have rapid, convenient and easy communication between the separate groups.' In general there is a lessened sense of community, and attendance at formerly popular gatherings has greatly diminished. The atmosphere in the villages is described by Mrs Thomas as listless. Although she notes, as I did, the friendliness and hospitality of the people, she is struck by their 'languid passivity' – a term that could never have been applied to them in the past – and was informed that they were depressed to a point of being unable to plan, cope with their problems, or act decisively.

In this way the Chakmas have been sacrificed to the common good. From my knowledge of comparable cases I expect that the situation will deteriorate and that in another thirteen years the Chakmas will have virtually ceased to exist as a people. It is particularly ironical that their sacrifice has been at least partially in vain. The great dam which, among other things, was supposed to control downstream flooding, has in fact contributed to it. Waters have risen higher since the completion of the dam than ever before because in heavy rain the lake collects water far more quickly than did the river. This is discharged rapidly, and with disastrous results, through the spillway.

Lastly, it is pertinent to ask for whom the Chakmas were immolated. It was not, as we have just seen, for the farmers who lived below the dam. Was it for the many poor Bengalis who lived elsewhere in the area? Possibly: for although they would not themselves use much electricity, they might benefit from the industrial development facilitated by power. There might be more and better jobs available to them, and they might be helped indirectly by increased productivity and wealth in their area. On the other hand the ripple effect is not inevitable: everything depends on the longer political and economic framework. Would the already rich industrialists profit from the power produced by the dam? Undoubtedly. Would the foreign interests associated with them also profit? Undoubtedly. It depends upon one's point of view whether one considers the anguish and destruction of the Chakma people to have been justified.

B. WESTERN COUNTRIES

8 Francis and Hilary
A Marriage

Francis and Hilary were married very young. Francis's father had
been killed in World War II and Francis had been brought up,
the only child, by a somewhat doting mother. She was not a
rapacious or a cannibalistic woman. She always claimed, and at
one level of her mind believed, that she wanted her son to be
independent of her, to marry early, to father happy children and
experience the joys of a family life she had scarcely known. She
came of an old Scottish family and combined a certain religious
inflexibility with rigid ideas of what a husband should expect of
his wife: loyalty, unswerving obedience, acceptance of all that he
did (except, of course, sexual infidelity or aberrations, which
should be met with resignation).

Francis was essentially high spirited and normal, but inevitably
he had accepted his mother's view of the relation between the
sexes. He had also accepted her evaluation of himself, which was
as biased as that of most widowed mothers of good-natured and
handsome only sons. Into the bargain, he had been to a boys'
school where he had learnt little about girls except some distorted
dirt.

Hilary was not equipped to counteract the combined impact of
Francis and his mother; if she had been, she probably would not
have married him. She was the gentle, diffident, and experienced
second daughter of a large family, who thought that Francis was
marvellous and that it was a miracle that he should have fallen in
love with her.

They got married and their sexual life was rather drab, but neither of them realized the fact. Their relationship was drab too, because they did not know how to get the most out of each other (both were constrained by false images of themselves and of their partner). Francis believed that the role of the husband was to be very much the master of the house, and, conversely, that the role of the wife was to be largely subject to her husband. He acted on these beliefs. It is not surprising that he had no idea of companionship apart from what he had learnt from his mother and this, as he matured, had increasingly come to mean separate development (as the South Africans say), linked by a few overlapping concerns. So he had his work, his sport, and his male friends, and she (he presumed) had her domestic affairs, her civic and/or good works, and her girl friends; the overlap occurred in bed, in the meals they ate together, in their joint social engagements, and in the child they eventually produced.

Hilary spent a great deal of time alone and this, coupled with her inadequate sexual life, made her dissatisfied. She was restless and unhappy – and felt guilty because of her unhappiness; she felt that she was being disloyal to her husband, that she didn't appreciate him, that she was a bad wife. Finally she was driven to consult the only authority she knew, the minister of their church. This poor young man didn't know much more than she did. To make things harder, he was attracted to her himself. In consequence, although he put it gently and even sweetly, he took a hard line. The wife was subject to the husband; she must obey him; she must control all frivolous and worldly thoughts and desires. Hilary was being tempted, he said. Francis was a fine young man, a regular communicant, all a wife could ask for; only the Devil could be making her dissatisfied. She must pray, thank God for her blessings, and so on. All this Hilary did and eventually reached a sort of tranquillity, though she felt no better inwardly.

About three years after her marriage Hilary had a visit from her younger sister, Beth. This young woman had been doing graduate work at an American university and had married a Canadian she had met there. The sisters had seen little of one another since they were schoolgirls. It was while her husband was on a botanical expedition that Beth took the opportunity to come to stay with Hilary for a month.

After two weeks Beth could contain herself no longer. 'What's wrong with you?' she exclaimed. 'You seem half dead.'

Hilary was at first shocked, then defensive; then she began to admit that marriage, for her, had difficulties and disappointments.

'Well,' said Beth, 'I think it's like that for everyone; nothing's perfect. But we find there's very little that can't be put right in bed. There's nothing like the profound intimacy of sex for correcting the perspective.'

Hilary said nothing for a few moments. Then she smiled rather sadly, saying, 'I suppose I've never had it.'

This admission was the beginning. For several days, in the intervals of caring for their babies, and doing housework and shopping, they questioned each other and compared notes. Bit by bit Hilary became convinced that her marriage, which (if this is not a contradiction) she had considered to be both standard and ideal, was neither. Beth had a very different life and so, it seemed, did most of her friends, though some of them made the most monumental mistakes – but here, too, they were different from Hilary because they admitted their mistakes and took drastic corrective action. Beth and her husband were lovers. They hated to be apart and when they were together they had a gay, wild, and companionable time interspersed with bouts of vigorous lovemaking. They shared. There was no caste difference, for them, between wife and husband; they were a team in which each did what he or she best could for the other and enjoyed doing it. Their child, and they hoped there would be more, was being brought up as a member of the same team.

Hilary slowly began to understand what she was missing and a small core of resentment began to build up within her. She became somewhat terse and difficult with Francis who, poor fellow, could not imagine what was happening. So he also went to the minister who, in turn, tackled Hilary, who sent him off with a flea in his ear. She has changed, he thought sadly, and so she had; she had become aware.

Beth was joyfully reunited with her husband and they went off together to establish a botanical research station in British Columbia and to raise a tough, healthy family. But the seeds Beth had planted in her sister's mind were germinating.

One evening, after several days of an atmosphere laden with muted bad temper, Hilary nerved herself to talk to Francis about it. He tried to brush it off, but she, for once, did not give in. 'You must listen to me,' she cried desperately, and it began to come out with a rush.

Francis reacted with hurt withdrawal and Hilary almost gave in, almost said, 'I'm sorry, darling, it's all my fault; I have been self-willed and egotistical. Forget it and forgive me.' But she didn't. Instead, she said, 'I'm terribly sorry if I have hurt you, but our marriage is at stake and I had to. I am somehow not becoming a proper person, and if I can't be a proper person I can't be a proper wife either, so I'm not just saying this for me but for you too. Please understand me and help me.'

Francis was moved and said he would, but all the same he felt threatened, as though some of his autonomy had been eroded. It was as though his freedom of action was in some way founded on Hilary's subservience. He was accustomed to and needed someone who would treat him like a god and so repair the ravages of self-doubt bequeathed him by his over-protective mother.

What Hilary wanted was the sort of life her sister had. She wanted to do things with her husband; she longed for them to participate in each other's lives as fully as possible. Beth and her husband were each autonomous human beings who were, nevertheless, interdependent. Hilary, on the other hand, had no adequate life of her own, and very little autonomy. She was dependent in almost all things on her husband's outlook and habit of life, but there was little interdependence. Instead of interdependence, there was interaction. Francis and Hilary responded, often with irritation or resentment, to each other's moods, but there was no mutual reinforcement, no common quest for common goals. Hilary felt this, but could not really convey it to Francis. If he glimpsed the truth, it made him anxious. He felt criticized and menaced and, since these are unpleasant feelings, he managed to displace them by blaming Hilary. It was she who was demanding and unreasonable; he had nothing to reproach himself for.

In consequence, Hilary's attempts to share her life with Francis, to involve him in her interests and to be involved in his, were abortive and short lived. Her concerns meant little to him and he was suspicious of her effort to enter his world. The more she tried, the worse their relationship became. Hilary became bitterly discouraged. At times she almost wished that Beth had never opened the door onto another world. Her awareness had brought her nothing but frustration and disappointment. She no longer enjoyed the spurious peace she had had in her early married days, and she had gained very little in its place.

But Hilary was becoming tougher. If she could not build a satisfying life with Francis, she would build one by herself. She began quite firmly to lead her own existence. If there was a film or a play she wanted to see, she went to it. She visited old friends. She left Francis's supper in the oven and went out to evening classes or to the local opera group. She paid for baby-sitters out of the housekeeping money. It was not a very dramatic rebellion, but it was a firm one. She stood up for her right to be independent, if she could not be interdependent, with good nature but without yielding to Francis's sulks or protests that things had changed; they certainly had.

Before long, as might have been expected, she became fond of a young man. She had met him at an English literature class. When the first heady excitement had somewhat died down, she suddenly became apprehensive and took sober stock. Her marriage, she realized, was in a precarious state. She also realized that she did not want it to collapse, that she still loved Francis and would rather have a good relationship with him than with anyone else. Francis, when she told him, was equally worried, but neither of them could really communicate with the other; there was too much resentment, self-pity, guilt, and anxiety for either to see the other with any clarity.

Once again Francis approached the minister, but this time the good man, declining to intervene, recommended a psychiatrist skilled in marriage guidance. Hilary and Francis both agreed, somewhat sceptically, to see the psychiatrist, but they came away impressed. He did not, of course, take sides; neither did he offer advice. Instead, he tried to help them to understand their own feelings and motives. As they began to see themselves more clearly they became able to throw away the distorting lens of emotional self-interest. Consequently, Francis began to see Hilary as she really was, while she began to come to terms with her role as a wife. They became able to discuss their joint and individual problems amicably and constructively. One day Hilary suddenly understood that what she had always wanted had begun to happen: they were sharing each other's lives.

Of course, these things took time and the changes were gradual, almost imperceptible. But as Francis's and Hilary's perception of each other changed, the character of their relationship changed also: they took a greater interest in each other's doings (Hilary did not renounce her new-found concerns) and they did much more together. Their relationship of interdependence is still developing.

The reader may have identified already the stages, the different types of relationship, unpeaceful and eventually peaceful, through which Hilary and Francis passed.

Initially theirs was a conflict relationship (since Francis restricted Hilary's freedom) of the type 'unbalanced/lower awareness of conflict'. Hilary received her education (in the sense in which the word is used here, to imply 'making aware') from Beth, and the relationship moved into the category 'unbalanced/higher awareness of conflict'. The role of the minister was to attempt to conceal the conflict, to establish something like 'pseudo-balance/lower awareness of conflict'. Hilary did not respond, however, and confronted Francis with her need for a relationship based on greater reciprocity, that is to say, balance. When he was unable to accept this new form of relationship, she in fact rebelled and took equality by force despite his disapproval and opposition. After a stormy period, a third-party conciliator, in the person of the psychiatrist, was able to change their perceptions of each other. It should be noted that the minister had also attempted to act as a conciliator, but at a stage of the unpeaceful relationship when conciliation could only mean reconciliation to an unhappy lot. Conciliation applied at such a stage is comparable to drugs that suppress the symptoms of a disease but do not cure it. Perhaps, though I do not know for sure, there was a period of bargaining as distinct from conciliation, but I suspect that the concessions and rearrangements almost automatically accompanied the change of perceptions. There was definitely, however, a phase of development in which Hilary and Francis, who had so nearly parted for good, restructured what had been separate lives into a joint existence.

9 Returned Prisoners of War and their Society[21]

One of the most interesting examples of large-scale social therapy concerned British soldiers who had been captured during World War II.

The great bulk of these were taken prisoner in the summer of 1940 when France fell, and early in 1942 when Malaya was over-run. Most of them were not repatriated until the summer of 1945. However, a few escaped or were exchanged before this time. These men, many of them the 'best' soldiers in terms of courage and initiative, proved to be restless and ill disciplined on their return. They were at odds with the army and with their families, and their record of delinquency, both civil and military, was serious. Clearly, the end of the war would present a major problem in terms of the resettlement of tens of thousands of prisoners of war. The word 'resettlement', rather than 'rehabilitation', was used to describe their problem for the precise reason that their condition was essentially one of unsettlement. The men were confused and restless. They found it hard to re-establish contact with family and friends from whom they had become estranged by the gulf of years of unshared experience. Many found it hard to stick at their civilian jobs; many marriages broke up; there was a high incidence of psychosomatic disorders. Fortunately, a number of senior military officers, who had themselves been prisoners during World War I, took a particular interest in the question and, by the time the ex-prisoners started to come back in large numbers from German or Japanese captivity, an army organization called Civil Resettlement Units (CRUs) had been created. Before describing this organization, it is necessary to diagnose the returned-prisoner-of-war syndrome.

Essentially, these men had been removed from their society and, having made an adjustment to a new society, had become alienated from the old one. To begin with they had moved from civilian to military life. This in itself, as I too had learnt, is a dramatic change. The average non-soldier plays many roles in his society: he is a husband, a son, a father, a worker, an employer, an employee, a neighbour, a member of various organizations, a citizen who votes and pays taxes. He belongs to a society composed of both sexes, young and old, whose members are engaged in an infinite variety of activities having many different goals. But the soldier, in his one-sex world, abandons most of his civilian roles. Of course he is still a member of a family, still a citizen, and so on, but military roles are so clustered about the main occupational objective – to destroy the enemy – that all others grow dim. The army provides work, clothing, recreation, food, entertainment, comrades with whom a strong male solidarity is forged, ritual, hierarchy and objectives within the hierarchy, and, above all, discipline and purpose. The old life becomes slightly unreal by comparison.

When a man's unit goes overseas and particularly when it moves into the front line, where his life depends constantly upon the vigilance and resourcefulness of a small group of companions, his identification and involvement with them become amazingly close. His roles are few, but clear cut, forged out of the exigencies of battle. His human relationships are those of the soldierly interdependence of comrades in arms within the structure of rank (a relationship can be thought of as behaviour within a role). His values centre on loyalty to the men on whom his life depends and for whom he would give his own life. Even when he returns unscathed from the war it is difficult for him to weaken these roles and relationships as he moves back into civilian life, reassuming his old roles and rebuilding his former relationships. Few men, however unmilitary they may be, have made the transition smoothly.

The former prisoners of war, however, had additional difficulties to contend with. Many laboured under painful emotions in which guilt for having been captured and resentment against those who had not suffered as they had were inextricably interwoven. A large number had been away from home for five years, with very little chance of communicating with their families. They relied all the more closely, therefore, on their fellow-captives for closeness and support. Prison-camp conditions were such that a man had only two alternatives: either (and rarely) he cut himself off from his fellows, becoming a lonely and usually sick isolate, or he was very strongly united to the group.

During their captivity these men were still at war. Their military duty was to make life as hard for their captors as they could and to escape where possible. They also had to preserve their health and morale in circumstances of discomfort and deprivation. This situation made for a singularly warm and close-knit community which was, moreover, highly democratic. Rank became much less important since it no longer related to the complex divisions of normal military existence (in any case, officers and men were separated in the German camps). Instead, the cohesion of the community depended upon freely given participation. Men learnt a new dimension of loyalty and unity which, despite their painful and often appalling circumstances, had great value for them. It was, however, a source of additional strain when they returned to a society in which these newly discovered values of human conduct were not recognized and in which relationships followed a norm that was more stereotyped, more lopsided (or perhaps less egalitarian), and less altruistic. It was bad enough for these men to be unable to convey what they had suffered. For many it was even worse to be unable to describe what they had learnt. Given, in addition, their inevitable separation from their society, the result was that they felt completely estranged. More particularly, they felt alienated from those who should have been closest to them, who – because they could not understand, and because one expects most from those one loves most – were now felt to have failed them utterly. Some men withdrew from the society they no longer related to; they left their jobs and their homes. Others remained, but in body rather than in spirit. This withdrawal did not happen at once. There was normally a jubilant reunion, but the excitement wore off after a few weeks, and a grey reaction set in. Some men escaped it by returning to the army, for although this was the organization almost all of them, theoretically, wanted to leave, it was also the one they understood. Its rules were practical and unequivocal. A man knew where he was in the army and many retreated to it from the unexpected emotional hazards of civilian life. Naturally, such behaviour tended to arouse perplexed resentment at home. Did he not love his family any more? Was there another woman? Had he changed? He had, indeed, but in a fashion it was hard to understand. An important task for the CRUs was to help not only the men but also their families to comprehend what had happened.

For these reasons it was appropriate that the army, through its Civil Resettlement Units, should take on the task of reconnecting these men to civilian society; it was trusted, and it was safe. Nevertheless, the nature of traditional military discipline was even more antithetical to the new 'democratic' insights of the prison camp than was society at large. It seemed vital that these insights be preserved since they apparently constituted the growing-edge of what was otherwise an utterly grim experience. Without what has been termed (by Eric Trist) the creative aspect of the casualty there would be much less hope for eventual resettlement. Therefore the part of the army that was concerned with resettlement would have to be, in certain fundamental ways, different from the rest of it.

Of prime importance was the principle of consistency. If what a man had gained from his prisoner-of-war existence was to be retained and strengthened, it was held, the whole ambience of the new experience must be directed towards that end. His capacity for freely chosen participation must be preserved; and for this reason there could be no compulsion. Accordingly, entry to the institution was entirely voluntary. It was argued by some that men who were disturbed could not tell what sort of treatment, if any, they needed, and that they should be made to attend a CRU, but the prevailing view was that this would constitute an inner contradiction which might vitiate the whole course of resettlement. For similar reasons, within the CRUs there was no formal discipline. This applied also, for the sake of consistency, to the clerks, cooks, and others on the staff who had not been prisoners of war. All programmes and facilities were voluntary; there was no penalty for non-attendance at any CRU activity. The aim was to create an environment which provided, on the one hand, safety, understanding, and stability, and, on the other, a sufficient degree of permissiveness to enable a man to experiment with his capacity for freedom and to extend it from the known atmosphere of the army to the more uncertain environment of civilian life.

At the peak period of need there were twenty CRUs containing, at any one time, about 240 men. The average length of a man's stay was four weeks, but, if it was considered desirable, men stayed longer. Many had serious practical problems and these were dealt with kindly and efficiently. There were welfare officers who assisted with uncomprehended problems relating to rationing (which covered furniture and clothes as well as food); with the spate of postwar regulations; with the difficulties inherent in scarce housing; and with the agonizing issues of broken homes or motherless children. Medical teams dealt with health problems occasioned by privation, war injuries, or strain; frequently, men who would have feared or scorned to visit a psychiatrist took advantage of an apparently physical condition to seek psychological advice. Employment problems were tackled in several ways. Vocational aptitude tests were given; Ministry of Labour officials provided information on jobs; and furthermore, local employers were enlisted to give short-term employment, called job rehearsals, to men who were then able to test their aptitudes and inclinations. There were workshops in which men often experienced a sort of occupational therapy; it can be comforting to do something with one's hands when one's mind is troubled. Sometimes an act of material creation restores self-confidence to a man who doubts his ability – since he cannot live happily at home – to do anything.

Men were sent to the unit nearest their homes so that they could visit their families at weekends and family members could visit the CRU, thus gaining further insight into problems of resettlement. This reaching out into the home, and indeed into the community as a whole, was perhaps one of the most valuable features of the CRUs. A man might not be able, alone and unhelped, to face the problems of readjustment to his family, but from the safe, secure base of the unit he might be able to transfer his dawning self-awareness to the home scene. Eventually, most men were able to return to their homes and resume happily their familial roles. The job rehearsals constituted, of course, an additional means of establishing connections with society as well as a means of trying out different sorts of work.

The community of the unit itself had a therapeutic character. The staff, officers and men, delighted in their remedial role, perhaps because it offered a complete contrast with their prime function of destruction over the previous years. Officers conducted group discussions which, though employing only a crude and early version of group-therapy techniques, gave a valuable chance of releasing tension and gaining awareness. Perhaps the most effective agents of therapy, their own and that of others, were the men themselves. As each fresh weekly intake of about sixty came in, a previous intake took care of them and felt great pride in helping with the process of reconnection.

If a man's view of his own society with its complex of roles, relationships, and culture patterns has lost its meaning for him, if its internalized values are seen as relative or worthless, it is reasonable to expect that his alienation will show itself in his relations with others. Likewise, if a process of resettlement is to have any real therapeutic effect, these roles and relationships will be restored and have a richer content. It should be possible, therefore, to estimate the extent to which a man has become re-settled by the character of his relationships with family, neighbours, employers, and so on.

Thus I anticipated, for I was serving as research officer to the CRUs, that if men were satisfactorily readjusted their relations with their associates might be expected to be less one-sided and less demanding, less dominated by their own driving psychological needs for reassurance or for proving themselves or whatever it might be. These relationships would be more open, more participant in the sense of the pattern we had attempted to build up in the CRUs, more relaxed, based more on mutual understanding and on an attempt to help. During the course of my research I had intensive interviews with 150 former prisoners of war, together with their families, neighbours, and, in most cases, employers. Gradually, several patterns of relations emerged. The men who were apparently most disturbed according to a variety of criteria – who refused to obtain work, who were anxious, aggressive, or depressed, who had separated from their wives, or who were receiving treatment for what had appeared to be psychological symptoms – had relationships with others that were dominated by their own problems. The other people in the relationships had little significance for them except as persons who aggravated or assuaged their pain; if one is completely dominated by one's own difficulties, one has little appreciation of the problems of others. Consequently, there was a kind of lonely rigidity about these men which only compounded their basic distress, for what they needed most of all was a closeness they were unable to accept or acknowledge. It was possible to identify several stages in the deterioration of such relationships and it seemed that in many cases an initial failure was experienced in a man's contact with his immediate family, which came to colour his attitude towards the community at large.

The local community was included in my study and I was interested to discover that those modes of behaviour that represented the most unsettled condition were also looked upon by the local community as being undesirable. It was notable, however, that the traditional culture of the community was characterized by behavioural conventions that severely limited the growth of richly interacting relationships. For example, the idea of cooperation between husband and wife in such homely tasks as house decoration, dish-washing, or gardening was despised. Each member of the family had his allotted sphere and to trespass into another, or to ask for help in one's particular task, was seldom tolerated. Modes of behaviour that have once served to organize society along harmonious lines often persist after their usefulness has declined and then serve only to inhibit flexible adjustment to changing circumstances. In the difficult conditions of postwar Europe it seemed to me fairly clear that many couples were in fact making life much more difficult for themselves by failing to make use of the potentiality of their relationship. For example, if a wife were unable to go out shopping for some good reason, the husband would not go instead, and the whole family would be reduced to eating unappetizing scraps for dinner. Likewise, the household might be upset for days while the husband carried out some piece of decoration on his own which could have been done in half the time if the wife had agreed to help. Relations with neighbours and other family members tended to be somewhat formal, based on a set of conventions that were almost stylized in their attention to traditional forms.

In contrast with the behaviour of these ordinary citizens, the behaviour of a certain group of former prisoners showed considerably more adaptability and cooperativeness than was normal for their neighbours who had not suffered captivity. In the families of this group there was, I found, an extraordinary degree of vigour and creativity, and I sensed that here were men who had really discovered how to get the most out of relationships, who had broken the bonds of conventional restriction that keep many from developing a rich and varied communion with a wife or a child. It was significant that these persons were much admired and perhaps envied by members of a community who did not emulate their behaviour but who were prepared to respect it, apparently seeing in it a desirable form of adaptation.

Statistical analysis of behaviour patterns in fifteen different types of relationship showed that the men who had developed the more participant type of relation were predominantly those who had spent some time in a CRU, whereas those whose behaviour was in varying degrees disturbed tended to be those who had not had this particular form of experience. There was a continuum in terms of the degree of flexibility and participation they showed in their relationships, from returned prisoners who had been to a CRU, through the control group of community members who had not been prisoners at all, to those former prisoners who had not volunteered to attend a resettlement unit.

Some conclusions may perhaps be drawn from this connective process of the CRUs and the subsequent degree of resettlement.

The initial trauma of military service caused a painful loss of contact with the home community, but at the same time it laid the foundations of a broader adjustment based on an understanding and acceptance of differences rather than on an identification with a particular set of norms. Subsequent experiences heightened both tendencies. The shock and the separation of captivity set men at a great emotional distance from their homes while the participant and democratic culture of the prison camp gave strength to values which (as shown by the control group) were much less valid at home. Thus when a man returned he was very far from his society. He was often so far removed from it that when an occasion of friction arose with his wife, employer, or neighbour, he had no means of bridging the gulf. He could no longer handle the tools of his own culture to reach a settlement and would quarrel bitterly and irreparably, leaving home or job, or breaking all communication with his neighbour. In one sense, the role of the CRUs was to bring him close enough to his society to make it possible for inevitable differences and quarrels to be settled peaceably, without rupturing relations completely. As a man became reconnected with his society he was eventually able to drop his protective mask and to view the world around him objectively, not as a mirage reflecting the shimmering distortions of his own fears and pains. Because the inner hold of the culture upon him had weakened, he was also able to adopt new and more realistic modes of behaviour, but this was not possible until the more painful effects of his captivity had been reduced. Up to this point, his newly won awareness did more to exasperate and frustrate him than to help him to adjust.

In this process there is a constant tension between the need to be close and the need to be, in some respects, detached; between the need to be involved in relationships, for without this nothing can be achieved, and the need to be able to view them dispassionately. Objectivity is essential, for without it we become so identified with forms and traditions as to lose all power of movement and change.

10 Employers and Employees: the Firm

This case concerns a commercial undertaking which, for the sake of anonymity and brevity, I shall refer to as the Firm. The Firm maintained, not far from the place of work, a residential estate for some 200 families of its 300 employees. The directors, who were genuinely concerned about the welfare of their people, had provided every sort of amenity: there were sports grounds, swimming baths, a school, a community centre, and many other facilities for recreation, entertainment, and instruction. Above all, the directors maintained a close personal interest in their employees. The general conditions of work and employment were excellent, as were working relations at all levels, and there had never been the slightest suspicion of labour unrest or overt dissatisfaction. However, despite circumstances as pleasant as goodwill and intelligence could make them, there was a subtle undercurrent of tension. Frank complaints were rare, and were never made against the directors themselves, but fantastic rumours would circulate from group to group, and there were veiled mutterings about favouritism. Many people seemed to be obscurely and unnecessarily uneasy, scared of speaking out, and there was a general failure to make use of the remarkable facilities provided.

I was a member of a group which was invited by the directors to look into the situation. The first task was to attempt to locate the origin of these feelings of unease, which seemed so at variance with the objective reality of an almost ideal situation. After several weeks of talking, and particularly of listening, I became convinced that the directors, in their attempts to create such perfect conditions, had come to assume too much importance in the lives of their employees.

Most employers are responsible only for work, but the directors of the Firm were responsible for home conditions as well. This led to rather complex attitudes towards them. At one level they were held in great personal regard. People wanted to please them and laboured hard to this end (though I sometimes had the feeling that their motives were tinged with a childlike need to please all-powerful parents). Many employees and their families were genuinely appreciative of all that had been done on their behalf, but out of these positive feelings grew others less constructive. The first was a sense that criticism was ungrateful and therefore to be suppressed. The second was a sort of dependency on the directors. There was one specific component to this dependency: people working for the Firm lived in the Firm's houses, but only as long as they were employed by it; thus if they lost their jobs they lost their homes and all the amenities they had come to value. At a period of general housing shortage this situation created great anxiety. In a community in which so much depended on a few important persons, people came to feel that any criticism was dangerous, for it might lead to dismissal and the loss of a house. This was perhaps rational, but the reasonableness was somehow undermined by a strange additional fear of rejection: losing a job and, consequently, a house – serious enough in themselves – symbolized rejection by the director–parents. There was also much concern about the way houses were allocated to employees. The directors made the allocations and jealously guarded the right to do so because, as they reasonably maintained, their ability to allocate accommodation affected their ability to hire, which was clearly their business. Housing, in fact, was a key issue in a practical sense and came to have an even wider symbolic significance in the director–employee relationship: a high percentage of the rumours and resentments concerned alleged partiality.

For all these reasons, many feelings were bottled up, becoming in the process morbid and irrational. It is not to be wondered at that people were less contented than at first sight they might have been expected to be. Since they could not express their fears, a gulf developed between them and the directors. Everyone tried to conceal the gulf. It was camouflaged by parties and politeness, but many people on both sides knew it was there and were pained by it.

My role in this situation was partly as researcher and partly as conciliator (as I now see it) or group therapist (as I would have termed it then). My job was to try to create a situation in which each side perceived the other more realistically. It seemed to me that, since the conflict had grown out of the particular relationship that existed between the employees and the directors, something must be done to alter the shape of that relationship if the mutual perceptions of the two groups were to alter and the conflict situation be changed.

A committee known as the Amenities Committee seemed to me the appropriate vehicle for this change. It was composed of employees, although its chairman was a director, and was supposed to deal with all issues affecting the community. It could, theoretically, have concerned itself with most of the difficulties around which rumours and resentments had grown up, but it was an atrophied organization seldom representing the feelings of its members and preoccupied usually with such harmless subjects as children's Christmas parties. The meetings were bland and innocuous social gatherings at which business of little moment was transacted. Tea was drunk, bread and butter and cake were consumed, and there was polite discussion of trivial issues. Nevertheless, it was empowered by its constitution to deal with important issues and so could be used to alter the structure of the relations between the employees and the Firm in such a way as to ease the present negative situation.

A common term in much contemporary discussion of conflict is confrontation. It was not much employed at the time when I undertook my work with the Firm and its employees, but in effect I tried to stage a confrontation between the two groups. They had, as I suggested, grown very far apart in terms of psychological distance. So far were they separated by a complex combination of anxiety and guilt on the part of the employees that they could not communicate. The monthly meetings of the Amenities Committee might have provided a setting for a confrontation, but they did not do so because the emotional gulf could not be bridged. My task, then, was to bring them to the point where they could confront each other, that is to say, express feelings towards each other, and, it was to be hoped, find some common way out of their difficulties.

I spent a considerable amount of time over a period of about two months talking with members of the Amenities Committee, individually and in groups, and collectively at meetings of the Committee. Initially, we discussed things very impersonally. The employees expressed the formal, almost official view that everything was fine; no one had any complaints. I did not press them, but as they came to know me better and ceased to fear that I was some sort of agent of the directors, they became more open. Concealed fears and inner resentments were voiced. The employees' view of the directors became clearer: as individuals they were kind and helpful; as a group they were unpredictable and touchy. Their deliberations were mysterious and secret; they were people to be placated.

At the same time, I also saw a lot of the directors. It was painful explaining to these good and idealistic people how, collectively, they were thought of by their employees. Their feelings were understandably hurt – it is always hard when good intentions are misunderstood – but they responded with a courageous determination to put things right. Nevertheless, it seemed to me that they too had a collective perception of their employees, which was that they were somewhat ineffectual and unreliable. Because of this view they were loath to permit the employees, through the Amenities Committee, the sort of responsibility that would have given the Committee real meaning and so served to allay the general psychic malaise.

Here revolved one of the familiar vicious circles of such situations. The Committee members would have liked to have had authority for allocating housing and dealing with outside agencies concerned with such matters as garbage collection and public transportation, but they knew that these were ticklish issues and were afraid to raise them. Other matters, mainly concerned with social occasions, were not central to the existence of the community and consequently were not treated with great seriousness by the Committee. The result was that the directors were convinced that the employees did not have the sense of responsibility or the understanding of the firm's problems that would enable them to make wise decisions on more important matters. (Suppose, said the directors, the welfare of the Firm – and therefore of the employees – depended on bringing in a skilled technician who would not come unless a house was provided. Would a committee of employees give him priority over a man who was less important industrially but who had more children, for example, or had been waiting a long time for a house?) Nevertheless, it is axiomatic that people who are without responsibility behave irresponsibly; they learn responsibility by its practice. An analogy can be made with the experience of former colonial peoples: when things went wrong after independence, their previous rulers deplored the fact that the people had been granted independence before they had learnt to govern themselves. But how, ultimately, could they learn to do this while still governed by others?

The process of bringing the Amenities Committee and the directors closer together reached a point where each side developed a degree of confidence in the other. Indeed, the Committee members, at last daring to express themselves, made a number of extreme and unrealistic proposals; but after they had let off steam in this way they became specific and practical, drafting a paper on the principles by which they proposed, if permitted, to allocate houses and to conduct other business. The directors had said that they would be very happy for the Committee to deal with many important matters, but that housing allocation must, for the good of the whole community, remain in their own hands. Nevertheless, when the eventual confrontation took place at a specially arranged meeting of the Committee and the directors, the directors accepted the well-presented and reasonable demands of the Committee for the right to allocate housing and to deal with external agencies. Both sides had drawn much closer together, being less anxious and more understanding about each other.

Following on these specific discussions there was a general rethinking of the function and structure of the Committee. The object was to make it more efficient and more representative, and to give it a more central part in the life of the Firm. The principle cause of the conflict had been that the authority of the directors spread into their employees' private lives far more than did that of most employers. As long as the employees lived in houses belonging to the Firm, this situation had, to some extent, to continue, but their new responsibilities shifted the balance to a considerable extent.

A different interpretation could be made of these events and now, at a distance of over twenty years, I am not sure which is correct. My role may have been simply to mystify, to obscure the conflict, to paper over the cracks of the intrinsically unpeaceful relationship, to create a Bantustan. A purist might well assert that in the capitalist system there is an ineradicable conflict between the workers and those who own the means of production. Perhaps what I did was to help the workers to become aware of a peripheral aspect of the basic conflict and to resolve it by the mechanisms I have described; in other words, to be lulled into a false sense of equality and to accept what should – to free men – be unacceptable. I might argue that this was a special case: that any profits the Firm might make were put into a charitable trust and did not enrich the directors or a body of shareholders. I think, however, that this is irrelevant; certainly, it did not affect the attitudes of the employees.

The reader must make his own evaluation; the case is presented here as an example of a situation in which a particular technique, rightly or wrongly, was applied.

11 Employers and Employees: the Factories

Since I have been involved only peripherally in industrial disputes in England and Pakistan (in the latter through my work with the Government Planning Commission), I am not presenting a specific case study. Rather, as in 'Colonialism and Neo-colonialism' above, I shall examine the general proposition that a relationship, in this case that of industrial worker and management, is inherently unpeaceful. It would certainly seem, from the daily reports of strikes, disputes, and disturbances, at least in the capitalist countries, that worker–management relations are far from peaceful. We must determine, however, whether there is that inescapable conflict of interest which, in my definition, typifies unpeaceful relationships. If the needs of labour, specifically as expressed by the unions that represent labour, are incompatible with those of capital, there must be a profound discord in Western society.

The view of management, essentially the representatives of the shareholders, is that there is no conflict; that there are 'two roles' but not 'two sides'. The following passage presents the argument briefly and urbanely:

'An important question which needs to be got out of the way at the start is whether or not management and the trade unions really form two sides of industry. This point is almost always in the back of people's minds and a great deal of unnecessary word-play takes place about it.

In the sense that they have different roles to play and different functions to perform they do form two sides. In the sense that they have a common interest in the prosperity of industry, there are not two sides. Although it is in the interests of both management and unions that industry should develop and grow, when it comes to deciding how the benefits of growth and development should be shared their interests are not the same, nor will they necessarily agree about the best methods of promoting growth. Essentially the role of the unions is to look after the interests of their members (in the long term as well as the short term), while management has to judge what is in the best interests of shareholders and customers as well as employees. The fact that their interests are bound to clash when it comes to deciding who gets what share of the cake all too often obscures the point that management and unions need to co-operate together to increase the total size of the cake and must co-operate if the economic objectives of the company and all the people in it are to be achieved' (Clarke, 1966, p. 1).

The ultimate sentence is the crucial one. It is undoubtedly true that a prosperous firm will be able to purchase a measure of industrial harmony by providing benefits for its workers: pay increases, retirement benefits, improved working conditions, recreational facilities, and the like. But is this tantamount to achieving the 'economic objectives' of 'all the people in the firm'? Even if it were, it seems possible that many, brought up in poverty and ignorance, would price themselves too low. Moreover, do social objectives always coincide? Undoubtedly some working conditions are more pleasant than others, but does an increase in pleasantness constitute a change in the structure of the relationship?

In the early days of European and American industrialization there was open and obvious exploitation of the workers. The workers sold their labour for a pittance while their employers grew wealthy, and they had no redress against victimization. The subsequent development of unions and labour legislation has given workers some protection, coupled with progressive improvement in their conditions of employment, but in essence the relation between employee and employer remains the same. The former sells his labour, making it over for a period during which it is controlled and organized by the latter, who possesses a number of sanctions he can apply to enforce his authority: fines, loss of bonus, reprimand, dismissal, and so on. Aside from taking part in union activity and in strikes, official and unofficial, the only protest open to the worker as an individual is to resign, an act that is likely to hurt him much more than management. In this respect the relationship is essentially unbalanced and could also be properly called asymmetrical, in that the worker has to peddle his labour in order to survive while the capitalist employer is under no compulsion to hire him.

Perhaps the most important clue in deciding whether the relationship of the industrial worker to his employer is, or is not, unpeaceful lies in the question of equality. If the workers received a sufficient proportion of the profits of industry to reduce progressively their economic inequality, the management claim that there is no conflict might be substantiated. But in England, as in most essentially capitalist countries, this does not seem to have happened. We should not be deceived by the higher standards of living and the reduction of abject poverty into thinking that the gap between rich and poor has been reduced or that the relation, where employment is concerned, has become more balanced. The following facts may illustrate, though I could not in a brief section attempt to prove, this contention.

In 1966 *The Economist* (15 January) estimated that 84 per cent of all private wealth was in the hands of 7 per cent of the population and that, of those, the wealthiest 2 per cent had 55 per cent of the riches. At the same time, 87·9 per cent of the population with holdings of less than £3,000 in fact owned less than £107. Furthermore, 'the rich not only have more money; they also make it multiply faster'; the poor do not invest while the rich do. This means that the rich not only have the money, but in addition own the country's productive system.

Until the publication in 1962 of Titmuss's *Income Distribution and Social Change*, it had been thought that the national income was being distributed on a more egalitarian basis. Titmuss's analysis showed, however, that there were powerful forces making for inequality. For example, the higher the salary the higher the proportion of tax-free fringe benefits. These were calculated as 11 per cent of the salary of a man earning £1,000 a year, but as 31 per cent in the case of a man earning £7,000 (*The Economist*, 27 August 1966). In addition,

'the British fiscal system is almost unique in the Western World in its generous treatment of wealth holders in allowing them to use family settlements, discretionary trusts, gifts, family covenants, and other legal devices for redistributing and rearranging income and wealth' (Titmuss, 1962, p. 361).

Such features to a large extent offset the progressive increase of income tax proportionate to income. Moreover, the taxes on wealth, such as surtax and excess profits tax, amount to considerably less than what is raised by indirect taxation (on, for example, tobacco and beer) and is predominantly paid by the poor majority of the population. Nor does it seem that the current situation, bad as it is, is an improvement over a worse past. Nicholson (1964) sees little change between 1937 and 1959, while Titmuss concludes that 'ancient inequalities have assumed new and subtle forms' (1962, p. 199).

This, indeed, is to be expected in a capitalist society where, despite successive Labour governments, there has been no serious confrontation with capital. As Blackburn observes:

'In societies of the capitalist type, where the ownership of the means of production is concentrated in private hands, inequalities of wealth are necessary to sustain the productiveness of the society itself. If the social process of investment and accumulation is left to private ownership then the fate of society as a whole is inextricably bound up with the fortunes of the rich. Once the productive resources of the community constitute also the private wealth of a section of the community, then inequality will be self-perpetuating. To preserve itself, capitalism must preserve inequality' (1967, p. 37).[22]

The system is strengthened because the worker, along with everyone else, depends on it. The higher the profit obtained by his labour, the more employment will the rich be able to create. In this sense, and given a situation in which the power of capital dominates, the interdependence referred to by the managers does exist; but it is in no sense, as might seem to be implied, a partnership. In effect, it would seem that the firm exists legally 'for the benefit of the owners of its property or assets and that employees have obligations to assist in achieving this end' (Ross, 1969, p. 15). The inferior status of the worker is thus further emphasized.

It would follow from these arguments that the relationship of management to labour in capitalist countries such as England is conflicted and therefore unpeaceful. I would further characterize it as unbalanced. The level of awareness of workers will now be considered in the context of labour disputes and the ways in which they are settled.

One might assume, from the frequency of labour disagreements and of strikes both official and unofficial, as well as from the size, strength, and resources of many trade unions, that labour was aware and militant. But it would appear, at least to a relative outsider, that the relation between labour and management has been greatly mystified and obscured.

A principal element contributing to mystification is that many unions, or at least key figures in unions, have, as it were, joined the establishment. Their leaders receive knighthoods or peerages, or join the cabinet. The unions, while continuing to press for the advantage of their members, do so within a framework acceptable to the economy as it is; that is to say, they do not aim at a degree of equalization that would affect the capitalist structure. Hence the great number of unofficial strikes and the frequency with which shop stewards are defied (as among Ford workers in February 1970). Management pamphlets, such as that already quoted, make it clear that the unions should be courted and that high union membership makes for stability, a strange and sad commentary on the decline of union militancy and further evidence that many unions have become part of the system.

A second element in mystification is the 'enlightened' policy of some managements: workers are offered generous terms that conceal the conflict of interest – and often entail, as a hidden cost, some erosion of their rights.

A third factor may well lie, in the future, in the joint management approach advocated by, among others, the Trades Union

Congress in 1966. This approach implies that employees at all levels would take part in all aspects of decision-making. But it is hard to see how, within the existing system, the power of employees could be increased. Ultimate control would remain beyond their grasp. They would possess only the illusion of power, enough to sap their enterprise and undermine the principles of collective bargaining that have served them in the past.[23]

It is elements such as these that contribute to low awareness on the part of the workers concerning their basic conflict of interest with the employers. This is not to say that workers are unaware of specific needs and injustices, and those are, of course, the cause of many disputes and much unrest. Nevertheless, the general sophistication of collective bargaining ensures that many of these needs are met – whereas the larger problems out of which they arise are forgotten.

All the same, I believe that there is an undercurrent of bitterness and resentment. Factory workers in general do not enjoy their work: it is boring and inhuman, it demands too little of them, it is controlled too impersonally, and they have too little freedom. In consequence, absenteeism from psychological illness and accidents has greatly increased (despite the National Health Service) in the last twenty years (Wright, 1966).[24] Even when workers appear contented, deep-seated anger may be unexpectedly aroused by seemingly trivial incidents. Blackburn (1967, p. 48) quotes the case of Vauxhall's Luton factory. On 17 and 18 October 1966, as reported in *The Times*, 'near riot conditions' broke out. This was only a month after the publication of an article in the *British Journal of Sociology* (Goldthorpe, 1966) describing a survey of the attitudes of car-assembly workers there which concluded – so far as management policy was concerned – on a note of restrained optimism.

The truth is probably that the level of awareness of workers fluctuates from time to time and varies from place to place. But on the whole it seems to be lower rather than higher.

I have scarcely mentioned the methods by which industrial disputes are settled. Apart from arbitration, which I do not discuss in this book, they are conciliation and bargaining, which I do. These are used in essentially the same way in labour relations as in any other sphere. Conciliation is an attempt to clear away the confusions and misapprehensions that stem from anxiety and resentment, suspicion, fear, and ignorance, emotions that so easily develop in conditions of conflict and, having developed, constitute almost autonomous forces impeding settlement. Bargaining is a process, often inseparable from conciliation, by which the parties to a dispute try to make the best deal for themselves, conceding as little and gaining as much as possible. Both unions and management are adept at bargaining, and, in addition, a whole profession of labour consultants have put their negotiating skills on the market. In fact a large proportion of the literature on labour relations (whether on psychological, economic, or management aspects) deals with bargaining. It is for precisely this reason, in my opinion, that worker–management relations are stuck in their present phase of unpeacefulness, with both low awareness and imbalance.

What happens, schematically, when a dispute arises, is as follows: the recognition of some (possibly minor) injustice, a by-product of the main conflict of interest, leads to confrontation, that is, a demand by the union and – possibly – a strike. This confrontation does not, however, aim at challenging the power of the management, merely at achieving a particular objective. Thus when the union begins to bargain without having gained equality it sacrifices its opportunity of resolving the essential conflict (see *Figure 3*). Bargaining carried out before confrontation has led to the establishment of a balanced relationship is not con-ducive to peace. If it is successful, in the sense that the particular issue is dealt with, two things may follow. Either the conflict reverts to one in which there are both low awareness and im-balance, or the Bantustan type of pseudo-balance is established. The latter would be especially probable where, as in the case of joint management procedures, the semblance of equality had been established. It may be objected that labour has, in fact, power, that the concessions gained countless times by the unions show that management cannot stand up to them. But, as I have tried to

Figure 3   *Typical 'settlement' of employer–employee disputes*

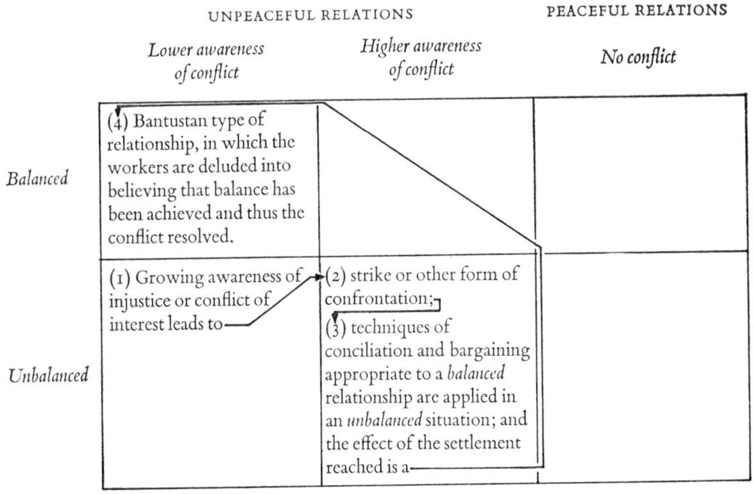

	UNPEACEFUL RELATIONS		PEACEFUL RELATIONS
	Lower awareness of conflict	*Higher awareness of conflict*	*No conflict*
Balanced	(4) Bantustan type of relationship, in which the workers are deluded into believing that balance has been achieved and thus the conflict resolved.		
Unbalanced	(1) Growing awareness of injustice or conflict of interest leads to—	(2) strike or other form of confrontation; (3) techniques of conciliation and bargaining appropriate to a *balanced* relationship are applied in an *unbalanced* situation; and the effect of the settlement reached is a—	

suggest, there is little evidence of a growing equality that would indicate that the wealthy minority, the owners of the means of production, are losing their power. The 'gains' of labour have constituted little more than reforms, deceptive revisions of an essentially unchanged system.

In my terms the only way of changing this unpeaceful relationship into a peaceful one would be to engage in confrontation on basic rather than peripheral issues; to continue (as might have been done if the general strike of 1926 had been successful) until the relationship with capital is balanced, until an egalitarian society is created and social justice firmly established.

12 Some English Villages and the Local Government[25]

There is an area of south-west England that some decades ago was one of the most prosperous in the country but is now one of the most backward. Villages that once possessed small industries and a variety of stores now seldom have more than one or two shops, while their populations have often dropped by more than 50 per cent and whole categories of persons, especially farm labourers and craftsmen, have almost disappeared. Standards of agriculture in these villages are now for the most part very poor, communications are bad, the populations are withdrawn and show little interest in the possibility of obtaining help from agencies that might assist them in improving their conditions.

I found instances of villages that had rejected the proposal for a bus service linking them with a neighbouring town, and knew of individuals who had never been outside the narrow boundaries of their own parish. These are not happy communities. People complained that progress had passed them by, that there were no opportunities for their children, that the county authorities never did anything for them. At the same time, social life was limited and impoverished, dominated by factions and feuds. This was the average, but there were some villages that were more pathologically fossilized, as it were, and others in which there was still a lively, vigorous social and economic life. Almost all the former were villages that had been most severely affected by population change, particularly during the last fifty years. The livelier communities had not shrunk, and indeed had often expanded. The reason why some villages had changed more than others was largely fortuitous – a new road had been built by the county authorities, an industry had been set up, the market value of a particular product had declined or increased. The social state of a village was not, in short, a precondition of the changes that had taken place, rather the reverse.

It seemed that the condition of these various villages, having arisen by a chance, became fixed in patterns of behaviour which were very hard to break. The villages that had suffered the greatest deprivation in terms of population, amenities, and openings for employment, were the most hostile to all the agencies, such as the county council and various agricultural bodies, that might have helped them to improve the state of which they complained. They had developed ritualized attitudes of hostility and suspicion to outside officials, even to persons such as a schoolteacher and a minister who, coming from elsewhere, held positions of responsibility in the community. I encountered an instance of a village teacher being burnt in effigy – a solemn and rather frightening expression of group hostility. In one village the boast was made that in the course of a two-year period during World War II they had got rid of no fewer than sixteen teachers in the one-teacher village school by making life unpleasant for them. One teacher told of a very uncomfortable period in her life when most of the mothers in the village gathered ominously outside the school every morning, waiting, she assumed, to invade if there was the slightest evidence of her ill treatment of the children.

Many of these villages demonstrated an interesting piece of social juggling. They had to elect a member to sit on the rural district council, the local government authority for a group of villages. This, however, was a body of which they felt the greatest suspicion and dislike, and no villager of any standing was going to jeopardize his position by sitting on it. In consequence they arranged that the person elected should be either someone who was thoroughly disliked, so that they could all dissociate themselves from what he did on their behalf on the council, or someone who was known to be feckless or foolish and unlikely to attend many of the council meetings. There was a relationship between the degree of hostility a village showed towards outside authority, and the extent to which the village community itself was split among hostile factions. It is not to be wondered at that the county and rural district authorities looked askance at some of these village communities.

I played a conciliating part in only one of these villages, which I shall call Thornley. I hoped, by using the same sort of approach I had employed with the Firm, to find a way to reduce Thornley's intransigent and self-wounding isolationism and to help it to develop the more relaxed and open attitude shown by the villages that were both more populous and more prosperous.

I approached my task warily, for the likelihood was that I too would be identified with the vaguely hostile outer world. Fortunately I had no official position of any sort. I did have one or two useful introductions to key people in the community, which enabled me, over a period of several weeks, to make a number of acquaintances, some of whom, in small ways, I was able to help. Before long, an excellent opportunity presented itself for trying to re-establish more realistic relations between Thornley and the authorities. This arose because the village had been allocated some new government housing – which was all to the good – but the rural district council planned to build the new houses on a site that the villagers felt, with a sort of angry impotence, to be highly unsatisfactory. When I asked them if they had made any protests, they replied, 'No, what is the use?' But I persuaded them to work out an alternative plan for locating their houses, and brought the county planning officer and some of his staff to meet, entirely unofficially, a body of village spokesmen. The two sites were examined, and that chosen by the village was pronounced the better.

This trivial incident opened eyes on both sides. It was a revelation for the village that the remote official world could be so helpful, understanding, and approachable. The county authorities, in turn, were astonished that a village thought to be so refractory that it was nicknamed 'black Thornley' could be so sensible and easy to deal with. This meeting appears to have contributed in considerable measure to subsequent changes in attitudes in Thornley. The main alteration could be attributed to the new conviction that the county council, and all that it stood for in the anonymous official sphere, was not hostile but friendly; and to the realization that things could be achieved through collaboration with it and other agencies. This led in turn to more forceful action on the part of the parish council, and to closer support – with corresponding advantage to Thornley – of the rural district council.

It was of particular interest to me that the social life of Thornley became less ingrown. Some unprecedented steps were taken: for instance, a demand was made to the local education authority for evening classes, and village excursions were organized to neighbouring places of cultural interest.

13 The Blacks and the Whites: USA[26]

What I would term a revolution of awareness is occurring in the racial ghettos of North America. It is not that the black Americans have suddenly become conscious of their miseries and of the injustices of their situation – of these they have always been aware – but that they have recognized the futility and fraudulence of their hopes.

For some time past their hopes had been based on the concept of integration. This meant, to most people, the gradual removal of barriers between underprivileged Negroes and the rest of the population; it meant that 'black' was to be fully integrated into white society, enjoying its privileges, pleasures, affluence, and responsibilities. The passing of civil rights legislation, the (nominal) desegregation of schools, the steady (though far from spectacular) increase in the number of professionally qualified Negroes, the appointment or election of a few to high office, the generally sympathetic view of educated whites – all seemed to give promise of better things on the way. Nevertheless, by 1964 there was a growing belief that things were not going to improve substantially, that the civil rights leaders were dupes, that the blacks were more effectively trapped than ever in the poverty of the ghetto, and that the few who had made it into the middle class had sold out to the white establishment, becoming lackeys of the evil society that had enslaved and brutalized their people. There was a strong disillusionment with the white liberals who had belonged to, indeed led, the various civil rights groups: they had not solved the essential problems, they had merely indoctrinated a few 'good' blacks with their own values and helped them to join the *bourgeoisie*.

In the mid-1960s the black people began to understand two things. First, that the Northern whites, to whom many had looked for support, were worse – because hypocritical – than the Southerners. 'We began to know what you are like', one of them told me, 'when we saw your faces on the television screen in shots of disturbances in the Northern cities; the ordinary 'decent' people were full of hatred for us, it was plain to see. We knew then how we stood.' Second, they recognized the inexorability of the ghetto situation. More and more black people were crowding into the inner cities to live, hemmed in there by the housing discrimination practised by the whites who had moved to the surrounding suburbs. Unlike the waves of European immigrants who had started in racial ghettos but managed to break out, the black people, coming late to the cities, found political organizations already in existence which jealously guarded against encroachment by this new influence. Moreover, those who claim that what the Irish or Italians have done the blacks could do also, ignore the effects of generations of slavery on the outlook of both the enslaved and the slave-owning races.

As bitter disillusionment spread, the comparison of the ghetto with the colony was made with increasing frequency and power. 'The dark ghettos are social, political, educational, and – above all – economic colonies', said Kenneth Clark. 'Their inhabitants are subject peoples, victims to the greed, insensitivity, guilt and fear of their masters' (Clark, 1965, p. 11). This forceful statement is worth examining. The ghettos are, for the most part 'ruled' by outside authorities, city councils composed of members belonging to a race that is, on the whole, hostile to the black. Police are appointed by these authorities to patrol the ghettos, like an occupation army, to maintain law and order; this is contrary to the function of most police forces, which are appointed by the community they serve in order to protect its citizens. Even garbage collection is organized from outside and carried out by white collectors who, as a glance at any ghetto street will show, care little how they do their job. Ghetto schools tend to be among the oldest, most dilapidated, and overcrowded in the country (no colonial power has ever cared much about the education of 'subject' peoples – if they got too much they might not be content to remain subject). Less is spent on them than on the schools in the suburbs; the teaching materials are antiquated and inappropriate; few good teachers are appointed to them, and even fewer remain long enough to improve things much. With the swelling black population of the inner cities, the schools are increasingly segregated and the unhappy atmosphere of failure prevalent in poor schools contaminates even the brightest children: in the eighteen months prior to December 1965, 67 per cent of black as opposed to only 19 per cent of white candidates failed the Selective Service Mental Tests. In a society in which employment depends increasingly upon education the ghetto youth starts life with a major handicap which derives, not from his inherent qualities, but from his insalubrious environment and the scant attention paid to it by the authorities that remotely control the conditions of his life. And ironically, to pile discrimination upon disadvantage, in 1960 the median earnings of a black college graduate were less than those of a white person with three years or less of high school.

General social conditions are notoriously bad. The relative gap between the maternal and infant mortality rates for blacks and those for whites increased greatly (though both rates for blacks have improved) between 1940 and 1965. And the 1965 estimate of 14,000 cases of rat-bite a year, mostly in the ghettos, caused a brief national scandal. The most serious social condition is undoubtedly poor housing. Most ghetto property is owned by white absentee landlords who charge exorbitant rents. In Chicago, for example, the blacks pay approximately twenty dollars more than their white counterparts, while in other parts of the country they pay either the same amount as whites for worse housing or more for identical housing; what has been termed the colour tax has been levied very widely. Here again control by external, as it were foreign, entrepreneurs to the economic detriment of a people strengthens the colonial analogy. Furthermore, the high rents for miserable accommodation tend to increase the feelings of futility and frustration engendered in general by ghetto existence. The children lack the pleasant atmosphere that might encourage study, and the parents who pay so much for so little have little incentive to save – how can they?

The general economic situation of the ghetto has further

colonial implications. The major businesses–like Unilever in West Africa or the great French firm Compagnie Française de l'Afrique Occidentale – are white-controlled. This means, to begin with, that most capital, as in the case of housing rents, goes out of the community. It also means, since many of the customers are poor, that various forms of exploitation and extortion can be practised. Not only are food prices apparently higher in many ghetto areas than outside them, but outlets catering to low-income groups in many towns charge more for the same item than do average stores; a study in Washington found that the average difference in price over a range of goods was 52 per cent. In addition, devious practices in advertising and high-pressure selling are common, such as the substitution of old goods for the new ones originally chosen by the customer. In some twenty states the iniquitous procedure of garnishment is practised, whereby the wages of an individual can be diverted to a creditor simply through court action, without a hearing or trial. One New York study showed that 20 per cent of the low-income families investigated had been affected by garnishment; for the most part such families fall unaware into this trap, their ignorance having been ruthlessly exploited.

Of still more consequence for the people than the exploitation they suffer is the effect of ghetto life upon employment possibilities. The ghetto community, poor, property-less, prevented from building up capital, can offer little good employment to its members. In consequence, black Americans are twice as likely as white ones to be in unskilled, low-paying jobs, and their unemployment rate is also double that of whites. Indeed, these tendencies seem to be increasing, for although the number of blacks in high-income jobs has gone up, and although the average black family income has grown, the gap between it and that of the average white family has increased, between 1947 and 1966, in terms of constant 1965 dollars, from $2,174 to $3,036. It must be remembered, further, that even if more high-level jobs were available, the poor schools and the sad atmosphere of ghetto life would disqualify many blacks from holding them. Thus Carmichael and Hamilton (1967) are justified in asserting that

F

'the core problem within the ghetto is the vicious circle created by lack of decent housing, decent jobs, and adequate education. The failure of these three fundamental institutions to work has led to alienation of the ghetto from the rest of the urban area as well as to deep political rifts between the two communities' (p. 155).

These inexorable circumstances convinced many in the mid and late 1960s that, as in the colonies, there could be no development without independence, or at least without the relative degrees of independence implied by different interpretations of the term Black Power. The ruling white majority, the colonialists, were too afraid of the blacks to want them to spread beyond the ghettos; they needed the cheap labour, they wanted their markets and their money.

There was also a psychological awakening. The black population became aware that for decades many had been untrue to themselves. They had sought to join their oppressors, to become members of an exploiting racialist society, to lose – so far as they could – their blackness. They had wanted the welcome of their white colleagues in the universities or professions – and of course the whites wanted them because it made them feel less guilty. The same thing had happened in the colonies. The white way was the only way to position (and, relatively speaking, power), and many joined (though mostly in minor capacities) the colonial establishment, governing their fellow-countrymen in accordance with the specifications of the colonialists, and at the end of their careers receiving a minor decoration from the appropriate alien king or president. The colonialists did not mind spending money and time educating this sort of 'white' black. He did much of their work for them, he was a lightning-rod for local hostility, and he was granted in return a measure of white fellowship. Actually some colonizers virtually turned a small number of educated and talented natives into members of their own society. The educated West African from a French territory was led to feel that the roots of his culture were in Paris, while the *assimilado* of Angola or of Mozambique was accepted as one of themselves by the Portuguese.

But this is perhaps the ultimate act of cultural destruction, for to pay for his acceptance the African had to be assimilated, that is, to adopt the customs, goals, values, and habits of thought of those who were brutalizing his fellow-Africans. In the same way, it came to be felt, the middle-class American black had betrayed his origins, and the white liberal who befriended him was a seducer. But if the educated black wished to escape from the confines of the black ghettos to the open opportunities of the white *bourgeois* suburb, it must be that his own community lacked the power to hold him. For centuries the Negro in the United States was powerless, a thing belonging to another human being, possessing no rights and no hopes except for ultimate salvation. His own African-ness had been eradicated; his name changed, his language lost, his songs and ceremonials prohibited. He saw himself at times, perhaps, as he was seen by the arrogant and fearful white man – as lazy, useless, stupid, and potentially dangerous.

The current revolution of awareness encompasses both the vicious circle of ghetto life and the attitudes of mind that would make many acquiesce in it, some escape from it, but very few perceive in black culture anything of value. The Black Power movement, echoing the nationalist and separatist movements of the mid-nineteenth century, attacks both the ghetto mentality and the ghetto socio-politico-economic structure. Black Americans have been deprived of their identity and made to use the corrupt, oppressing society as a model, but to be black is beautiful. In much the same way that Leopold Senghor built up the concept of *négritude* and Kwame Nkrumah that of 'African personality', so the new black militants are active in forging a sense or a quality of blackness to give their people an identity, and so the strength to establish themselves as a community without reliance on the hateful values of an oppressor race. This is the psychological corollary of their political goals.

Politically speaking, Black Power can mean anything from control of the United States by a black minority to greater involvement of the black community in its own community affairs. A moderate compromise approach would claim that black communities should have the same degree of self-determination as comparable white areas. Thus Roxbury, the Boston ghetto, should be given the same autonomy as the adjacent town of Cambridge which is of similar size. In this way black communities would have control over their own municipal services, including, most importantly, schools and police, and would have some say on questions of housing and commerce.

Is this approach, in effect, simply advocating apartheid? I pursue this question in Chapter 21, on 'Development', but may perhaps briefly anticipate the arguments here. If my understanding of ghetto conditions is correct, apartheid in fact exists and is a bad thing – as is any ill-balanced separation of groups, or indeed any separation accompanied by fear, hatred, and suspicion. The Black Power solution (I am not referring here to its most violent or extreme expressions) goes some way towards the establishment of a more balanced relationship between the black and white communities, which might, it is hoped, constitute a basis for the resolution of racial conflict, that is, the stage of development, in which both groups work together towards common goals and, eventually, genuine integration. By this I mean such a degree of openness of the communities to each other that differences diminish, blur, and finally disappear. But we have far to go.

14 The Students and
the Professors[27]

My generation of students had no conception of the issues with which contemporary students are concerned. The privileged young men at Oxford (and for that matter, I suppose, at Cambridge) may have felt awed reverence or amused contempt for their teachers; they may have obeyed the rules or flouted them. The system, however, they accepted. Though they often had close personal friendships with the dons, they did not question the authority of the university and the colleges. Everyone knew that old Professor So-and-So was eccentric to the point of lunacy, that Dr Such-and-Such was an alcoholic, that Dean The-Other had not done a stroke of work for twenty years and was a homosexual to boot, but that was the essence of the place. Despite, or even because of, these odd characters, the institution moved majestically through the centuries. It was detached, benign, authoritarian – though once one entered the ruling group it was the most remarkable democracy, the truest company of scholars in the world. It made much of its money, or was reputed to, out of slum property. It was supremely powerful in the city and could remove a case involving an undergraduate from the city magistrate's court to try and sentence him (often very severely) itself. It could have undesirable (which in this context usually meant extremely desirable) women expelled from the city boundaries. It was rumoured that the university proctors had nominal power to inflict the death penalty, but did not exercise it for fear that it would be removed; they wanted to retain it, people said, to exercise their right just one last time on a supremely suitable subject. It was snobbish, but then so were most of the students in a quiet, upper-class fashion. It was trivial in that an inordinate amount of time, money, and attention was given to sport, entertainment, and ritual. It was archaic in its medieval survivals (the whole college system, for example) and its failure to adjust to the modern world; but so, of course, was most of English society. To use the contemporary term, its teaching lacked relevance: you could not get in without knowing a classical language, and obligatory Hebrew had not long been discarded; there were no sociologists, and only one psychologist (though he was called the Wilde Reader in Mental Philosophy); there were some anthropologists, but they were hung up on what we then called primitive society.

This is how it was and we never questioned it. We might have been disappointed or exasperated by the symptoms, but we never dreamed of rebelling against the system that produced them. Most of us loved Oxford and still do, for there were great things as well as the anachronisms and the absurdities – but this is not sufficient ground for acceptance; the fonder one is the more one should wish to erase imperfections. Today's students have a different vision of their institutions and their role in them. This much we know from what is happening all over the globe. By the same token, because the university world was a peaceful one thirty years ago – even five years ago – we can infer that my experience at Oxford was representative, as far as general student attitudes are concerned.

Awareness of things as they are includes the recognition that they could be different. I, as a student, was not really aware of my university environment because I accepted it as given. It was a part of the environment of my family, of the culture in which I grew up. But the young men and women of today are, it seems to me, wiser and stronger. They are able to detach themselves from their circumstances enough to evaluate them and attempt to change them. In consequence, universities throughout the world are in a state of ferment. Students have been responsible for the removal of oppressive governments in Korea, Turkey, and other countries, and they nearly succeeded in France. Since the Berkeley 'revolt' of 1964, they have assailed traditional university structures and procedures in the United States. The history of student activism is, of course, as old as the universities themselves, but the upheavals since the end of World War II, the surge of the colonial territories towards freedom, the social and economic changes that have everywhere shaken the patterns of class privilege and entrenched positions, have influenced the attitudes of young adults towards society in general and particularly towards that aspect of it that most directly impinges on them – the university. It has been said that American youth, politically apathetic in the 1950s, was spurred towards its present militancy through involvement in civil rights and the agonizing issues of the Vietnam war. This is no doubt true, but it may well be that unrest on the American campuses is a part of a more general awakening; this much is perhaps shown by the honoured place accorded to Mao Tse-tung, Ho Chi Minh, and Che Guevara in the activist pantheon.

The young people maintain – and who shall say that they are wrong? – that established society is, to borrow a term from one of the texts of the progressive movement, one-dimensional (Marcuse, 1964). And this criticism applies equally to Russia and America, to France, Korea, and Argentina. One-dimensional society exists to serve an élite (though, as in the United States, the elite may be the majority of the citizens) whose goals can be expressed in terms of money and position within the social structure that, circularly, provides the goals. The rules of this form of society are meaningless except in terms of self-maintenance. They are the rules of games people play to get ahead of each other legitimately, and they have little to do with love or truth or the growth of the spirit. The military–industrial game is one of the most successful, and the skilful player wins the most coveted prizes. Much of scholarship, organized religion, and conventional morality both supports and is shaped by the goals and games of one-dimensional society. The political form does not really matter very much; dictatorships of the Left or the Right as well as democracies – all deny freedom to people to grow along other lines. To play other games, or rather, not to play games, but to live spontaneously and openly, is anathema to the one-dimensional society. It sneers angrily, but perhaps a little anxiously, at the medallions and flowers of those who demonstrate their nonconformity in this way. The one-dimensional society, or the Thing, as it is sometimes termed to emphasize its inhumanity, is really much happier with genuine crime – so long as the crime pays. Whatever it may prate concerning freedom and democracy it will support the most vicious tyrant. The one-dimensional society, without a glimmer of conscious hypocrisy,will protect what it terms the freedom of its own people by promoting the oppression of someone else's people. One of the chief games is the creation of false needs in order to sustain the vast industrial complex, and we achieve status to the extent that we satisfy these needs for new and better appliances, larger homes, or whatever it may be. In so doing, moreover, we lose much of our freedom, especially our freedom to experience widely, for we sacrifice our intellectual and emotional range by succumbing to the ad-man. As Marcuse (1964) points out, it is only those who are 'outside the productive process', particularly the students, who still possess the psychic integrity to rebel; the rest, as the students maintain, have already sold out to the establishment – however liberally we talk, we play its games.

Universities are both in and out of society. The hierarchy of rank, the divisions between students and faculty, tenured and non-tenured, administrators and teachers, exemplify society's high regard for status based on playing the game (in this case the academic game) according to the rules. In an angry statement entitled *The Student as Nigger*,[28] a university teacher (who clearly has not sold out) shows how students are treated in at least one institution as an inferior kind of animal, stupid, ill-behaved, unreliable. This is very far from the medieval concept of the community of scholars in which respect was accorded only to learning and wisdom. Ironically, however, universities are frequently accused of medievalism by their detractors.

The universities truckle to the one-dimensional society, it is said, through the very nature of their academic programme. They train scientists, administrators, and economists for the industrial complex. In their laboratories they carry out research the results of which will be applied to guided missiles and nerve gases, to the creation of meaningless needs, and to a thousand other purposes supporting the Thing. They train intelligence agents, they analyse the politics and practice of defence (which of course means war). Their social scientists find ways of making people more eager as producers and consumers – to what end? To keep the system turning more rapidly: to what end? To get more and more people embroiled in it. Furthermore, much of the university research and teaching that is not directed towards maintaining or serving the system is, it is argued, futile or trivial. It deals with topics that are so abstract or remote as to have no 'relevance'. Relevance is a key term. That which has no relevance gives the student no clue to understanding the social, psychological, economic, or political problems around him. The academic counter-attack states that the students' demand for relevance is anti-intellectual; that the study of Thucidydes, for example, can illuminate most human and political problems. The students answer that it can, but that it is usually so taught that it does not. In general, they are not against courses dealing with theoretical or, one might say, academic topics, as long as these are taught with skill and knowledge and as long as more directly applicable courses are also available. In short, the poor teacher is always irrelevant, whatever his field; the good one is always relevant.

The universities have become factories turning human beings into productive units for the system, thus helping it to grow in strength and complexity. It is hard to do anything outside the system; after one has been in it a few years, by the age of thirty, say the students, one is corrupted by it. The pressures on the young American of today to enter college are almost irresistible, but once enrolled he is subjected to what many feel to be the idiocy and insult of the rules, to the irrelevance of the teaching, and to moral subversion through the alliance between the university and the one-dimensional society. It is for this reason that Paul Goodman calls the students the largest exploited class in the country. They are needed by the system and so they must be made to need the system. But sometimes things go wrong. The very efficiency of the factory may be its undoing, as it was at Berkeley. The vast, impersonal, mechanically efficient organization with its busy, impersonal professors and its ant-like students had lost sight of the fact that it was still dealing with human beings; that contact and closeness and sharing have as much to do with learning as has the ingurgitation of knowledge.

If this were all there was to say about society, and in particular about universities, things would be even worse than they are. But the universities are still somewhat divorced from the Thing. The average professor is less caught up in the need-machine, less concerned about status, more interested in ideas, and more involved in causes than is his brother in a great corporation. He is more sympathetic to youth, even though he is more directly threatened by it. He is not, unless he is an administrator, really an organization man. Of course there are some professors who see activists as dirty, dangerous, and anti-intellectual vandals who wantonly destroy all the universities have stood for and protected. People in high places who feel like this do things that evoke a violent response from their students: a good formula for rebellion is awareness on one side and incomprehension on the other.

Nevertheless, even in the most rigid and archaic universities, the chances of successful rebellion are considerable. The shock of student violence has jolted most university administrations into increased awareness – *satori* can be a collective experience of institutions as well as of individuals. The moment of conflict tends to bring about a narrowing of the communication gap so that students and faculty can at least talk to each other. When this happens the students become less demanding, more reasonable, while those who enjoy violence – for in such circumstances a few always emerge – fade into the background. On the faculty side, it is the liberal members who have for the most part, up till now, had some ascendancy. In this respect, universities tend to be more responsive than most communities, where the threat of violence may easily strengthen forces of reaction and repression, leading to the establishment of minutemen or vigilantes, and the heavy arming of the police. It is of course best if faculty and students have not drifted so far apart that rebellion must substitute for communication. Violence is essentially a poor technique. It always harms the innocent and encourages the cruel. Its value is as a sort of shock therapy, something to be used when nothing else will serve, but painful, wasteful, and unpleasant.

It must be admitted, however, that peaceful relations between faculty and students depend on more than tolerance and good communications. What began as dissatisfaction with faculty–student relations a few years ago has now developed a new dimension of disillusionment embracing the wider interrelations of universities, governments, and at least some branches of industry. Where governments are deemed exploitative or imperialist, and industries as serving their ends, it is not enough to try to improve faculty–student relations since the low quality of these is in part a result of the character of the wider relations. To the extent that the faculty succeed in conciliating the students, moreover, they may simply be creating a Bantustan relationship of pseudo-balance. Ultimately, therefore, positive peace will return to the embattled campuses only when the role of the university in relation to the wider society has been redefined.

The present confrontation must lead, first, to easier and more balanced relationships between different groups within the academic community – and I mean not only between students and faculty, but also between junior and senior faculty, research students and supervisors, clerical staff and administrators, etc. – and, second, to a different type of relation between the university and society: institutions of higher education must be freed from dependency on industries that might use them for anti-human ends, and at the same time they must be concerned not only with scholarship but also with the application of scholarship to the relief of suffering.

In what follows, I shall discuss only one facet of university reform: the student–faculty relationship. It is not that I consider this to be the most important, but it is the one I know most about.

II

In this section I discuss three of my own educational experiences. I offer these as illustrations of the type of development in the student–professor relationship that may contribute towards peace on the campus.

In 1952, when student unrest was regarded as something ludicrous that took place in such undisciplined parts as Egypt or Venezuela, I was a thoroughly orthodox Oxford academic. In that year I took charge of the Department of Education and Psychology at the University of Exeter.[29] The main task of this department was to offer a year's course of teacher-training for graduates – approximately, the American MAT. Possession of the diploma that was issued on, as it was neatly put, successful completion of the course, was an important prerequisite for many teaching positions and most of the students received a government grant to take the training. I quickly began to discover that the majority, certainly the brightest, of the students considered this to be a year of fatuous futility, though awareness that things could be changed had not dawned on them. They had to learn, in about twenty weeks of actual course work (the rest of the time was spent usually doing practice teaching in schools), the rudiments of such diverse topics as religious instruction, the philosophy of education (whatever that is), the school in society, the history of education, classroom management, sex education, the way to teach their own subjects, the physical and emotional development of the child, educational psychology and educational testing, physical education, and school drama – a doughty mass, both unpalatable and indigestible. At the end of the year it was vomited out in a series of examinations. The students told me they could get by with a crash programme of cramming facts, which were promptly forgotten after the test, a couple of weeks before the end of the last term.

The pretentious and overcrowded curriculum was not, however, the most offensive thing. Far worse was the general way in which the students were treated. I should make it clear that this is not a criticism of my colleagues, delightful and sensitive people, but of the conventions of teacher-training as they existed nearly twenty years ago and may still exist, so far as I know, in some places. The student was a student. He was there to be instructed, an open vessel into which the superior knowledge of his lecturers was to be poured. His questions were not welcome, he was orated at rather than talked with, all his classes were compulsory and there was hell to pay if he did not attend. The ironical thing was that the end-product of this hierarchically autocratic process would be a full-fledged educator, a professional colleague of his teachers. It struck me as incredible that people should be prepared for the formidable responsibility of teaching by an authoritatian process that gave them no responsibility for their own education. How could we expect them to switch immediately from being the taught (a condition the average student had been in for seventeen or eighteen years) to being the teachers? The training we gave, it seemed to me, should be in the nature of a transitional process. And the most important part of this should be that people who, at the end of this process, were expected in the most significant way to behave as adults, should be treated as grown up.

In practical terms this meant that the classes were made optional: if one intends to treat people as if they are mature – which is the best way to make them so – one must trust them to do what they need to do. It meant further that the students were brought into the process of planning their own programme. We also abolished examinations. We found that the prospect of examinations tied people emotionally to the student level, and confined them intellectually to the study of textbooks and the idiosyncrasies of examiners when they should – if properly stimulated by the faculty – be embarking on a voyage of exploration. We wanted people to read, to be interested, to range widely in their thoughts, but we did not expect them to be educators deeply versed in educational theory and philosophy. It seemed foolish to talk to students of academic status when they were working to acquire in a very short time the knowledge necessary for teaching. Those who are scholarly learn in a scholarly way; those who are not apply what they discover to their new situation and become worried and upset if they are compelled to treat their training as directed towards examinations and detailed information, rather than to the actualities of the job. We felt it unnecessary for a man to know Plato's *Republic* in minute detail but believed he should have a chance to know and discuss what wise men had written, and to relate their theories to the hard facts of his life and work. It was also pretty clear that a man's ability as a teacher was not subject to proof or disproof by an examination. We were in a position, on the other hand, to assess his progress and aptitude for teaching most realistically through work in tutorial classes and seminars, the essays he wrote, the practical teaching he did, and a great deal of informal contact.

A related step was to do away with differentiations in the final award given to the students upon completion of the course. Previously a few of the best students had been given the grade of distinction, but we discovered that these very students felt they were singled out inappropriately from friends with whom they had been working during the year in the joint effort of learning how to do a valuable job. They felt that the idea of special awards produced an element of competition that gave the wrong emphasis to the purpose of the course.

We streamlined the curriculum as much as possible, cutting formal lectures down to a minimum, and relying more on tutorials and seminars which seemed more suitable settings for the type of learning we hoped would occur. I believed greatly in the group-discussion method for exploring sensitive and delicate issues and I found our seminars of incomparable value in establishing communication with our students. This is important, because we were working experimentally, and depended greatly upon the reaction of the consumers for what we decided to do in the future. In fact, no major development occurred without prior discussion with a number of student groups. At the end of each year we spoke with the students in detail about the session's work, and the procedure for the following year was built to a very large extent on their criticisms and suggestions. Nothing was retained that did not pass the severe test of their approval.

I became differently involved with similar issues in the much more militant setting of an American university in 1969. There I was asked to assess the teaching programme of the Harvard Graduate School of Education in the light of the needs of the times and of the general tensions of the university world. I undertook this with a student colleague, himself a well-known activist.

Although we were concerned with the way in which the School taught its students, we were in fact inquiring into the nature of this particular academic community – what divided it and what held it together, its various parts, the areas in which communication was good, and those in which it was bad. Take, for example, the question of relevance. Although some faculty members argued that teaching could be related to current topics of moment without loss of scholarly rigour, others reacted to the word as though it were a betrayal of all they prized in academic life; to them relevance implied the sacrifice of scholarship to expedience and they felt that pressure for relevance endangered the freedom of the academic to study what he would. The same sorts of argument were aroused by proposals that the School should be more actively concerned with the community (here it should be emphasized that a professional school at a more purely academic institution could well have a different relationship with the community), and that it could afford to recognize types of excellence not demonstrated by the conventional criteria and so recruit and graduate new types of people for the many new kinds of job that are emerging in the cities.

One of the most serious cleavages was between those faculty members who believed in colleagueship with their students and those who maintained that students were students because they were substantially different in knowledge and experience from their teachers and could not be expected to share in the sorts of responsibilities implied by the concept of colleagueship. The students themselves, or most of them, claimed these responsibilities, with varying degrees of fervour, as privileges or as rights. They wanted, for example, to be involved in the School's policy-making and administration through membership of various committees, and they wanted the right to initiate courses on topics of their own choosing which should be recognized by the School for credit towards degrees. The students tended to feel that in general the faculty were against them and that any concessions were in the nature of a student victory. They were not, however, just serving their own interests. The best of them had positive feelings for the School and felt that they could make a contribution to it by presenting their own particular point of view and experience.

Here, clearly, were the seeds of discord. In what circumstances would they germinate? The main difference between this and my Exeter experience was that the Harvard student body (and a considerable portion of the faculty) had become aware, not only that some things were imperfect, but that they could do something to change them. The awareness of the students had created a degree of distance in which some unpredictable incident (it is not incidents that matter but the context in which they erupt) might have caused open conflict. I must emphasize here that we were dealing with one of the most intelligent and civilized communities in the world and that the dangers and eruptions I speak of are to be seen in that perspective; nevertheless, I noted the beginnings of student–faculty and faculty–student mirages.[30] The student mirage of the faculty was of rather dry and cowardly scholars who, secure in their position, had removed themselves from issues that really mattered. Some, as individuals, were all right, but viewed collectively they were, at best, apathetic and unaware; at worst, reactionary, hostile, and entrenched in privilege. The faculty mirage of the students was of potentially (not actually, for everyone in the story is most urbane) destructive anti-intellectuals who wanted to take over the School and who would make a terrible mess of it. The faculty mask was of tolerant liberal scholarship. The student mask was of committed involvement. There was in fact very much in common between the two groups, but there is always the danger that, in a situation where interests appear to conflict, the divergent masks and mirages, the unequal awareness, can create a situation of increasing violence.

A major part of the recommendations made by my student colleague and myself reflected the Exeter situation, though the setting had of course greatly changed. It seemed to me that there were two groups of people, the one nominally faculty and the other nominally students (though in fact there was a considerable overlap, since a number of students had also faculty appointments), who had a great deal to contribute to each other as long as the distinctions between them were not too precise. The two together could constitute a true community of scholars; separately they could damage each other. The task was to bring the two groups together, and the divergent groups among both students and faculty, if not in unity (which is not always possible or desirable) then in comprehension. Essentially, the faculty and students of a professional school of education are concerned with the same thing. Means had to be found to express this common purpose and to allow dissenters to dissent. There was consequently some concentration on the role of students in the policy formation of the School and in the initiation of courses, and on student–faculty relations. At the same time it was necessary to consider quality: to recognize that poor teaching was irrelevant whatever the field; that poor teaching that was also irrelevant, in the sense of failing to illuminate the contemporary scene when it might have done so, was even poorer; and that poor teaching does much to impair student–teacher rapport. Quality is therefore of vital importance in establishing peaceful relations within the universities.

But quality is hard both to define and to achieve. To illustrate this point, and to draw together the several arguments of the previous pages, I describe an experimental learning (not teaching) procedure of my own.

I have for several years given a seminar entitled 'Social and Educational Problems of Developing Societies'. When I first gave it, I had a theory to explain a number of things relating to a wide range of topics and my teaching was built around this framework of ideas. But then I came to see the limitations of the theory and began to feel that my job was less to offer concepts than to open up a large and interesting field where there was something of concern and excitement for everyone. The students were mature people and always at least half of them had had overseas experience. I realized that it would be valuable for everyone, including myself, if this wealth of experience could be shared. But things didn't work out as well as I had hoped. The main reason for this was, I think, that I had not sufficiently thought through either my role or that of the students. I aroused expectations that I was going to teach rather than discuss, but I then tried to get the students to take the initiative. As a result, the students who had come expecting to be taught something fairly precise were disappointed. On the other hand, those who would have liked a more open approach did not have quite enough freedom. This caused a certain measure of anxious frustration and I was not sure what to do about it.

My inquiries into the School's teaching programme impelled me to look more deeply, however, at my own performance. I began to see that seminars like mine were, or should be, very different from classes in which didactic teaching took place. A man teaching calculus, for example, has to impart a body of knowledge that is fairly precise. Whatever his technique of transferring this knowledge from himself to his students, the nature of the knowlege will be the same. But with fields like development, or with topics such as urban politics, conflict, or the school in society, there are many problems and issues that can be approached from many different angles, rather than a fixed body of information that is encompassed by a specific discipline. No single person can approach all the issues from every point of view; the most he can do is to constrain the field, as I had done earlier, by attempting to fit it into a particular theory. It would be far better, it now seemed to me, to allow the lights of varied experience to play over the arena, to brighten as many dark places as possible, to illuminate problems from different sides simultaneously. A seminar group such as mine, with its varied talent and experience, could offer *to* all its members *through* all its members a unique learning experience. The corporate wisdom of the group far exceeded the wisdom of any single member, certainly including myself. The problem was to stage-manage the production and the sharing of this wisdom. A dominant role by the director of the seminar could, as I well knew, make it impossible. I also knew that the teaching that most students had experienced had shackled them. In theory they wanted to have a say in what and how they learnt; in practice they were worried by the opportunity of doing so. Some had even said that they were made anxious by being treated as colleagues engaged in a joint effort at understanding – but perhaps this, too, was because my role was somewhat mixed. The way out of these difficulties, it seemed to me, was for the seminar to be run by a study board formed from the seminar members and including my faculty colleague and myself. This board would ensure that there was the most effective sharing of talent, that the needs of individual members were satisfied, and that key areas in the field were identified and covered.

This was done. At the first meeting it was made quite clear that this was not to be a didactic course taught by myself. I was primarily to be the broker for the skills of the seminar members. I would also, of course, bring my own experience to bear on the discussions, but as a contributor to a common learning experience in which I shared, rather than as a teacher. I would be available to any student who had a particular interest with which I could help, but in general the work of the seminar would be carried out by its members. I made it clear that there would be no grades and no formal requirements in the sense of examinations or papers. The only demand to be made on students was that they should contribute actively to the common learning of the group. These points were explained at the outset, and clearly enough to enable those with a different learning style to leave.

After a couple of weeks of preliminary exchanges on the broad shape of the problems facing us, a satisfactory procedure was evolved. The group split into six working parties averaging five members. Each party worked on a particular topic for presentation to the whole seminar at one of its weekly sessions. The working parties also sent a spokesman to sit with me on the study board (or Steering Committee, as it came to be called), which also met weekly to view the progress of the seminar and to bring forward suggestions for its improvement.

I have described this experience – certainly most rewarding for me personally – because I feel it represents an approach suitable to the present troubled world of the university. It gives the students responsibility for things that matter to them; for things, therefore, that they are qualified to make choices and decisions about. By the same token, an appropriate colleagueship is recognized, a membership of a company of scholars. As far as a faculty member is concerned, he has, at least in my experience, just as much chance to contribute usefully to the learning process as in any other context; I have been perfectly satisfied with my role as entrepreneurial contributor. Viewed from another angle, the faculty member is not as excluded as he is in some of the 'free university' courses that dissatisfied radical students organize. Lastly, how effective is this as a learning procedure? I can only confirm that the quality of discussion and presentation was excellent, that the range was great, and that the students expressed considerable satisfaction with the procedure.

The experiences I have described could come under the heading of development, since they were intended, among other things, to lead to improved relations between professors and students. Not all students, however, would view them in that way. The more militant are hostile to reforms that appease the students, obscure the continuing conflict, and create, in fact, a relationship of pseudo-balance. They argue that as long as the universities form part of a corrupt society, in the sense that they draw their support from it and in turn serve its interests, they are to be destroyed rather than reformed. Thus universities constitute an accessible and vulnerable target for young revolutionaries. Whether the militants are right in their assumptions, or whether – as I hope – the universities can be reformed and weaned from dependence upon the forces they detest, time will reveal.

1. I would also recommend Black (1966) and Geiger (1967) for the light they throw on relations between the poor countries and the rich.
2. The most telling expositor of the psychological evils of colonialism has been Fanon (1965, 1967). Mannoni (1964) has some interesting if perverted insights.
3. Lord Macaulay, in his famous 'Minute' in favour of English education, dated 2 February 1835. The 'Minute' is extensively quoted in Mahmood (1895). See also Woodrow (1962).
4. These facts concerning Ghana and Brazil are elaborated by the Haselmere Declaration Group (1968). See also Dumont (1966), Kamarck (1967), Worsley (1967), Jalée (1968). Nkrumah (1965) gives telling examples of neo-colonialism in practice and is one of the earliest analysts of the system. See also Green and Seidman (1968).
5. From only five of the wealthy countries does more than 1 per cent of the GNP (a proportion widely accepted as a not unreasonable target) flow to the poor ones. The USA is eleventh in the list when countries are ordered according to the percentage of their GNP flowing to poor countries in investments and in aid: it gave ·65 per cent in 1968, a decline from ·75 per cent in 1960 and ·84 per cent at the height of the Marshall Plan. The average contribution through official channels of 15 rich nations has declined from ·54 per cent of the GNPs in 1960 to ·39 per cent in 1968 (the US figure is ·38 per cent). The Pearson Report considers ·70 per cent a suitable target for 1970 (Commission on International Development, 1969, pp. 145–8).
6. For a discussion of related ideas see the same author's contribution to Roszak (1967).
7. This chapter is based on Curle (1968); see also Curle (1966).
8. Based on Curle (1962).
9. The following books, among many available, provide good background material on the two wars under consideration. On Pakistan and India: Lamb (1966), Lakhanpal (1965), Chowdhury (1968); on Nigeria: Schwarz (1965), Coleman (1958).
10. Lord Macaulay, see note 3 above.
11. An excellent source on South Africa, from which I have drawn my statistical information, is Van den Berghe (1965).
12. This argument has been well made in relation to South Africa by Julius Lewin (1963, pp. 107–15). The much earlier arguments of Alexis de Tocqueville (1850) and those of Brinton (1957) also apply.
13. Such situations readily spawn military takeovers; see Murray (1956).

14. The growth of inequalities as an accompaniment of development is also illustrated by Williamson (1965).

15. Some of the most graphic descriptions of this kind of situation are to be found in the works of Chinua Achebe (especially 1959 and 1961) and in Turnbull (1962). Redfield (1941) and Durkheim (1930) have, of course, contributed greatly to the analysis of such situations.

16. This case was cogently argued by Galbraith (1961).

17. *The Arusha Declaration and Tanu's Policy on Socialism and Self-reliance* (1967) is a vitally important document. It shows how one formerly colonial country has charted a development course which steers away from the rocks and shoals of both neo-colonialism and slavish imitation of the West.

18. There is further discussion of the issues considered in this chapter in Curle (1960 and 1963); Government of Pakistan Planning Board (1956); and Mezirow (1963). For a general background to community development in the Indian subcontinent, see Mayer *et al.* (1958).

19. Sources on this area include Robertson (1898) and Schomberg (1938).

20. The only source I know of is T. H. Lewin (1869).

21. The work on which this chapter is based is recorded in Curle (1947). See also Wilson (1946), Wilson, Doyle, and Kelnar (1947), and, for a more general discussion of aspects of the therapeutic technique, Jaques (1948). Guttman and Thomas (1946) discuss an analogous problem.

22. The chapter by Blackburn (in Blackburn and Cockburn, 1967) from which this passage is quoted is a devastating account of the inequalities of British society. I derived from it much information relevant to my theme.

23. For a critique of this approach see Ross (1969, pp. 86–92).

24. According to Wright (1966, pp. 90–1), absence owing to certified incapacity increased in Britain between 1953–4 and 1963–4 from 13·2 million days to 17·66 million, and absence owing to accidents from 12·66 million days to 18·8 million.

25. The work on which this section is based is discussed in Curle (1952 and 1954–5). See also Mitchell (1950).

26. Perhaps the best single modern source among a vast number is the *Report* of the National Advisory Commission on Civil Disorders (1968). Facts quoted without acknowledgement in this chapter are derived from this source. Mention must also be made of Myrdal (1944). This great work, though not of course so up-to-date, is amazingly comprehensive. The mood of the American black population is expressed with great fire and artistry by Cleaver (1968), while *Daedalus* (Fall, 1968) gives a comprehensive overview of many of the outstanding problems. See also Skolnick (1969, pp. 125–76).

27. So much has been written on this topic that I hesitate to quote any sources. The following, however, offer a range of useful material on student unrest, especially in the United States: Cohn-Bendit *et al.* (1968); *Comparative Education Review* (special issue on Student Politics, Vol. 10, No. 2, 1966); *Crisis at Columbia* (Cox Commission Report, 1968); *Daedalus* (Winter,

1968); Lipset and Wolin (1965); Skolnick (1969, pp. 79–124). Interesting proposals aimed at establishing a new type of university which would not be subject to criticisms that may be levelled against most existing models are made in the 'College of the Potomac' (1968) and in Goodman (1962). For the view of the radical faculty, see Roszak (1967), and for the qualities of the radical students, Keniston (1968).

28. By Jerry Farber. This brilliant and embittered article was very widely circulated in mimeographed form in the USA. I saw it in 1968, but do not know where or when (if at all) it was published. A book of the same title, which enlarges on the theme of the article, has been published (Farber, 1969).

29. My attempts to influence the procedure of teacher education at Exeter are described in Curle (1955b).

30. My employment of the words 'mirage' and 'mask' anticipates the discussion in Chapter 19 below, in which they are defined (see the section on 'Psychological Aspects of Conciliation', p. 209).

PART II

The Practice of Peacemaking

Introduction

Elements in Peacemaking

The terms conflict management and conflict resolution are commonly used to describe the processes involved in changing unpeaceful relationships into peaceful ones. I hold that these terms are certainly appropriate for the stage of bargaining or negotiating that must normally be a part of the business of reaching a settlement and achieving better relations, but that other terms are required to differentiate other stages that commonly occur. I identify the following approaches to, or components in, peacemaking.

Research

By this I mean simply the investigations and researches any would-be peacemaker must pursue in order to master the facts of the particular unpeaceful relationship. If one gets involved with delicate and complex issues without understanding the specifics (however good one may be on the theory) one's ignorance will quickly become apparent; it is then unlikely that one will get very far.

Conciliation

This is activity aimed at bringing about an alteration of perception – the other side is not as bad as we thought, we have misinterpreted their actions, etc. – that will lead to an alteration of attitude and, eventually, to an alteration of behaviour. Conciliation has to be carried out by someone who is not caught up in the turmoil of emotions that usually besets the participating parties to a quarrel; the conciliator normally has to be a third party. His task may be thought of as the psychological aspect of peacemaking, for he will be concerned as much with creating an atmosphere in which a settlement can be reached as with the terms of that settlement. His job is to lower the temperature, to provide a moment of calm in which reason can reassert itself, and to present a different interpretation, another point of view, a possible way out of an impasse, a face-saving device that will enable an unpopular thing to be done. Conciliation oils the machinery of negotiation with trust and prevents the tragedy and loss that occur when one nation bludgeons another into submission and then imposes terms which sow the seeds of a future confrontation, as in the case of Germany after World War I.

Bargaining

This is the process of negotiation, or 'horse-trading' as it is commonly termed, through which two conflicting groups try to reach a settlement in which each gives as little as possible and gains as much as possible. When the parties are unbalanced it is likely that the settlement will be correspondingly lopsided and so perpetuate the unpeacefulness of the relationship. In a more balanced situation, however, successful bargaining can lead to circumstances in which both sides can live without mutual impairment. Successful bargaining leads essentially to a resolution of conflict and to the establishment of a peaceful relationship, that is to say, a balanced relationship in which the advantages of one side are not gained at the expense of the other.

Development

I use this word to represent a phase in peacemaking that is characterized by a restructuring of unpeaceful relations to create a situation, a society, or a community in which individuals are enabled to develop and use to the full their capacities for creativity, service, and enjoyment. Unless development in this sense can take place, no settlement will lead to a secure and lasting peace.

I have deliberately employed the term development in order to link this stage in peacemaking intrinsically to development in economic, social, and political spheres. Since much of my experience has been with 'developing' nations, I am particularly concerned with the persisting conflict and turmoil so many of these nations display. Such conflict is attributed by some to a lack of development (in economic and political terms), but I believe it is also a product of faulty development, which has created un-peaceful relations rather than healed them. For in the 'developed' world, too, a development of relationships as defined above is obviously required. Thus there is a clear need for a restructuring of the relations between the black and white communities in the United States; and indeed of the relations between the rich and the poor in that and many other countries.

I must make it clear that by a restructuring of relations I do not mean bringing about subjective changes of attitude among the poor and weak which might make their condition more acceptable to them. Nor do I mean effecting superficial improvements in their circumstances which might be sufficient to divert their attention from the deeper conflict of interest. On the contrary, when I talk of a restructuring of relations between the rich and the poor, for example, an essential first step would be the bringing about of a progressive reduction of the gap between the two until something like parity, or at least the political equivalent of it, had been achieved.

The process of bringing about a balance of power – in economic, political, and other spheres – is usually part of what I refer to as confrontation (see below). Development, in the sense of a re-structuring of relations, is essentially a later phase. When confron-tation, by reducing the disparity of power, has led to successful bargaining, then development can take place. It is the consolida-tion of a peaceful relationship through collaboration and co-operation, and the mutual adjustments these demand.

To these four processes of peacemaking I would add education and confrontation as making a contribution that is in some ways even more important to the eventual establishment of peaceful relationships.

Education

Among communities of 'ignorant slaves', such as the Faqir Mishkin, no change will occur, no move away from passive unpeacefulness, until there is an increase in the level of awareness of the fundamental conflict of interest. This will come about through, in the widest sense of the word, education.

Confrontation

This term is used to cover all the techniques by means of which the weaker groups in unbalanced relationships attempt to change the character of those relationships, specifically to make them more balanced. Ghandian non-violence, civil disobedience, protest, sabotage, the various non-violent alternatives to war, and confrontation as practised by the students of today and by the black Americans – all are included. Revolution is, of course, the classic mode of confrontation. It may seem strange that a study of peacemaking should include such violent or potentially violent methods. It is not my intention, in fact, to prescribe violent solutions. Nevertheless, we are concerned with methods of changing relations, and one way of attempting to do so is by violence.

The possible interrelations of these different elements of peacemaking are discussed in Chapter 15, 'The Sequence of Peacemaking'.

It may seem that values intrude unduly in what follows. Indeed, this whole essay is based on a value that I term peace: that is, a condition in which the relations between nations, and between groups within nations, and between individuals, and perhaps in the future between planets, are such that no unnecessary violence, physical or psychological, is done either actively, or passively through a failure to do what might have prevented it. This admittedly is a value, but one with which I imagine few would disagree. If it is accepted, then much that is subsequently advocated will be seen, I believe, to follow logically.

Note on Conciliation and Bargaining
In the chapters on conciliation and bargaining I may be criticized for ignoring or dealing inadequately with a large number of well-tried peacemaking approaches. In fact, the greater part of conflict-resolution theory is concerned with this area and includes, for

example, studies of mediation and arbitration, the role of the United Nations and the International Court of Justice, games theory and simulation, arms control, and escalation strategies. But I have not intended to summarize, still less to supplant, the enormous amount of work done in those fields. All I have tried to do is to suggest that in the movement of a relationship from a condition of conflict to one of peace there is a stage when the functions of conciliation and bargaining are essential.

Let us take conciliation first. Whether we are concerned with a precarious marriage, uneasy labour relations, groups at odds with each other, or international disputes, the problem of improving bad relations is sharpened by suspicion, distrust, faulty perceptions, poor communications – what in a later section I refer to as the mask-mirage phenomenon. The deterioration of relations is accompanied by a worsening of the psychological ambience to a point where, especially in times of war, perceptions are so distorted that peace initiatives are doomed to failure almost before they are launched. Conciliation is essentially an applied psychological tactic aimed at correcting perceptions, reducing unreasonable fears, and improving communications to an extent that permits reasonable discussion to take place, and, in fact, makes rational bargaining possible. (It does not always follow, of course, that a bargain will be struck because objective difficulties may remain even if all the subjective obstacles have been removed.)

Conciliation is a function that may operate within any peace-making context. It is a psychological technique, or rather the rudiments of one, which I believe may be refined and developed as a therapeutic technique. Any negotiator, to the extent that he is successful, and whether he is working on a large scale or a small, whether he is an arbitrator, an intermediary, or a mediator, whether he represents a government, an international agency, an organization, a profession, or simply himself, is also engaged in conciliation. I do not discount any of the many approaches to achieving settlement of disputes; I merely suggest that unless they include an element of conciliation they are unlikely to be successful.

Conciliation involves individuals, both those who conciliate and those who are conciliated. Governments can exert influence and apply pressure, but only individuals can carry out the delicate task of helping other individuals to see more clearly the agonizing and confusing issues on which they must make decisions. It is my belief, in fact, that the fewer ties an individual has with a government (which is always seen as a potential exerter of pressure) the more effective he will be as a conciliator; hence, the section on private diplomacy (p. 225). In practice, of course, in the majority of cases the conciliator has some public position, and there are also, as we shall consider, certain advantages in this.

It need hardly be said that conciliation is a third-party activity. Only in exceptional circumstances can individuals involved in a quarrel be sufficiently detached to view the attitudes of both their enemies and their own side with objectivity. If they could, moreover, they would probably be suspected, for different reasons, by both friends and foes.

The chapter on conciliation, though fairly long, does not pretend to do more than give examples of what this function of peacemaking might imply, and try to show some of its psychological roots.

Conciliation and bargaining, more often than not, are overlapping and inextricably interwoven. It may also happen that the sequence is reversed so that bargaining comes first and conciliation second (or rather, successful bargaining – unsuccessful bargaining often precedes conciliation). For example, an unpopular solution may be imposed on two conflicting groups by powerful external forces, but the parties to the quarrel, now that the grounds for their dispute have been largely removed, may begin to lose their fear of each other and move gradually forward to the stage of development. It is for these reasons, perhaps, that most writers treat the two stages as though they were one. The following differences, however, may be noted:

1. Conciliation deals primarily with subjective phenomena; bargaining with objective.

2. Conciliation tends to be carried out at an individual level; bargaining is more a matter for organizations (governments, unions, etc.).

3. Conciliation is a third-party function; bargaining is more likely to be carried out by the principles in the dispute.

4. Conciliation is the beginning of a psychological settlement; bargaining leads to a material settlement.

Bargaining is the stage usually reached by the parties to an unpeaceful relationship after they have been brought together somewhat through conciliation. But bargaining itself may be divided into two phases. First comes the rather desperate haggling, the proposals and counter-proposals through which, in times of crisis, each side jockeys for position either before or during the early stages of negotiation.

During this phase many of the psychological themes carry over from the stage of conciliation (which means in effect that conciliation must continue). Throughout the process of crisis bargaining, in fact, fear and distortion are overriding elements of the situation – conciliation has reduced them merely to the point where it may be possible to begin discussions, however wary and hostile. Nevertheless there is a shift of emphasis; there is some common attempt to consider rational solutions to joint problems. And a cooler atmosphere may be created in which solutions that were previously rejected, because they were perceived differently, can be accepted.

The second type of bargaining is more rational. It may still be dominated by fear that the other side will try to cheat, but this is a not unreasonable fear which might, so to speak, be computerized. The stress is more on the long-term struggle for advantage or for maintaining balance, which might be exemplified by the negotiations for Britain's entry to the European Economic Community or by the USA/USSR Strategic Arms Limitation Talks.

I have dealt almost entirely with the first phase of bargaining because I am particularly concerned with the question of how contestants can be brought to the bargaining table in a spirit of constructive compromise. This is by far the most important step in the transition to peace.

I might perhaps have dealt with the second phase of bargaining – with the sorts of arrangements that are arrived at and the sorts of stratagems that are employed to reach them – but was held back by several considerations.

First, to do so would have meant opening up the whole vast issue of how governments regulate their relationships. This is not an area of which I have any particular knowledge while it is, on the other hand, one that has been most extensively documented.

Second, my subject is unpeaceful relationships, whereas a great deal of second-phase bargaining takes place in the course of normal international relations. Even in cases of serious conflict much of the venom must have been drawn from the situation before such bargaining can occur.

Third, in my opinion the truly critical phase in changing an unpeaceful relationship into a peaceful one occurs during the preliminary exchanges, through which the contestants to the dispute are brought to the point of negotiations genuinely aimed at settling it.

Fourth, most conflicts in the world today are on a relatively small scale in the poor countries. On the other hand, a great deal of work on conflict theory refers almost exclusively to relations between the great powers and to the cold-war situation. I have not dealt with these at all in this book, and the unpeaceful relationships with which I have been concerned are on a smaller scale.

The actual solution adopted, the actual bargain accepted, depends upon circumstances too varied to permit of generalization. I would stress only that, in the context of my arguments, a valid settlement must be one that is based on, and maintains, a relatively balanced relationship. Any other solution will push the relationship back to a previous stage of unpeacefulness, leading to a subsequent second round of hostilities. A related general point is that the effectiveness of conciliation and bargaining as peacemaking techniques depends upon the stage at which they are applied. They are appropriate to conflict situations only when there is a balance of power; for if the discontented slave is brought by conciliation to be contented with his lot, conciliation has in this case merely prolonged an essentially unpeaceful relationship.

It is important to note at this point that conciliation may fail or bargains may be broken because of factors quite outside the control of the peacemaker. Thus changes in the domestic or military situation may lead to the repudiation of agreements reached in an earlier context; or the influence of external powers may prevent a settlement between two contestants (or perhaps promote an unsuitable one). Indeed, in any quarrel more are embroiled than the two principals. In the Nigerian civil war, for example, the complex calculations of interests that determined the giving of support by the United Kingdom, the USSR, France, Portugal, South Africa, and other countries, and the withholding of it by the USA, greatly affected the course of the conflict and, at various stages, the chances of settlement.

Finally, I should re-emphasize the difference between bargaining and development. The former creates conditions in which two groups are prepared to coexist without overt hostility. The latter implies a much more positive collaboration for mutual benefit. Although bargaining continues at the stage of development (just as does conciliation at the stage of bargaining), many other functions, institutions, and types of individuals are now involved.

Types of Peacemaker

We are accustomed to think of the peacemaker as someone who, through wisdom, experience, and goodwill, brings warring nations to the conference table. This is, indeed, an important peacemaking role, but many additional modes of peacemaking are outlined in this volume, and it is very unlikely that one individual could be concerned with, let alone responsible for, more than one or two of them. It is not a single Promethean human being who guides the slave from ignorant apathetic subservience to awareness and revolt, leading to equality and – by way of subtle bargaining – to constructive collaboration. The educator in awareness is a revolutionary. The man who stages the confrontation in which the slave, newly aware of his position and identity, faces his master, is likewise a revolutionary. The conciliator who attempts to change the perceptions of warring groups about each other is an outsider to the dispute whose skills are grounded in the social sciences and in psychology. The bargainer who arranges the settlement once the conciliator has done his work may be a politician or an administrator (though a dash of social science will help him), and he will probably be a member of one of the parties to the quarrel (unlike the third-party conciliator, though their roles overlap). The man concerned with development may be almost anything, since it involves such a broad and varied field; essentially, perhaps, he will be a politically wise statesman, but any number of specialists will be concerned with the details – economists, educationists, political scientists, and many others.

Many of these peacemakers, if it is proper to lump together so many different people with so many diverse functions, will be activists. They will take the initiative in changing relationships, just as did Fidel Castro and Che Guevara in the Cuban revolution when they stirred the rural population to take control of its political destiny. Those concerned with the development stage will be politicians and planners attempting to implement their ideas. The bargainer will be a tactician trying to get the best deal. Only the conciliator will be ideologically neutral, and that only to a relative degree. His role can perhaps be likened to that of the psychoanalyst in that his task can be carried out better by listening and interpreting than by taking the initiative; but he is not committed to passivity and in the interest of reaching a settlement he may find many ways of exerting pressure.

15 The Sequence of
Peacemaking

We are now in a position to draw tentative conclusions concerning the relationship between type of conflict and type or types of peacemaking approach.

Much of the literature on conflict resolution deals, in effect, with what I have termed bargaining, a process that is important, but not exclusively so, in establishing peaceful relations between states or between employers and employees, these being the fields in which most work has been done. I believe, as stated above, that there are three additional processes, the four together forming a sequence: research, conciliation, bargaining, development. Some of these processes will be less crucial than others and there may also be some overlapping, but there tends to be at least a shift in emphasis from research to conciliation and then to bargaining and then to development. This progression applies principally, however, to conflict situations that are relatively balanced and in which there is some awareness of conflict.

Where the conflict situation comprises an unbalanced relationship, the peacemaking sequence is less predictable, and the techniques of education and confrontation will be required to stimulate awareness and to achieve the degree of balance without which conciliation and bargaining can be used by the powerful as tools of pacification. In cases where the strong partner in the relationship takes the initiative in peacemaking (as did the Pakistan government with regard to the villages, through the agency of Village AID and the Basic Democracy system) the element of bargaining becomes much less important. Research is still necessary, but now much greater emphasis is placed on conciliation, both to solve the practical problems and to take the relationship

183

a stage further. By these means the relationship gradually changes into one that is more balanced: the people can express their will, they elect their own representatives, they have the relative degree of freedom enjoyed by the people of a democratic society who can, in the last resort, overthrow the government and choose a new one.

A very different situation prevails in cases where the strong partner not only does not help, but actively opposes attempts by the weak one to redress the balance. Top-dog intransigence must lead, eventually, to underdog militancy. At this stage the only peacemaking technique open to the underdog may be confrontation. The rulers, whoever they may be – the rich nations, the tyrannical or insensitive government, the professors, the whites, the landlords – must be forced to look at the underdog, to change their perception of him and hence their behaviour towards him, and ultimately to make the relationship more balanced. The actual technique employed may be violent or non-violent, but the principle remains the same. The masters, faced with potential (or indeed actual) revolution, have two alternatives. Either they can try to crush it, rooting out the ringleaders, imprisoning or killing them, and intimidating the rank and file; or they can attempt to use the tools of conciliation and bargaining. In the latter case they try to avoid trouble by making concessions which will assuage the people's hunger for freedom without actually giving it to them. They attempt to produce the appearance of balance without the substance. This technique might be called sweeping conflict under the carpet.

Many studies of conflict have been concerned with the preservation of negative peace, in the sense of the simple absence of violence. Fewer have been concerned with positive peace: the building of creative and cooperative associations between groups and nations. To conceal conflict not only does not contribute to positive peace, but makes it harder to attain. It falsifies the position in a fashion that makes it more difficult to put right. Moreover, it militates against the condition of 'peace' it aims to promote; it merely postpones the eventual explosion, which is likely to be all the more violent for the suppression and the delay.

It can be seen, then, that the combined techniques of research, conciliation, bargaining, and development are appropriate to conflict situations in which the two parties have a balanced relationship and can in fact negotiate because one of them does not have a preponderance of power. The various techniques of confrontation are appropriate to the weaker party in an unbalanced relationship because he is trying to reach a greater degree of parity. Once he has achieved this he will become able, through the conciliatory efforts of a third party, to enter into rational discussion of the situation, or he will be in a position to bargain – but he cannot do these things while he is weak. His overtures would be rejected, or he would be unable to strike a fair bargain.

The strong party who engages in bargaining holds all the best cards. In particular, he is usually strong enough to do a great deal of damage if he wants to. He can also offer some attractive propositions which may well be accepted with relief by people who, though angered by injustice, fear the consequences of opposition and are ready to accept compromise.

Thus, from the point of view of the government or employer wanting a quiet life, it seems to be sensible policy to apply to one sort of conflict the peacekeeping technique suitable to another. In fact, such a policy prolongs the conflict; it might be termed a technique of non-resolution which postpones open violence, but it may be felt to be justified if the violence is postponed for a long enough time.

What we have just been considering applies to unbalanced relationships in which there is some awareness of conflict. When awareness is low, the situation is different. This is negative peace in the sense of passivity or submission; it is apathetic acquiescence in crippling, inhibiting, degrading, and limiting circumstances. Revolutionary governments of peoples unaware of their miserable conditions have, of course, tried both to change these conditions and to raise the level of awareness through community education and other methods of information and propaganda. But where continued ignorance is in the interest of the rulers, the education must be carried out by anyone who has sufficient nerve. The purpose of such education is to move the conflict into the stage of awareness;[1] and at that stage the object of the weaker party is to move it into a stage of greater balance; and thereafter it is to be moved into the stage of development. This progression is shown in *Figure 4*.

Figure 4   Peacemaking approaches appropriate for different sorts or stages of conflict

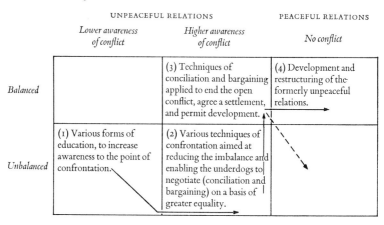

| | UNPEACEFUL RELATIONS | | PEACEFUL RELATIONS |
	Lower awareness of conflict	*Higher awareness of conflict*	*No conflict*
Balanced		(3) Techniques of conciliation and bargaining applied to end the open conflict, agree a settlement, and permit development.	(4) Development and restructuring of the formerly unpeaceful relations.
Unbalanced	(1) Various forms of education, to increase awareness to the point of confrontation.	(2) Various techniques of confrontation aimed at reducing the imbalance and enabling the underdogs to negotiate (conciliation and bargaining) on a basis of greater equality.	

Notes: (a) The peacemaking sequence may, of course, begin at any of the stages of conflict.

(b) The broken arrow would illustrate, for example, that a minority group, having striven for greater equality, is satisfied with a measure of self-government short of independence; even so, the relationship would clearly be more peaceful than it was previously, with an acceptable degree of imbalance.

Among the case studies, only that of the Firm (p. 126 above) demonstrates anything approximating the complete change from an unbalanced relationship with low awareness of conflict to a peaceful relationship of development, but the shifts were somewhat blurred and inconclusive. Moreover, the people involved, far from being ignorant peasants or *Lumpenproletariat*, included a large number of educated and sophisticated persons. Nevertheless, their circumstances were such that few of them had articulated to themselves the conflict in which they were engaged. My discussions with them, though consisting mainly of their answers to my questions, did have an educative effect as a result of which they formulated the issues. They became more aware of their situation and more intent on doing something to change it. Some of the subsequent meetings with the directors had, indeed, the character of confrontations. These, because of the goodwill and under-standing of the directors, led to a process of conciliation and bargaining in which the directors tried to ensure that their interests would not be damaged by any concessions they might make. Finally, there was a restructuring of the relationship be-tween the employers and the employees, and various steps were taken to ensure harmonious growth in the future.

Figure 5 shows a different progression. It illustrates graphically the technique of pseudo-resolution by which an appearance of balance is created. It will be noted that this involves applying methods suitable for the resolution of one type of unpeaceful relationship to the resolution of another.[2] The end-result of the sequence shown here is the Bantustan, as depicted in *Figure 2*. Other examples of pseudo-resolution are the integration move-ment in the USA and the privileges granted to the Angolan *assimilado*. In the American case those who promoted integration were certainly well intentioned, but they succeeded in blurring the conflict; it is for this reason that the blacks have turned so bitterly against the white liberals.

Figure 5   Negative peacemaking by obscuring conflict

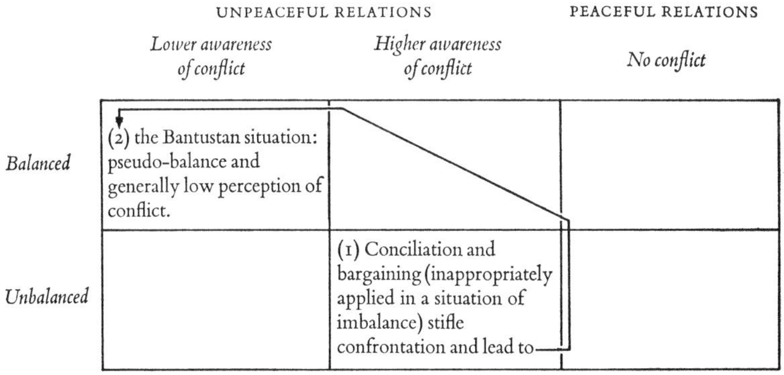

The only way in which the unpeaceful relationship shown in *Figure 6* can be transformed into a peaceful one is by a reversal of the process: the pseudo-balance must be recognized as imbalance; there must then be confrontation; this, if successful, will lead to conciliation and bargaining – and thence to development. It will be noted that the conciliation-bargaining techniques are pushed up into their proper case.

Figure 6 Reversal of negative peacemaking

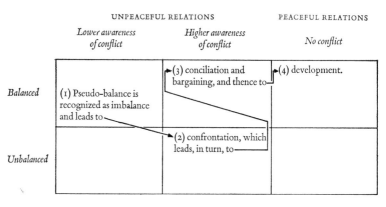

In relationships of alienation, the most useful peacemaking technique is conciliation. This aspect of peacemaking is largely psychological and it is appropriate to situations in which, to a greater extent than is normal, one-sided misperceptions are dominant. In addition, however, some developmental reordering of the relationship might be needed to prevent relapse into this form of social paranoia. Thus it might be advisable to devise a charter for advisers, elaborating and confirming the nature of their relationship with their counterparts.

The most important conclusions to which our discussions have led us are these: peace means more than the absence of open strife; to reach the phase of development, the ultimate stage of peacemaking, it may be necessary to pass through the stage of confrontation which may, although there are alternatives, be violent; our understanding of the nature of peace determines our approach to peacemaking.

Chapters on education and confrontation follow the chapter on research, since to be effective as peace-making techniques they should precede the stages of conciliation, bargaining, and development.

16 Research

The brevity of this chapter would seem to indicate that its subject scarcely warrants separate treatment. However, research is a necessary and distinct function of peacemaking and, although there is little to be said about it, it should be mentioned independently of the other functions.

It is particularly important for third parties embarking on tasks involving conciliation, bargaining, and development to be primed with correct information. This should relate especially to the issues and the actors. The would-be peacemaker who is not fully informed is liable to make ignorant and impolitic remarks which swiftly disqualify him, in the eyes of the parties to the conflict, for the role. Exceptions should be made for individuals, such as Fisher (1969), who have a particular technique, and for social scientists working in situations of controlled communication, as described by Burton (1969), whose very ignorance of the details of a conflict enables them to be more objective and to generalize more effectively. But, on the whole, information about the situation in particular and about conflict in general is indispensable.

I have on several occasions found that a period of unobtrusive study has prevented me from making what might have been disastrous errors. For example, when I was first about to visit Thornley, several friends suggested that the best informants about the situation would be the minister and the schoolteacher. Fortunately I made long-range inquiries of people who knew the village and discovered that these two people were extremely unpopular. Had I been known to have been consorting with them it is likely that many other doors would have been closed to me. In the event I was lucky enough to meet someone whose cousin, a respected young farmer, was a leader of unofficial village opinion. He provided a very good point of entry for my work and after a while I felt that my reputation had become sufficiently secure for me to risk a visit to the teacher!

In much tenser situations involving international violence or the threat of it, comparable but more difficult investigations have to be made. If it seems desirable, for example, to approach people at the highest level of government, then one must choose with the utmost care who is going to introduce one. If one's 'introducer' is out of favour or espouses unpopular or unorthodox views, one will suffer by association. If he is not influential enough he will not be able to arrange for one to meet the president or the prime minister; or again, if he is too important or too arrogant, he may try to deal with the matter himself. If his views of the situation are greatly at variance with one's own (a fact that may emerge in discussion) he may effectively sabotage one's efforts. Thus knowledge of the people, of the factions and the power structure, is vital, not only at the beginning but indeed increasingly as one becomes more deeply involved and meets many individuals in a variety of situations. A few close friends, the equivalent of the anthropologist's informants, who can keep one in touch with the shape of unfolding events, are invaluable.

An understanding of the nature and character of the conflict, its antecedents and ramifications, is obviously necessary for the peacemaker if those he deals with are to be assured of his credibility and seriousness; but it is also part of his stock in trade as a peacemaker. The time may come when a peaceful solution to the conflict will depend on the information he has to convey, or on his interpretation of some piece of information. In the troubled circumstances of war desperate emotions are aroused, which distort understanding. An objective presentation of facts that have been misinterpreted, or even not known about, may bring peace nearer.

In this sense, research is a continuing function of peacemaking, though it may be most important at the outset. Peacemaking, we should remind ourselves, is, apart from everything else, a demanding intellectual exercise.

17 Education

Education in this context means education for awareness: the awareness of the slave that he is a slave. (The masters are not considered in this chapter; they are educated through confrontation.) There are two strands to this education. The first is to develop the perception of the ignorant peasant, the *Lumpenproletariat*, even of the prosperous and successful lackeys of the rich, until they realize that they are imposed upon, used, and exploited; the second is to make them aware that they are not helpless. Given this understanding they can begin to hope, and hope is the most revolutionary force in the world; it drives men to a desperation they did not dare to feel when they believed themselves to be impotent.

Education for awareness, hope, and desperation is not easy to impart. Moreover, it is resisted by apathy, ignorance, and fear; it requires a tremendous mobilization of nerve for the weak to abandon what security they have and to pit themselves against the strong. It is resisted also by the frightened self-interest of those who, by serving the rulers, have shared to some small extent in their power and risen above their fellows; if they were to turn against their masters they would lose everything; it is hard for them to recognize that their chains, though gilded, are nevertheless chains.

Formal education plays an indirect and indeterminate part in creating revolutionary awareness. Most educational systems throughout most of history have served the élite, reinforcing in their children the ideology of their class and strengthening their sense of superiority. Members of the lower orders who attended these schools became imbued with the attitudes of the élite, for if affluence and power seem associated with certain beliefs it is hard not to adopt them.

Similarly, in the colonial territories the imperial powers established school systems patterned on those of the metropolitan country. The principal purpose of these was to produce 'educated natives' who knew enough of the British, French, or Dutch way of doing things to fill subordinate positions in the administration, the police, the agricultural department, education, and the armed services. In the mission schools the main purpose was to save souls, but the effect was much the same: the boys (for few girls were educated) learnt that subject people can acquire power only by sharing (slightly) in that of their masters. They also acquired competitive materialism, that great contribution of the rich to the poor nations, which is bestowed by the very structure of European education even if transmitted by unworldly members of a religious order. From this point of view, education blunted awareness.

There is, however, another side to the matter. As Benjamin Franklin observed, 'nothing enfranchises like education'. Even the most rabidly colonialist education imparts certain useful and ideologically neutral skills and a quantum of valid information. Many of today's revolutionary leaders received most of their formal education in schools and colleges set up by or modelled on those of the colonial powers. At least they were taught to read, a dangerous ability, since those who possess it can progress from laudatory versions of British history, such as were staple fare in great African schools like Achimota, to Marx or Fanon. In addition, they gained a view of the world spreading far beyond the boundaries of their village.

Of course, if any nation wishes to awaken the awareness of its own people the educational system, properly reshaped to expunge the colonial legacy of inappropriate subject-matter and unsuitable method, can prove a powerful weapon for change. It has been used in this way in Tanzania and Cuba and may be so used in Pakistan, where a great effort is being made to erase the effects of more than a century of British education.[3] Also in Pakistan, as in many other countries, community development techniques have served as a tool for achieving education for awareness. Admittedly the lessons have largely been economic, technical, and administrative, but they have inevitably been associated with political awakening. This has frequently been demonstrated in Pakistan by the growing independence of the small farmers and their defiance of their landlords.

Perhaps our main concern is, however, with what can be done to educate for awareness in an essentially hostile environment where the ruling group, as in South Africa, South Vietnam, and many Latin American oligarchies, is intent on preserving the *status quo*.

The aim of these few paragraphs is to suggest that there is no soft or easy way of educating for awareness. To depict an extreme case, ignorance, inertia, powerlessness, and fear of enraging the rulers are matched against power, ruthlessness, interest in maintaining things as they are, and a cult of superiority. I can see no alternative to hard, dangerous, and largely unrewarding effort by people who have dedicated their lives to the task.

There are two main components of this work. The first is education in the more usual sense of imparting information, and of attempting to create the intellectual tools required to compare political systems, to perceive class structures, to recognize injustice and, finally, to be self-conscious and aware. But this new knowledge must be backed by the confidence that something can be done to alter the situation. Thus the second component of education is demonstration. The teacher must show that it is possible to stand up to authority. And if it is impossible for him to argue with, refute, or castigate the rulers in some open confrontation because they will not listen to or meet him, he may be forced to more clandestine acts of opposition. Che Guevara's mission in Bolivia constituted an educative demonstration of this sort. In terms of actual damage to the Bolivian régime, its significance was paltry; but in showing the people that even a small band could defy the might of the state it was invaluable.

The way of the revolutionary educator may not always be so hard or, it is to be hoped, so violent, but there can be no avoiding its difficulty.

After education, confrontation. Education begins to change the power structure by conferring awareness, that most powerful of all weapons, on the underdog. Indeed, if the whole of the oppressed and previously ignorant population were to become aware overnight, they would be invincible. Things do not, of course, work out like this. The first groups who become aware and whose awareness leads them to the stage of confrontation are usually small and their power is correspondingly limited. But once the confrontation begins it speeds up the process of education. The two move forward together; but the initial element of education must logically have preceded confrontation.

POSTSCRIPT

Since completing this book I have read *Pedagogy of the Oppressed* by Paulo Friere (1970). This, more than anything else I have read, is directly and penetratingly concerned with education for awareness, as a tool for moving societies towards peace.

18 Confrontation

Aims and Possible Effects

Confrontation, in my terminology, is the stage at which the weaker party to an unbalanced relationship attempts to achieve equality with the stronger so that they may both, on this basis, reorder their relationship. An example would be the relationship between the United Kingdom and India. There was a long struggle for India's independence during which the followers of Ghandi acquired sufficient political and moral, though not military, force to make continued British rule inexpedient. The British withdrew, but have remained on friendly terms with India, where there are now more British residents than there were during the imperial era. (There are, of course, many examples where the granting of nominal independence to the one side has been merely a cloak for its continued economic and political domination by the other. India, in my opinion, is not one of these.)

The case is different when the top dogs have no overseas base to withdraw to. When they constitute the ruling group of the country whose underdogs are confronting them, the alternatives are more stark. They may crush the opposition; or they may be crushed and annihilated by it; or they may reach a settlement by which they abrogate some of their power, but remain essentially in command. The third of these possibilities is the way of evolution rather than revolution, in which there is a gradual shift in the balance of power. Evolution normally occurs as a consequence of periodical confrontations, each one pushing the ruling group a little further. Nevertheless, apparent evolutionary changes may be little more than defensive actions by the rulers, who are hoping thereby to pacify the opposition without yielding essential points.

Of the other possibilities, the stamping out of revolt is clearly not a step towards peace; and the liquidation of the ruling group is not, in my opinion, a satisfactory alternative. I consider peace to be a positive relationship between persons or groups. If a married couple live in disharmony I would not say that peace was established by the murder of one by the other. But whereas it may be possible for a husband and wife to be reconciled, both continuing in their previous roles as spouses, this is hardly possible in much larger groups. The *campesinos* and the ruling oligarchies of some Latin American nations could not, after confrontation, persist peacefully in their earlier roles since it was those very roles that had caused the original unpeacefulness. The only solution in such a case is for the form of social control of the oligarchy to be brought to an end. The question that remains is what happens, as individuals, to the former members of the oligarchy? If they are imprisoned, exiled, or shot I would say that in some respects peace has not been attained, for peace implies increased opportunity for all to realize their potential. Dead people have no potential. Ideally, then, the new régime should find ways of incorporating individual members of the oligarchy, of using whatever talents they possess, and of educating their outlook – that is, of converting them. This may be an unattainable goal; so may peace. But unless we set our sights high we shall not achieve all that we could achieve.

The overthrow of the top dogs by the bottom dogs may also nullify peace, as I conceive it, in another sense. There may simply be a reversal of roles, as illustrated below, and one unbalanced

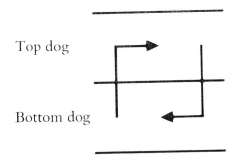

Top dog

Bottom dog

relationship is merely replaced by another. The roles remain the same, only the incumbents change, and the cycle of conflict is condemned to continue. As Yeats put it:

> *Hurrah for revolution and more cannon-shot,*
> *A beggar on horseback lashes a beggar on foot.*
> *Hurrah for revolution and cannon come again!*
> *The beggars have changed places, but the lash goes on.*[4]

Few revolutionaries seem to have been aware of this danger. However, Amilcar Cabral, the leader of the very successful liberation movement in Portuguese Guinea, is quite specific on this point (Cabral, 1969, pp. 84–90).[5] If, he says, with the eventual complete eviction of the Portuguese the Africans simply assume their administrative and managerial roles, the colonial tyranny will only have been replaced by another (as has happened in some other post-colonial countries). Spartacus, the heroic slave rebel of antiquity, on the other hand, did no more than reject slavery for himself and his followers, and claim equality with the masters; indeed, he wished in turn to be master; he had no desire to alter the system by which some could be masters and some slaves.

Violence

There are many arguments for resorting to violent confrontation, or rather violent tactics, if moral confrontation – that is, facing the top dog with the plight of the bottom dog, proclaiming his responsibility, and demanding justice – is ineffective. The most compelling is that the rulers will respond to nothing else. In an unpeaceful relationship in which the wellbeing of one group is contingent upon the misfortunes of the other (a clear case of conflict of interest) the rulers are unlikely to yield to persuasion. One can only attack them, defeat them, and rebuild society along new lines. Southern Africa and much of Latin America provide examples, among others, of systems in which the oligarchies would seem impervious to anything except armed assault. Even so, the only fully successful revolutionary movement in Latin

America has been in Cuba; it is not easy for the oppressed to topple the oppressors.

Other arguments for violence are based more on the psychologically desirable effects it can have on the underdog than on practical necessity. Violence purges; it creates a sense of identity. But Fanon, who supports this view, himself presents case studies of psychiatric patients suffering from the effects of 'purifying' violence (Fanon, 1965). Thus one Algerian, whose mother had been killed by the French, felt driven to kill a white woman and did so as she begged on her knees for her life; but this experience made him sick rather than whole. A violent, definite act, as opposed to less direct forms of opposition, may do much to build morale and create confidence. It may focus strength and attention on the struggle and encourage those who might otherwise have remained passive to join in.

A further reason for violence, also developed by Fanon (1965), is that in circumstances (such as colonial liberation) where freedom has been achieved without violence, it is only half-achieved. Deals are made, compromises are arranged, and, although there is a nominal transfer of power, the dead hand of the former colonial ruler retains its grip. I have seen enough of neo-colonialism to concede the force of this argument.

On the other hand, there are many disadvantages to violence. When carried out against powerful and well-organized rulers it is often extremely costly in lives. It is, moreover, by no means always successful. Many revolutions have failed, and those that are most justifiable are those that, because of the ruthlessness and rapacity of the rulers, are most likely to fail.

Jacques Ellul, a French Catholic sociological writer who has entered the controversy concerning violence (in which many of his co-religionists, including priests, take the opposing view), maintains that there are 'laws' that prevent violence from having positive results (Ellul, 1969, pp. 94–104). These are: that there is continuity in violence in the sense that one act leads to another, so that violence begets violence; that violence is reciprocal in the sense that the response to violence is further violence; that there is a sameness about violence, so that however high its goal all practitioners are reduced to the same level; that the man who uses violence will go to any lengths to justify both it and himself; and that there is a close link between violence and hatred. Such arguments may be chewed over endlessly; I merely quote them as examples of reasoning which it is as hard to disprove as to substantiate.

A more compelling argument to me is that violence leads to death, or at least to physical or psychological harm. Some may maintain that violence ennobles the perpetrator, but no one can say that in regard to the product of his violence – a man dead or maimed. If peace signifies a condition in which the potential evolution of each individual is more readily realized, then violence is its antithesis. Thus we could not with a clear conscience resort to violence as a step towards peace unless we were sure that we were eradicating a cancer that could never grow again; but could we be certain that it might not, perhaps, grow the more readily because it had, as it were, been pruned? We should also have to be certain that in attempting to erase it we were not ourselves infected. Some advocates of violence hold a millennial view of history, believing that one episode of surgical violence can lead to everlasting peace and is thus justified. I can hardly believe that, in our present stage of social evolution, this can be true. Kaliayev, in Camus's play *Les Justes*, says on this issue: 'We are killing to build a world in which no one will ever kill. We accept criminality for ourselves in order that the earth may at last be full of innocent people.'[6] But the lesson of that play, and of *L'Homme révolté* (Camus, 1951), is that violence is justified only if he who inflicts it himself lays down his life.

The arguments against violence appear to me, all in all and bearing in mind a temperamental predisposition to non-violence, stronger than those in favour of it. The problem is to define a course of action which will be as effective and less questionable in its ultimate results.

Moral Confrontation

I give this name to the sort of confrontation that has been initiated in many cases by students and by black Americans. (In other situations they have employed the tactics of revolutionary confrontation, which I shall discuss next, as well, occasionally, as violent tactics. But moral confrontation and revolutionary confrontation may be combined.)

Moral confrontation aims not to destroy or overthrow, but rather to change the perceptions of the ruling group, to raise its level of awareness until it understands what it has done and accepts responsibility for the damage it has inflicted. And, of course, a full acceptance of responsibility will lead to a reapportionment of power and a restructuring of the relationship.

White sympathizers of black Americans have often expressed pained surprise, tinged, at times, with resentment, when the blacks have staged an angry confrontation with them. Are they not, after all, the people who have espoused the Negro cause, promoted civil rights, and issued clarion calls for equality? Surely they, if anyone, understand the Negroes. But the blacks themselves have been aware of the armour of white superiority (to do things *for* people rather than *with* them signifies contempt) and have striven desperately to pierce it with barbs of understanding.

The confrontation, in which furious accusations and insults are flung by the blacks at the passive, bewildered, but determinedly meek whites, has the effect of a sort of crude shock therapy. Assumptions are cast in doubt, preconceptions are challenged. People who believed themselves to have been always on the side of the blacks, to have been 'colour blind', suddenly realize that they have been blancocentric, really believing that the blacks needed them. If they are people of goodwill, this *satori*-like perception will be succeeded by their serious efforts to comprehend more deeply, and to eradicate in themselves the source of racial superiority with which whites are so deeply imbued. When such effort occurs, the confrontation is continued in a dialogue which may lay the basis for further understanding and, eventually, for effective common action.

When, on the other hand, the confrontation takes place with people who are essentially hostile to or frightened of the black population, they will be confirmed in their suspicions and the unpeaceful relationship will be pushed one stage further along the road to violence.

The confrontation, however, is more than a device for educating (or sometimes alienating) the whites. It has an important psychological value for the blacks. The expression of hatreds long suppressed – though not, I would maintain, necessarily by violence – does something to restore the sense of identity or pride. Moreover, it may well be necessary to ventilate these feelings, hidden for centuries out of fear, if others warmer and more tolerant are to emerge. It may be psychologically necessary for the expression of hatred to precede love. And the black people may find it easier to have true friendship for the whites when they have come to terms with their own identity and purged themselves of the desperate feelings that were obscuring and confusing that identity. Only then may it be possible for the identity of awareness to succeed the identity of belonging (see pp. 215–16).

In the case of the students the issue is neither so difficult nor so desperate. Nevertheless, the shock tactics of student confrontation have proved necessary in many universities to open the eyes of the professors. The largely symbolic act of a temporary occupation of a building has impelled the professors to self-examination, whereas they have remained unmoved by more orderly protests or petitions. Ironically, those who have remained deaf to constitutionally framed demands tend to react with umbrage to unconstitutional ones: Why could not the students have raised these matters through the proper channels?, they ask. We would have been most sympathetic to any reasonable suggestions. But, as I have already noted, professors tend to be concerned about the young. When inescapably faced with evidence that their students are discontented, they apply themselves seriously to the problem.

There was even a certain element of confrontation in the case of the Firm. It was very muted and polite, but the change in the relationship did not begin until the directors and representatives of the employees faced each other and the employees did what they had never done before: they said what they thought about things.

In a situation of moral confrontation one group, the underdogs, is essentially saying to the top dogs: Look at us and see us as we are rather than as it pleases you to see us; realize that you made us like this; do something about it. There is a threat in all confrontation. In fact, moral confrontation can lead easily to violence, but it is essentially a sub-violent technique for forcing awareness on a dominant group which is incompletely aware both of its own underlying attitudes and of its effect on the dominated group. It is an important tool in the peacemaking kit, but a dangerous one, since it may inflame the ruling group, heightening the hostility of the latter and leading to the abandonment of the non-violent approach.

Unlike the technique of conciliation (which, of course, is not appropriate in such circumstances, for conciliation could only mean blurring the contradictions and concealing the conflict), confrontation calls for a unilateral awakening rather than a mutual change of perception; the other side is already aware. Neither is confrontation a third-party activity: it is carried out directly by people who constitute one party of the relationship; they challenge the other party to change its behaviour.

Revolutionary Confrontation
In revolutionary confrontation opposition is pushed to the point of absolute rebellion, though without violence. If the rulers cannot be brought to recognize the evils they condone and so to remove them out of conviction, life must be made so intolerable for them that they change the system out of necessity, or have to accept the change thrust upon them.

There are examples of effective revolutionary confrontation (or civilian or non-violent resistance, as it is variously termed). The best-known is, perhaps, the Indian independence movement under the incomparable leadership of Ghandi. During World War II in Holland, Denmark, and Norway an amazingly effective non-violent resistance was waged against the German occupiers.[7] Non-compliance with orders and regulations, complete failure to cooperate, strikes, go-slows, intentionally stupid mistakes, intentionally bad work involving unidentifiable sabotage – such behaviour and activities were much harder to deal with, German generals told Liddell Hart after the war, than were guerrillas (Liddell Hart, 1969, pp. 239–40). When the Germans were dealing with armed resistance they knew where they stood and could take steps to crush it. But when a whole population passively defied them there was little they could do. Admittedly the German occupiers were not compelled to withdraw by these tactics, but they were considerably incommoded by them, whereas guerrilla activity was not very effective except to create confusion immediately before an Allied landing.

An extraordinary and little-known episode occurred in 1944 in El Salvador (see Lakey and Parkman, 1969). The dictator Martinez was forced to resign and flee into exile by almost entirely nonviolent action. Martinez had successfully put down an attempted army rebellion in April of that year. Later that month students took the initiative and distributed a leaflet which read:

'Decree for a general strike including hospitals, courts, and public works . . . The basis of the strike shall be general passive resistance, non-cooperation with the Government, the wearing of mourning, the unity of all classes, the prohibition of fiestas.

By showing the tyrant the abyss between him and the people, by isolating him completely, we shall cause his downfall. Boycott the movies, the national lottery. Pay no taxes. Abandon government jobs. Leave them unfilled. Pray daily for the souls of the massacred. The Archbishop has been humiliated.'

The students went on strike. Bus and taxi drivers joined them, so did civil servants. Stores closed, the doctors treated only emergency cases, the banks shut. Even the churches shut in sympathetic protest. Eventually, on 8 May, 40,000 people demonstrated in the National Palace. Three days later, urged by all his advisers, Martinez left. His successor gave amnesty to all political prisoners, ordered the freedom of the press, and organized general elections.

Revolutionary confrontation has recently received systematic study. Sharp identifies three types of what he terms non-violent action. These are *protest*, *non-cooperation*, and *intervention* (Sharp, 1969, pp. 109–11).[8] Under the heading of protest come marches, sit-ins, renunciation of honours, protest literature, the 'haunting' of officials, and so on. Non-cooperation covers all types of strike (general strikes, go-slows, work-to-rule agreements, etc.), boycotts (including economic boycotts, rent refusals, social boycotts), and political non-cooperation (including revenue refusal, boycott of elections, boycott of government employment, civil disobedience, and mutiny). Intervention includes sit-ins, obstruction, invasion, and parallel government.

Some would add active sabotage to the intervention category. There are two main disadvantages to this. In the first place, an act of sabotage gives the enemy a clear-cut target on which to concentrate his energies whereas the non-cooperative activities of thousands of men, women, and children pose a diffuse and indefinable problem. Second, it is not always easy to discriminate between violent and non-violent sabotage: blow up a factory at night and the watchman is killed; blow up a bridge and a busload of children hurtles into the river; carry explosives about and there is an incident in which uninvolved outsiders get killed. But these are perhaps dangers that can be guarded against. In favour of sabotage it can be said, in the first instance, that, as the Dutch discovered, those engaged in less active forms of civilian resistance are greatly encouraged by a material and tangible consequence of opposition, such as a wrecked power station; the effects of their own protests or non-cooperation are so hard to identify that unless something can be seen to be done somewhere, it is easy to lose heart. The second advantage is, of course, that carefully selected sabotage can cause great damage.

There is no doubt that an effective campaign of revolutionary confrontation demands a population having a high level of awareness, which is the basis of morale, and a high level of organization, which is the basis of defence against an enemy with all the physical power. Thus in the South African resistance efforts of the 1950s, as Miller points out (Miller, 1965, pp. 282–3), only 1 per cent of the black population was involved with the revolutionary African National Congress, and its organization, with virtually no full-time staff, was deplorable. It is understandable that the attempt failed.

Lakey (1969) lists the *building of an effective organization* as the second of five stages of what he terms a 'Strategy for Non-Violent Revolution'. The first stage is *cultural preparation*, which corresponds to any stage of education in which awareness is created. The third is *propaganda of the deed*. He cites as an example the intention that the Phoenix should sail to North Vietnam with medical supplies: if it is allowed through, a step has been taken to accept human rights for all; if it is stopped and its crew prosecuted 'the injustice of the system is further revealed'. In either case a heartening demonstration will have been made. Next comes *political and economic non-cooperation*, which he defines in much the same way as Sharp. It will be salutary for impatient revolutionaries to see that what might be considered as genuine resistance comes so late in the sequence, for *intervention and parallel government* is placed last. Under intervention, Lakey includes the occupation of factories and administrative buildings. By parallel government, he means 'that ordinary functions are taken over by the revolutionary movement' either independently or in some form of collaboration with existing authorities. This has happened in part on a number of occasions, as when, in India, taxes were paid to the Indian National Congress and when, in St Petersburg in 1905, after the civilian insurrection, the municipal government had to have its orders endorsed by the Soviet.

The Effectiveness of Confrontation

I do not know of any instance when an oppressive indigenous government has been overthrown by non-violent revolutionary confrontation and then replaced by a government of the revolutionaries. There are, however, examples of a particular tyrant having been overthrown (El Salvador is one), of particular policies having been abandoned, and of certain aspects of a system having been changed. Indeed, as Lakey points out (1969), it is seldom necessary to proceed to his fifth stage: satisfactory concessions have usually been made before that point is reached.

Reference to concessions brings us back to the point made at the beginning of this chapter, about evolution. (Let me define. By evolution I mean that the existing system is modified in accordance with the demands made by its opponents. By revolution I mean that the existing system is overthrown and replaced by one devised by its opponents.) Most governments of Western Europe have gone through a process of evolution to reach what is, in general, a fairly high level of democracy, that is to say, a relation between the governors and the governed in which there is little conflict of interest and, since the electorate can oust the rulers, not much imbalance of power. In the majority of cases this evolution has been jolted forward by revolutionary action such as the French revolution, and the revolutions of 1848. In a number of cases, non-violent revolutionary confrontation, corresponding to Lakey's fourth stage – for example, the Peterloo Massacre or the Tolpuddle Martyrs – has had the same effect. But most evolution occurs as a result of normal democratic processes. Even in democratic countries, however, circumstances may arise – as currently with regard to issues of race and defence in the United States – when the norma legislative and administrative procedures are inadequate. In many particular institutions (academic, industrial, or bureaucratic) of otherwise healthy societies, moreover, the mechanisms of evolutionary adaptation may fail. In such situations some form of confrontation may be necessary. Strikes and various related techniques of exerting pressure constitute theoretically, if not always in practice, revolutionary confrontation in this less extreme context. If the workers can make so much trouble for the management that the management is prepared to negotiate, it means that the workers have achieved balance in the relationship.

As a general rule, however, the need for, and the dangers in, confrontation, especially revolutionary confrontation, increase in proportion to the strength and ruthlessness of the tyranny. That is to say, the greater the imbalance of the rulers and the ruled and the sharper the conflict of interest, the greater the need for confrontation.

Confrontation, if successful, leads to a complex period of conciliation and bargaining. Indeed, Schelling points out that confrontation in itself involves a process of bargaining. The revolutionaries can confront the ruler with 'chaos, starvation, idleness and social breakdown, but he confronts them with the same thing and, indeed, most of what they deny him they deny themselves. It is a bargaining situation in which either side, if adequately disciplined and organized, can deny most of what the other wants: and it remains to see who wins' (Schelling, 1967, p. 352).

Finally, it should be observed that confrontation, and particularly revolutionary confrontation, which is probably the most hazardous of all peacemaking stages, is not a necessary precursor to the stage of conciliation. Many disputes on all levels, from the international to the interpersonal, develop in relatively balanced relationships.

19 Conciliation

Many of a man's feelings about others derive from his feelings about himself. Since these feelings are often intricate, contradictory, and not fully grasped at the conscious level, his attitudes towards others are correspondingly obscure and irrational. One reason for a man's relative ignorance of himself is his fear of what self-awareness might reveal. Thus he conceals from himself by various psychological techniques, described in Freudian terms as repression, the shameful longings and sense of guilt that originated largely in early years. To compensate for this he develops a mask, a persona, which represents how he would like to perceive himself when he looks in his mental mirror, and how he would like others to see him. In fact, of course, the more conscious we are of these hidden elements of the mind, the more we are aware of our motives, the less frightening they become. As is well known, one of the main objectives of many psychotherapeutic techniques is to reveal what was hidden or half-hidden and what, half-perceived, seemed more terrible than it is. Mental health is closely related to self-knowledge.

The complement to the mask is what I would term the mirage. The popular belief is that mirages are beautiful visions of palm trees and water, but anyone who has travelled in deserts will know that they live up to their dictionary definition of a false image. Mirages are shimmering stretches of livid waste. In my terms, the mirage is what we see when we squint through slits in the mask. To the extent that we depend upon the mask for self-protection (especially in the sense of protection from one's self), we see a mirage of others. That is to say, we see them as much in terms of their response to our psychic needs as in terms of their character and qualities objectively appraised. If they accept us at what might be called our mask value, thus strengthening our defences, we view them favourably. If they do not, they make us anxious and they become unpopular. At this point, through the psychic trick of projection, we are apt to attribute to them the very flaws we dimly sense in ourselves and are attempting to conceal from ourselves and others by the use of the mask. To project them onto others is an excellent way of getting rid of them.

The way in which mechanisms of individual psychopathology get extended and transferred is obscure, but such transference certainly occurs. Thus the white races of both America and South Africa attribute to the black people a range of qualities which together build up the mask of a person whom it is justifiable to enslave and dominate: the black people are childish, sly, lazy, useless, unreliable, immature, happy-go-lucky, content to remain as they are, lascivious, violent, and so on. For similar reasons, white South Africans are much distressed to hear stories of African initiative or success and try to discredit them. To believe them would be to jeopardize their mask-mirage mechanism and hence, in this context, their political supremacy. Thus the protagonists in a war will almost invariably say: '*We* are a peace-loving people and are always ready to listen to reasonable proposals for a settlement, but *they* are not interested in peace, *they* wish to crush us; *our* soldiers are honourable men who fight fairly, but *theirs* are no better than barbarians; *they* bomb churches and schools, but *we* protect civilians.' One of the tasks of the conciliator is to point out that if both parties say the same thing and believe it (which is usually at least in part the case) there are grounds for hope, because neither side can be quite as bad as the other believes it to be.

There is a mask-mirage situation in most of the examples given in Part I. The directors of the Firm were sure of their liberalism and benevolence and saw their employees as ungrateful and irresponsible; the employees saw the directors as capricious, arbitrary, and easily offended. The students saw the professors as fusty, archaic scholars who had betrayed their learning to the establishment; the professors saw the students as destructive and wanton vandals who would tear down the edifice of scholarship. The professors saw themselves as the guardians of a great tradition while the students saw themselves as adjusting that tradition to the present day. The faculty in Ghana also saw themselves as the protectors of academic freedom, and viewed the government as composed of vindictive, self-seeking politicans who would destroy the university in order to promote their own ends and appoint their own incompetent friends; the government saw the faculty as lazy, grasping, hypocritical, neo-colonialists, living in unsuitable luxury paid for by a poor country, and perverting the flower of its youth in addition. The government saw themselves as the builders of a new African culture, as the flail of imperialism in all its forms. The foreign advisers saw themselves as wise and altruistic (had they not left their comfortable chairs to work in these barbarous places?), and their counterparts as incompetent, ungrateful, and not entirely straightforward; the local counterparts responded by regarding the advisers as ignorant and conceited, and a thoroughgoing nuisance to them, who were quietly getting on with the job with little fuss and less reward. And so on.

In all instances there is a reluctance to change such attitudes. Mask and mirage are interconnected to the extent that to alter one almost inevitably involves altering the other. My view of my enemy is related to my view of myself, therefore I cannot change my attitude to him without a corresponding change of attitude towards myself.

The concept of awareness takes these ideas a step further. At the personal level the degree of awareness corresponds exactly to the degree to which the mask is put aside. Although perhaps everyone employs a mask on occasion, the extent to which an individual depends on his mask certainly varies according to his capacity to perceive and accept himself, if not truly (for what does that mean?), at least as he is seen by others.

I have been particularly concerned, however, with awareness as applied to the individual's position in society and to the nature of that society itself. To start negatively, the Faqir Mishkin and the black South Africans, or many of them, have very little social awareness. I mean by this that however unhappy they may be they do not perceive that change is possible and that they themselves can bring it about. They are both powerless and ignorant, a mixture that is the perfect prescription for slavery. In fact, they lack awareness of their own potentialities. As Lenin said, 'the slave who is aware that he is a slave is already half-free'; but awareness leads to a grim struggle until freedom is complete. Awareness can be a powerful force in bringing people or groups at variance with one another to a settlement of their differences and a change in their relationship, but some reciprocity is essential. If it is only the slave who is aware of the degrading and infamous miseries of slavery, if the master considers slavery to be natural and proper, the slave will have to struggle hard for his freedom. During the conflict, relations between the two may seem infinitely worse. Relatively friendly and tolerant masters become hardened against the rebels; callous and intemperate masters grow more extreme. Slaves who, in dependent ignorance, accepted crumbs of their master's charity and doted on his children begin to hate bitterly and without discrimination. But the ultimate end of the battle, without which there can be no peace save the quiet of extinction, is when the masters become aware as well as the slaves.

The American, unlike the South African, blacks, are already engaged in the battle but only recently has it been fully joined. Only in the 1960s did a substantial number of the black American population really become aware of the extent of racialism in the Northern States, of the incurability of ghetto conditions without radical changes, of their own betrayal of their people and themselves by attempting to 'join' the white middle class, of the heritage they had ignored and forgotten, and finally of their power to act. Awareness, on the part of students, of the character of the university, and of their place in it and their place in society, is likewise recent. A point of special interest with regard to the prisoners of war is that they had acquired a level of awareness of certain capacities in themselves and of flaws in society which impeded the recognition of those capacities, but their awareness had been acquired in such traumatic circumstances that they were often driven to pointless and self-destructive activity. These examples suggest that one of the conciliator's main tasks is to create an equal level of awareness on both sides.

The concept of awareness gains a further dimension in relation to the concept of identity. A man's sense of who he is is clearly related to his sense of what he is. Nevertheless, identity has to be thought of differently from awareness. In certain respects, the sense of identity may stifle awareness. Thus at one level our sense of identity depends on what is commonly called an identification with various social, cultural, or racial categories or groups. For instance, the white Anglo-Saxon Protestant, the WASP, owes part of his identity, his self-view, to the fact that he is just that, while his individual identity is sharpened by living in a particular town, having a particular job, belonging to a certain association or political party, and so on. Looked at in this way identity is like a mask: it is something one can present to the outside world saying 'this is who I am'. But it is objective and external, unlike the mask, which is a cover for what is subjective and internal. Identity shows affiliation, the mask purports to show the qualities of what is appropriately called personality – persona, it should be recalled, is the Latin for mask. Like the mask, identity protects us from uncertainty and anxiety. It is the white South Africans' strong feeling of identity, coupled with a sense of almost sacred mission, that strengthens their ruthless rule. Likewise, the foreign advisers, the directors of the Firm, the university faculties, and many others tend to have a sense of identity implied in their position, making them somewhat less flexible and more sure of themselves than they might otherwise have been, and consequently less inclined to compromise anything that might lead to a change in their identity.

The consequences of a lack of identity can be devastating. The problems of the American blacks and of all former colonized peoples have been compounded by the fact that alien domination, in some cases deliberately, has damaged their sense of identity. This was done in a most systematic way among the slaves, whose African background, language, names, songs, dances, and observances were all erased. Henceforth they could create an identity only within the categories of the foreign society to which they had been dragged. Since they were a menial race with no rights it was hard for them to develop a proud sense of identity. Many accepted the white man's disparaging evaluation of them and felt that their only salvation lay in emulating him and attempting to creep into a humble corner of his world. Much the same sort of thing happened to many educated Africans and Asians. They were not deprived of their own culture, it is true, but they came to despise it. The whites held power and the only way in which an African or Asian could share in it, however inadequately, was by aping them. All that was 'primitive' and 'native' had to be discarded in favour of another civilization which, however, they never entirely entered. Among peoples who have suffered in this way, black Americans and former subject peoples, there is a concerted effort to revive a sense of identity based upon their own cultural heritage and to escape the thrall of what was alien. In both India and Pakistan, for example, there is a powerful move to abandon English as the language of government; and in Tanzania an African language, Swahili, is the national tongue.

While loss of identity leads to insecurity and social disintegration, identity as I have defined it may lead to other evils: rigidity, intolerance of others, and, on a national scale, chauvinism. There is, however, a further sense of identity which need not imply these things. Perhaps I may illustrate this by referring to an episode in my own life. At the age of nineteen I spent several months in Lapland and lived with various Lapp communities. At first the alien culture jarred on me considerably simply because it was alien. The Lapps were always gentle and cooperative and never did anything unpleasant, but their ways were different from those to which I had been accustomed, and what we learn in childhood acquires a universal validity, almost a sanctity: what is different must be wrong. My lack of ease did not last long, however. One day I awoke feeling perfectly at home and have never since experienced a similar disquiet. But my adjustment to life in Lapland was counterbalanced by my subsequent maladjustment to life in England. For weeks after my return I was unaccountably moody, avoiding my friends and wandering aimlessly alone, trying to understand what was happening to me. Gradually I began to realize. Although I had fancied myself as flexible, liberal, and objective, I had possessed a deep identification with the habits of my own culture. This caused my initial resistance to the Lapp way of life. In fact I had soon come to accept it, feeling that it worked and was perfectly valid in its own context. But this meant that the values of my own society were not absolute but relative; that I had an identity not simply as an Englishman, but as a member of a wider community of people. That I had always *known* this made no difference; now I *felt* it. And so, in a peculiar way, I became a stranger, because I had accepted the way of life of another land.

Slowly I rejoined, as it were, the society of my friends, but in a sense things were never quite the same again. I was never quite at home, never able to feel the deep inward sense of absolute rightness which makes real patriots. This did not mean that I had lost touch with people, that the old friendships had faded. On the contrary, I now felt that I was able to make better contact with others because I could accept more varied modes of behaviour. Indeed, in my subsequent life I have lived and worked in societies as divergent as those of the Middle East, Pakistan, West Africa, and the United States of America without feeling alien, but also without being strongly identified with the nationalistic symbols of any of the peoples among whom I have lived happily.

In some respects the prisoners of war in the case study had gone through a similar though more complex and much more drastic change. It was essentially a process of breaking down an old sense of identity and acquiring a new one. The slave, it is true, got a new identity, but it was partly borrowed and wholly tarnished by the intolerable context of the slave relationship. The prisoners of war and I, on the other hand, had suffered a change that enabled us, if circumstances were not too harsh, to move more freely, to form more and varied relationships, to be less bound by old forms, and to make more effective use of our capacities.

I term the first type of identity the identity of belonging; it is an important but limiting tool. The second I call the identity of awareness. Here the awareness should refer both to the inner life of the individual and to his consciousness of society. By bringing identity and awareness together the argument is swung back to its beginning and we can summarize the significance of these concepts for the task of conciliation.

If peace is to be brought to an unpeaceful relationship, both participants must see themselves and each other for what they are as human beings. The tensions of a quarrel go a long way towards making it still harder to solve. The worse it gets, the greater the suspicion, the fear, the uncertainty. One national leader said to me, in a time of emergency, about his opposite number: 'I thought I knew him well. We had been friends. Now I don't know. I must have been mistaken; he must have been deceiving me all along.' The more those involved in an unpeaceful relationship are aware of their own motives and of the effects upon them of the pressures of the situation, and the stronger their sense of their own identity as autonomous human beings rather than as belonging to or representing some group or nation, the more likely are they to be able to reach accord. But the psychological pressures often work in the opposite direction. The very existence of an unpeaceful relationship makes people feel anxious and insecure. They then tend to rely on the protection of the mask to assure them that they are good and on the mirage of the other side which depicts it, the enemy, as bad. When there is an unpeaceful relationship between definable groups, and especially in times of war between nations, the leaders are compelled by their position to serve as a symbol of unity and, by the same token, of identity. They are forced into a role which makes it increasingly hard to appreciate the other's point of view, to make concessions or conciliatory advances, to reduce the general level of unreason. On the contrary, they are impelled to take the tough line, to be unyielding in their demands, to emphasize the wickedness and untrustworthiness of the other side and the virtues of their own.

It is the task of the conciliator to find ways of stemming the psychological current so that, however briefly, the mask can be dropped, the mirage forgotten, awareness heightened, and the sense of identity broadened beyond the bounds of nationalism.

THE PRACTICE OF CONCILIATION

Conciliation could be defined as the psychological prerequisite for restructuring a relationship so that its tendency towards unpeacefulness is reduced. It implies the possibility of change although

216

the precise nature of the change comes more within the facet of peacemaking I have termed development. Conciliation can occur without the involvement of a third party. Two persons or groups may come to see each other differently and so decide that they were behaving with unnecessary caution or hostility and hence become more relaxed and increasingly amicable. Indeed, in many relationships, including international ones, there is a constant fluctuation between being more and less friendly, more and less cooperative, more and less open, more and less distrustful. But in certain circumstances the swing is all in one direction. As nations move towards war, for example, the fear and rage build up an emotional pressure making it increasingly hard for either side to revise its opinion of the other – except downwards. In these conditions, too, things are done out of alarm or resentment which seem bound to arouse dislike and suspicion. When affairs reach such a pass, communications between the two principals are so bad that only a third party has much chance of promoting a rational consideration of the quarrel.

Nations, of course, have diplomatic and governmental machinery for communication and can make good use of it until things get too bad. But in some situations there is no proper machinery for making representation. The villagers of Thornley, for example, though having representation on the appropriate official body, discarded it as a means of affecting their destiny. The employees of the Firm, caught in a psychological trap, made inadequate use of the inadequate machinery at their disposal for expressing their collective opinions. The prisoners of war were simply 120,000 individuals. The Pakistani villages had only the fossilized *panchayat*. The intervention of an outside element, myself in the first two instances, the CRUs in the third, and the Village AID organization in the fourth, was probably necessary to effect a change. It could be argued that these last two elements were not in fact third parties, that Village AID was part of the government of Pakistan and the CRUs a facet of British military society. But I think that this would be a misconception. Both of these institutions represented entirely new features of official life; there had never been anything like them before and they could very properly be considered as performing a linking or reconciling function, such as could normally be carried out only through an external agency, between society as a whole and those who were alienated from it.

It is interesting to compare these two institutions. The CRUs were planned with considerable psychological and sociological acumen to perform the function of reconnection or resettlement (or, as it might have been termed then, conciliation), but Village AID performed this function incidentally to its main purpose of stimulating rural development. Clearly, an agency that is specifically designed to carry out a particular task is likely to perform that task better than one that is not so designed, but community development, of which Village AID is only one example, has been singularly successful in many areas of the world as a conciliating agency. A main reason for the conciliating success achieved by both the CRUs and Village AID may lie in a central feature they had in common: namely, the voluntary, participatory character of the activities they promoted. They were organizations that encouraged enterprise and initiative but, unlike the traditional structure within which they grew up, without any compulsion. In both instances, many have suspected (and in some cases rightly) that the whole thing was an elaborate fraud. Thus the prisoners of war began by being extremely suspicious of the claim that all activities in the CRUs were voluntary and that there was no normal military discipline – no punishment, for instance, if a man returned late from leave. They would gingerly test the sincerity of the claim by carefully posed questions and minor rule infractions. When, after several of such sallies, the heavens failed to fall, they would begin to believe in the claims of the institution and start to relax. I once witnessed a dramatic example of the length to which a Village AID official would go to preserve the consistency of his role. This official, like most senior members of the organization, was an established civil servant and a magistrate. One evening, as we stood on the steps of his headquarters in East Pakistan, two men ran forward and, bending swiftly, kissed our feet. They then proceeded to present a petition. They stated that they had been defrauded and that they had been advised by the magistrate in the next town up the river to ask my friend to investigate the case. He, however, after hearing them carefully, refused. He told me that it had taken him nine months to convince the people that he was working with them; that, although a government servant, he was not engaged in a plot to defraud them, to imprison them, or to extort more taxes. At last they had come to believe that he was working with and for them, and many important projects were being started. If, however, he had even momentarily assumed his other role of a law officer who investigated, judged, and sentenced, the hard-won confidence would have been destroyed at once. It mattered little that the cause might have been wholly just; the sincerity and integrity of his position would have been doubted and his capacity to work effectively with the people undermined. Both the CRUs and Village AID encouraged independence and autonomous initiative, but offered enough support and guidance to reduce anxiety.

Here the similarity between the two organizations ends. The CRUs were devised communities aimed at helping their temporary members to come to terms with the wider society. Their affiliation, in terms of both structure and purpose, had much in common with other therapeutic communities which for the most part served to help psychiatric or other patients to adjust to normal living. Village AID, in contrast, was geared to improving the quality of rural life through agricultural development and the like, and the fact that a bridge was built between the worlds of the official and of the village was a by-product of the process. But there was a certain sharing of ideas. Enthusiasts of both community development and therapeutic communities possessed, their detractors maintain, a certain mystique. Although both claimed justification in social science, their key principle was perhaps more an article of faith than a scientific opinion. They both held, essentially, that human beings are cooperative creatures, that they achieve their full stature through participation in community processes, and that sickness both produces and is a product of conditions in which the possibility of participation is diminished.

In some of our cases there was no conciliation. Although an enormous amount of effort has been expended on attempts to improve race relations, these are too pervasive and structured to permit formal conciliation. Much has been done to mitigate conditions in specific communities, but there are no bodies representing the black and the white populations as a whole on behalf of which conciliation could be carried out. Moreover, levels of awareness vary so greatly that it would be difficult to bring about widespread changes without an equally widespread campaign to educate the whites on the nature of racism. There are few white educated Americans who would admit to harbouring any racial prejudice; there are equally few who do not exhibit what the blacks would identify as symptoms of racism. Together with education, development must play a major part in the amelioration of race relations. Some sources of unpeacefulness in this sphere can be eliminated only through changes in the structure of the relations between races. This will be considered later. The same sorts of problem make it difficult to improve relations between the richer and the poorer areas of the world.

There was no conciliation in the dispute between the University of Ghana and the government of the country. The body that might have been expected to play the part of conciliator was the Council. This was the governing body of the University and was composed of a few academics and a somewhat larger number of distinguished outsiders, including – in my time – two Cabinet Ministers, a judge, one of the traditional chiefs, and a well-known lawyer and journalist. These outsiders were much involved with the work of the University and at the same time were for the most part close to the government. In less volcanic circumstances they would have been ideally constituted to act as conciliating intermediaries. However, the political future, if not the liberty, of all prominent men in Ghana was in jeopardy at that time (at least one member of the Council was later imprisoned and another was forced to flee into exile) and the Council members were anxious to avoid being further embroiled in a possibly dangerous situation. The conciliator, simply because he tries to explain the other side, may be thought to favour it – and at that stage no Ghanaian could afford sympathies with the 'neo-colonialists'.

When conciliation is carried out by, as is normally the case, one individual or a small group of people rather than an organization, the questions of neutrality and trust are equally salient. No one will trust a would-be conciliator if he is thought to be involved in some way with the other side: how can his protestations of impartiality be believed? Even when there is no objective reason to suspect the conciliator he will be watched carefully to see whether his actions are consistent with his description of himself. The task of the conciliator is especially hard in an international conflict, for which reason this aspect is described separately and at length in the next section, but even in much less tense circumstances it is far from easy. Some of the difficulties can perhaps be illustrated from my own experiences working with the Firm and in Thornley.

While studying the problems of the Firm I was in fact employed by a research organization and so could properly be described as a third party, but my organization was under contract to the Firm to supply my work and other services and I lived in the area of the Firm and in the Firm's housing. Thus, although an outsider, I could also be regarded, and often was, as an agent of the directors (people who go around asking questions are always suspect in tense situations), or as one of the regular middle-level employees. The first thing I had to do was to take every opportunity of explaining who I was. This was relatively easy. The second and much harder thing was to behave in such a way that my explanation was accepted. I schooled myself to speak always with sympathy and understanding of any person or institution connected with the Firm and I succeeded so well that, when I once made an ironical statement about someone who had nothing to do with the Firm, my companion looked at me with a very shocked expression and remarked that he had never heard me talk like that before.

Since I was, so to speak, a member of the Firm community, having come to live there with my family, I inevitably had personal as well as professional relationships. But it is as unsuitable for a conciliator to live among the members of the community he is working in as it is for a physician to treat his own wife and children. One's friendships are interpreted as representing one's point of view and allegiances. In fact it is not until one has completely established the impartiality of one's goodwill that one has really earned the right to personal friendships. I spent weeks going around and talking to people, to the directors and their top management, to employees of every level, to their families, to teachers in the schools. I would explain my inquisition carefully, saying that I was an employee of an independent research agency which had been asked by the directors to conduct a survey of social relations. I asked relatively few questions. I certainly presented no questionnaires and I took no notes at the time of a meeting. Primarily I listened to people talking about the Firm, telling what it was like to be a member of the community, and what they felt about different people and committees.

It was strangely difficult. The conciliator, unlike the psychotherapist, is not a figure of authority. Indeed he abdicates whatever professional authority he might have had in order to be acceptable, that is harmless, to both parties; he must lay down his own weapons in order to visit both camps. He feels very vulnerable, knowing that his position is delicate and that he is more likely than not to make himself unpopular with one side and quite possibly with both. The risk is inherent in his role because as soon as he stops being merely passive and attempts to change perceptions he is tampering with masks and mirages, those prized mechanisms of defence. But it has to be done. He must suggest explanations or interpretations which inevitably raise fear and anxieties in some. Thus he makes himself a sort of lightning-rod for powerful feelings; if he is successful, strong emotions are aroused and he is, or feels himself to be, in danger of being struck.

Conciliation is essentially a lengthy and stressful job and for this reason a conciliation effort in the international sphere should comprise at least two people. The conciliator cannot help feeling the powerful tug of contradictory loyalties. He feels paranoid because he is close to people who are feeling paranoid. He feels exposed and defenceless and he is tempted to get some sort of security by aligning himself with some faction.

In the Firm, the process of peacemaking started, as it usually must, with a period of fact-finding. It moved into a stage in which I attempted to change perceptions by interpreting the feelings of the employees to the directors, and vice versa. This led into the related stages of bargaining, that is to say, working out a rearrangement of responsibility which would be satisfactory to both sides, and development, that is to say, restructuring the relationship. The last two phases are discussed in later chapters but are mentioned here to suggest what may be the most usual peacemaking sequence, though it is also true that there is a great deal of overlapping and that conciliation has to continue to the end. At this point I should pay tribute to the directors of the Firm. They were well aware that in sponsoring my work they were exposing themselves far more grievously than I was to anxiety and stress. What they did is proof, which in fact no one who had known them would need, of their courage, truthfulness, and dedication.

Work in Thornley followed a similar pattern, though the emphasis was more on research than on conciliation, bargaining, or development. My task was easier in that I lived some miles away from the village. It was harder in that the villagers, unlike the Firm's employees who were used to all manner of strange people doing incomprehensible things, had never heard of surveys or social research. Their suspicion of outsiders compounded the difficulty.

First came the problem of entry. The most superficial study convinced me that if I began with the wrong contacts I would never get anywhere. Luckily, as I have explained, I met the right people.

Next was the question of my role. I was determined to be as accurate as possible and yet to present my interests in a way that would be both comprehensible and acceptable. I did not want to use words like anthropology and sociology, which would undoubtedly make the villagers uncomfortable. Nor did I wish to imply that I had just come to study them. I have always been perhaps over-squeamish about social research for its own sake, and see no reason why people should satisfy my own curiosity unless it is in some way advantageous to them. One of my psycho-analytic colleagues used to remark that to demand information from someone without making some return is like asking him if one might cut out his appendix in the interest of science. I therefore explained myself by saying that I was interested in the history of rural areas from the point of view of the light it might throw on their contemporary problems and possible solutions to them.

I think that my explanation was more or less accepted, but I still had to demonstrate that I was friendly and well intentioned and was faced with a number of situations that I regarded as being, at least in part, in the nature of tests of my real feelings. My help was sought in several instances and I think that the assistance I was able to give did a great deal to establish me as a friendly person in a community which tended to dislike strangers. There were also attempts to win me over to one faction or another. For example, the schoolteacher and her brother tried to enlist my sympathy 'as an educated man' against the villagers, and this caused me some embarrassment. Since Thornley's relationship with the outside authorities was, in my terms, one of alienation and incomprehension, in which, therefore, there was no problem of mirror-images, I did not have the additional difficulty of having to establish my legitimacy with the other side as well.

In conclusion, conciliation is concerned with masks and mirages. The conciliator must constantly strive to understand why people see both themselves and each other as they do and how their perceptions can be changed; in what ways and for what reasons awareness is impaired and how it can be increased; what is the damage to and limitation of the sense of identity. The efforts he makes to establish himself are only preliminaries to the carrying out of a complex psychological task.

Where the task of peacemaking is carried out corporately by a large and complex organization, say a therapeutic community such as the CRU, the different skills of many people are woven together to make a cumulative impact. The psychiatrist, physician, social worker, and labour officer all play their specialized roles; there are many therapeutic activities: group discussions, job rehearsals, workshops, occupational therapy; there is the whole directed ambience of the unit. Eventually, through the CRUs the former prisoners became reconnected to their families and communities and so, in the process, to society as a whole, because they were much more aware of the issues they were facing.

But single individuals or small teams, what can they do? They must have an understanding of the particular situation so detailed that they can discuss it intelligently with the main actors, otherwise nothing they say will carry weight. They must also have a general knowledge of conflict situations, of how people react to them and of how they may be resolved. They need qualities combining caution with courage, warmth in personal relationships with coolness in reaction. They must be able to listen sympathetically and to discipline themselves so that their own opinions are kept in the background; yet they must be able to state a point of view cogently when it is likely to be important.

But however skilful the conciliator may be as an applied psychologist, conciliation is only one part of the whole process of peacemaking. Conciliation provides a respite in which the contestants are rather more likely to listen to each other, are somewhat less suspicious of each other, and are a bit better informed about the feelings of the other side than they were. It does not of itself provide the structure of an improved relationship or a process of negotiation by which this is agreed upon.

PRIVATE DIPLOMACY

Scope of Discussion

This section deals with a small but perhaps not insignificant aspect of diplomacy and international relations. It examines the part that may be played in the conciliation of conflict by persons without any official position. Clearly, what they can do is different from, and in many respects less effective than, what is done through official channels, whether governmental or international. In particular, they can exert no pressure, make no threats, offer no promises; and they cannot bargain. But the fact that they are not representatives of a particular organization may nevertheless give them a degree of freedom and a measure of acceptance that permit them to make a distinctive contribution to the situation, supplementing regular diplomacy. Here we shall explore the scope and limitations of formal or public, and informal or private, diplomacy.

First I must make it quite clear what I am talking about. For the purposes of this discussion a private diplomat is someone who is not attached to any government or to any organization, such as the United Nations or the Commonwealth, which has a political function. In countries where there is a considerable amount of movement between public and private life, as in the United States, for example, where many university professors have done their stint as ambassadors or other high officers of state, it may be hard to say who is and who is not eligible to be a private diplomat. Obviously the diplomat should not be a government servant at the time of his mission, though presumably this would matter little if he worked in something as innocent as a department of pre-school education. But whether or not a private individual who has once held a public position should engage in private diplomacy depends on several factors: the prominence of his former post; the extent to which he is still associated – if only in the minds of others – with official policy; the similarity of his official to his private role. It is not at all inappropriate, however, for the private diplomat to belong to a non-political organization such as the Society of Friends or the International Committee of the Red Cross, or to be associated with an academic organization, such as a university, which is thought to value objectivity and scholarship. In effect it may be very hard for him to operate entirely independently of organizational support, both moral and material.

It might be argued that representatives of small nations with a reputation for neutrality could serve the same purpose as private diplomats, and do so better because they would command greater resources. This is indeed partly true, and I would not in the least wish to minimize their usefulness, but the fact that they are representatives rather than individuals makes some difference. They do not speak for themselves. They have to report back to a government and, however friendly a government may be, it is a collectivity: one cannot feel towards it as one might do towards an individual. Thus, however popular the official diplomat may be there is a part of him that cannot be treated as a person. It is because the private diplomat is completely free of official

226

obligation and can be treated wholly as an individual that his position is unique. (Of course he has to establish his credentials as a private person who can be relied on – this will be considered later.) It should be added, in relation to the possible role of neutral states, that in many situations there are very few that are acceptable to both sides; in the hectic atmosphere of international strife, neutrality is easily compromised. In one of the world's most bitter recent disputes, virtually none of the world's polities was, for one reason or another – often extremely far-fetched – suitable to sponsor a *rapprochement*. To conclude, by a private diplomat I mean in general someone who engages in the mediation or conciliation of conflict under personal or non-official auspices.

Second, I am concerned here only with disputes that have led to, or are likely to lead to, armed hostilities. I include both inter-state and civil wars. As we have seen, there are other forms of conflict – less lethal international quarrels, labour disputes, marital disagreements, and so on – in which one may be able to identify some of the same elements as in armed conflict, and in which some of the same techniques of settlement may be employed. I am confining myself to hostilities, actual or probable, because when killing starts there is a marked jump in fear, unreason, suspicion, and desperation, with which it is particularly the task of the private diplomat to deal. I shall attempt to show that conciliation becomes psychologically more difficult as soon as blood is shed and that the main task of the private diplomat is to reduce the psychological hardening.

The purpose of the private diplomat, in this context, is to promote a settlement of a violent unpeaceful relationship that is in a balanced stage. But conflicts are often brought to an end by indefensible settlements in which one side yields everything and the other gains everything, in which injustices are perpetrated which merely lay the foundation for a subsequent round of violence. Herein lies a dilemma for the private diplomat. He is bound, since he is involved in the situation, to have his own ideas about the nature of a possible settlement, but all settlements have political implications and if he espouses one solution more than another he jeopardizes his political neutrality. His most appropriate role is to work for the establishment of conditions in which a settlement can be sought and eventually found, rather than to try to determine the nature of the settlement. However, he is not going beyond his province in promoting a settlement that is not a surrender by one side, but an agreement reached through direct or indirect negotiations in which the essential interests of both parties are borne in mind.

Limitations of Formal Diplomacy
Before examining the possibilities of private diplomacy, we should glance at some of the limitations of official diplomacy. Its greatest strength and its greatest weakness both derive from the same fact: namely, that it serves a government. When the government concerned is the government of a powerful country its diplomats can be very persuasive: they can suggest terms that will be most advantageous to those who will accept them and most damaging to those who will not; they can sponsor complicated bargains and trade-offs to promote their nation's policies; they can put pressure on smaller countries to support them in the United Nations and elsewhere.

At the same time, they are clearly recognized for what they are: the agents of a country whose policy is likely to be suspected in direct proportion to the power of that country. However experienced they may be, their views will be taken to reflect official policy as much as personal wisdom; and however much that wisdom inclines them to contradict policy, they must keep their opinions to themselves. Hence, though many of their discussions may be private, being held in secret, they cannot conduct private diplomacy because they are public persons. In a former era, when travel was slow and before the invention of radio, ambassadors were really plenipotentiary. They were dispatched to the far corners of the earth to settle disputes, forge allegiances, and establish trade pacts, and, because it might take months before their dispatches were answered, they had considerable power to take decisions and, within a broad framework of principle, to make policy. But today, no ambassador is more than minutes from his superiors at home. His spontaneous freedom of action is severely limited. If what he does is unpopular with the government to which he is accredited, he will be derided as a lackey of his government or perhaps as a sinister purveyor of purposefully bad advice. If what he does is popular, he will get less credit than he may deserve because his lack of independence is recognized.

For these reasons the good professional diplomat may, in certain circumstances, be a less valuable influence than his goodwill and intelligence would suggest. His personal popularity may be great, but it is known that he must express the official views of his government and that he must report back on any significant meetings or discussions in which he has participated.

I do not intend at all to belittle professional diplomats, but to point out some inevitable limitations of their official position. There is much that they can do, and do well, but there are some roles that it is hard for them to play; herein lies the *raison d'être* of the private diplomat.

There are, however, some harsher things that may be said, not about diplomats but about the policies they are bound to promote. Many nations have developed what might be termed a foreign affairs establishment composed of an influential group who declaim the traditional point of view to the rest of the world, a composite rationalization of erroneous beliefs about other nations, of strategic considerations, economic self-interest, and chauvinism. The ambassador's reports may do something to modify this view, but it is more probable that he will have little choice but to express it to some extent himself, and perhaps in the end to accept it. This traditional view of the rest of the world is closely related to the domestic political scene. Approaches to foreign policy issues are 'good' or 'bad', depending on how far they conform to the traditional view. In terms of vote-catching at home this consideration is far more important than the character of any particular situation or the solving of a specific problem. Most statesmen are more interested in remaining in office than in contributing to the solution of international difficulties and so their efforts in this direction are likely either to be half-hearted (unless the foreign issue is transformed into a domestic one, for example through war), or to be undertaken in terms of the traditional view rather than in terms of the realities of the situation. Since the diplomats have to do what the politicians tell them, their chances of successful initiatives are further curtailed.

All of these limitations apply even when the official diplomat is playing an ostensibly neutral third-party role in attempting to mediate a disagreement: he is still doing what his government has told him to do, and what his government tells him to do, however altruistic, is still in the best interest of that government. This is a fact of international life. Naturally, when relations between two states are good, that is to say, when the sum total of their actions amounts to mutual advantage, there is much the official diplomat can do to maintain and improve communications. But to the extent that relations are bad, the effectiveness of the official diplomat will suffer. The domestic political apparatus will become involved, with all the subsequent pressures and distortions, proportionately to the deterioration of the relationship. When conflict actually breaks out, the role of the diplomat is virtually at an end; another group, the military, is entrusted with working out a solution.

I would not include in these strictures on official diplomacy criticism of diplomatic missions sponsored by the United Nations and other international agencies such as the Commonwealth. The work of Gunnar Jarring in the Middle East, for example, or of Arnold Smith in Nigeria, is strengthened much more than it is circumscribed by its auspices and has proved to be of inestimable value. Nevertheless, even international agencies may be felt by one party to a conflict to be partisan, and the diplomat is both less free and more visible than his private counterpart.

Limitations of Private Diplomacy

The disadvantages of private diplomacy are that, as Young puts it, non-governmental organizations 'tend to be weak in terms of too many important resources'. They lack salience, technical resources and services, and are deficient in both 'relevant information and diplomatic skill' (Young, 1967, pp. 108–10). Of course if the private diplomat were a bumbling amateur impelled purely by a sentimental hope that good intentions would compensate for a lack of ability and experience, there would be no point in writing these pages. It is assumed that we are considering as private diplomats only persons who are as subtle and experienced as the average public diplomat, although not necessarily in quite the same way, and as well informed, not in the sense of having access to intelligence reports, but in the sense of knowing the people or comparable situations elsewhere, and perhaps in addition having a high degree of relevant academic competence, for example in international law, government, economics, or sociology. It is also assumed that they possess the salience to gain access to key people – as we shall see, the importance of the private diplomat rests primarily on his ability to exert influence on a few policy-makers. But salience is a combination of skill, adequate information, and good contacts rather than of accreditation.

So far as technical services and resources are concerned the private diplomat is admittedly at a disadvantage. If he has to do his own typing, make his own travel arrangements, organize his appointments, and so on, he will be able to devote relatively less time and energy to his main task. If, in addition, he is short of money and has to forgo the advantages of a hired car and first-class travel on long journeys, his work will suffer further. Not having a well-informed junior to keep him up to date with the latest relevant developments he will have to spend much of his own time in keeping abreast of affairs. These drawbacks, however, are difficulties rather than disqualifications.

Advantages of Private Diplomacy
To compensate for the difficulties there are some positive advantages:

1. The private diplomat who establishes himself as such, and who, it need hardly be said, possesses sufficient salience, will be respected as someone who tells the truth about the situation, proffers disinterested opinions, and conveys information without bias. Because he is a free agent, not obliged to report back to anyone else, representing nobody's policy, having no personal or party axe to grind, he can be regarded as a human being rather than as

someone whose individuality is subordinated to his position. It is easy for people to talk freely to him, even to make admissions of failure or doubt which could not otherwise be expressed without seeming to indicate a weakness that might be taken advantage of. Key people in the countries concerned may indeed find it easier to talk to him than to some of their own people, because in the eyes of their own people they have a political role, which must be unequivocally maintained if their position is not to be eroded. By the same token, if the private diplomat expresses unpopular opinions, they are likely to be listened to more carefully than if they were suspected of being part of a political power game, in which case there would be a tendency to reject them out of hand (for example, when one party to a conflict asserts that the other party's troops have suffered reverses, this statement, even if true, is immediately and categorically denied by the second party). In short, because he has no political part in the conflict, the private diplomat may be able to establish relations with the leaders which enable them to relax to some extent and to discuss the real issues rather than – as is often the tendency – the political by-products of the issues.

2. This is a corollary of the first point. Since the private diplomat is not the agent of a government whose home affairs are bound to influence its policies as regards the solving of foreign problems, he is free to concentrate on seeking for solutions that work rather than ones that satisfy the electorate, the foreign affairs establishment, and the business interests of a particular country.

3. Private diplomats can, and indeed usually do, take the initiative. It is impossible for an official third party, whether national or international, to intervene in some conflicts unless requested to do so by the governments involved (e.g., the United States could not have intervened in the Nigerian civil war unless asked by Nigeria). But there is nothing to stop a private diplomat from involving himself whenever he feels there is a reason to do so. His good offices may, of course, be rejected – that is a function of the situation and of how he handles himself. On the other hand, they may be welcomed by a state which is concerned about a

situation but prevented by pride or caution from appealing for outside assistance in tackling it.

4. Since the question of protocol does not arise, the private diplomat can move around inconspicuously. His diplomatic role is often concealed and protected by his personal role as a member of a religious group, for example, or as a lawyer, a professor, or a physician. I know of one complex and large-scale effort of private diplomacy, lasting more than two years and involving several people, many journeys, and a number of fairly dramatic events, which never received any publicity whatsoever.

5. Private diplomats are usually in a position to visit both sides of a dispute, an advantage that official diplomats are unlikely to have, in conditions of civil war especially.

6. Private diplomats can be disavowed or ignored by governments. This apparently negative feature of their position is advantageous because it also means that governments will more readily make use of them, knowing that they can discontinue contact at any time without diplomatic repercussions.

7. The privacy of the private diplomat does not mean that he is isolated from other groups concerned about the conflict he is working to solve. As I have said, the private diplomat does not supplant, but supplements, other types of effort. It is only to be expected that he will find ways of collaborating with concerned international agencies and governments as well as with private organizations other than the one he may belong to. Indeed, the private diplomat ideally becomes a part of a team of individuals and institutions working on a particular problem, each with his special skill and qualification.

The Role of the Private Diplomat

The private diplomat may have any number of different roles. At his most passive he just conveys messages from one side to the other. A more active part he can play is to take information to each side about the statements and actions of the other, and to interpret them, that is, try to change perceptions where these are distorted through faulty information or sheer ignorance. This role is very important because, in the psychological conditions of conflict, distortion and misunderstanding grow like mushrooms and do much to impede settlement. A still more active role the private diplomat may have is to make or discuss specific proposals for negotiation, about scaling down the level of violence, cease-fires, truces, and so on. Lastly, he plays a psychological role which, it has already been suggested, is the essence of conciliation: he may be able to contribute to an easing of tension, a cooling of temper, so that rational decisions become more possible.

Ideally, the private diplomat should do all of these things. In practice he will probably have to begin with the humblest and most inactive role. As a simple message-carrier he has not yet come into his own: he is being both tested and used. If he can take a message and bring back an answer without publicity or partiality he will win some trust and his role may expand. But initially he must accept the idea that he is simply a pawn. If it is to the advantage of one side to convey a particular impression to the other side, and if he is a suitable messenger, his usefulness will be exploited.

The Conflict Situation

The milieu of violence, or threatened violence, in which the private diplomat has to work is difficult, strange, and painful. However hard and even nerve-racking the task of conciliation may be in other types of dispute, it is not being carried out among people who are trying, or who are likely to try, to kill each other, or who believe that another party is intent on destroying them. War makes the situation different in kind, not just in intensity.

The first characteristic of a violently unpeaceful relationship is that each party to it appears, at least to the outsider, to be highly unreasonable. Take, for example, the extreme case of a large powerful nation assaulting a smaller weak one. However absurd it may seem to the outsider, the large nation's propaganda will assert, and most of its people will soon come to believe, that it is threatened by the small nation which has sinister designs on its independence and has already perpetrated atrocities on its people. The act of war is the crudest of physical acts and can be justified only by the crudest psychological means. In order to engage in it one has to believe in the wickedness and dangerousness of the enemy and in the virtue of one's own side.

The conciliator, of course, is not under the compulsion to prove to himself and world that what he is doing is right and so he is able to see both sides of the matter. But if he is foolish enough to point out to one side that the other is not really as bad as it is painted, or that it too has some sort of justification for its behaviour, he will become so unpopular that he will probably be unable to do any good. The reason for this is that in such situations certain aspects of truth are very dangerous: if people begin to doubt the absolute wickedness of the enemy or the complete justice of their own cause, they will not be able to go on fighting with such fervour and the enemy may therefore win.

It would seem that in most societies there is an influential group which believes in settling disputes by force. It asserts that aggression must be punished, that opposition must be nipped in the bud, that force must be met with force, and so on. This group is inevitably strengthened by all the apparatus of wartime propaganda, even when, rarely, more peaceful elements are also mobilized by the bloodshed. One result of this influence is to limit the freedom of a leader who may wish to attempt to negotiate or to make concessions that might lead to negotiations. In such efforts the leader is also limited, of course, by the conclusions that the enemy, equally constrained both psychologically and politically, might draw: Is he weakening? Is he beginning to crack? Perhaps the time has come to push harder! The self-defeating consequence is that moves towards peace, lest they seem to imply softness, must be accompanied by negating toughness.

One of the elements that tend to perpetuate conflict is, apparently, a sense of guilt towards those who have been slain. Paradoxically, it emerges as a determination to kill more young men: 'We owe it to our dead to continue the fight until we achieve our war aims.' In such circumstances even to consider peace, except under conditions that the other side could not accept, becomes both irreverent and treasonable.

Because these attributes of conflict situations obviously apply to

235

both sides, and because a conflict is a system involving both sides and their supporters, what each side does tends to intensify the intransigent irrationality of the other.

The Position of the Leader in Conflict Situations[10]

The leader who has to operate in these desperate and difficult conditions is subjected to many pressures, external and internal.

Perhaps his greatest difficulty is to reconcile what he does in foreign affairs, and particularly in the conflict, with the demands of domestic policy. He can probably never do what he would have chosen to do if there had been no opposition or potential opposition to keep quiet. To this extent he is impelled to define policies, to make accusations, and to promulgate doctrines he does not wholly subscribe to – but it is humiliating for a man to feel he is forced to say what he does not quite believe, and so eventually he may come to believe it. What a man believes as a protection for his ego rather than out of logical argument and conviction he will not readily surrender because of the threat to his self-image.

Leaders are lonely; the more grim their circumstances the lonelier they become. No man responsible for the conduct of hostilities can be expansive or relaxed. All his relationships are dominated by the exigencies of the struggle. The sensitivity of his position demands that he be very careful with whom he associates and on what terms. He may fear assassination and so withdraw even more from general contact. In any case he is insulated by protocol from most of his people; it is a strange irony that the greater a man's responsibility for his people the less he is in touch with those for whom he has responsibility.

Various implications may be drawn from the fact of the leader's loneliness. Unexpectedly, although he is at the apex of his nation's services he may be ill-informed, or, rather, his information may be significantly slanted. Because of his position his subordinates are often tempted to tell him, as far as possible, what he wants to hear. In addition, they will tell him what they would like him to know about the aspect of the war effort for which they are responsible. In consequence, leaders are frequently unrealistic or over-confident about the course of events. Naturally the truth may be forced upon them by circumstances, but often not before terrible blunders have been made.

As a result of his isolation and of the efforts of his officials to please him or to present themselves in a favourable light, the leader often develops an inflated sense of his importance and wisdom. It may be also that his view of himself (and consequently of others) is greatly influenced by his personal pathology. In these ways the leader's insulation from his environment is increased. The implication is that leaders are under pressures that make it harder for them than for many other people to change their minds, to listen to moderate counsel, and to pass objective judgements on the circumstances in which they are involved. The main function of the private diplomat is to make these things somewhat easier. A positive factor is that a high proportion of leaders are very intelligent and conscientious men who are deeply concerned about the conflict they are waging, but even so they do not escape from these pressures entirely.

The Practice of Private Diplomacy

If we assume that the private diplomat has not been invited to help by both contestants in a war (and it is highly improbable that he will have been), his first task is to make contact with the people who might influence decisions regarding the struggle – notably, of course, the leaders of the two sides. Unless he already knows one or both of them personally he will need introductions to them, and it is very important that he find the right person to make these introductions: an introduction from someone who is losing favour or who has 'unsound' opinions could make the mission founder as soon as it was launched.

The diplomat should, therefore, spend a period quietly studying the current power structure of one of the sides until he can decide upon a suitable person to approach. This person must be sufficiently accessible to give the private diplomat a good chance to explain himself and also sufficiently important to be able to pass him on up to the top. He might, for example, be a junior minister or a senior civil servant. The private diplomat's approach to the potential introducer must be very delicate. First of all, he must establish his legitimacy, though in an institutional rather than a personal sense – that comes later. He identifies himself as belonging to an acceptable institution, such as a university, a church, or a charitable body, and gives a general outline of his objectives. Since the eventual purpose of the mission must be to help the leaders to enlarge their perceptions of the situation, the initial presentation must involve questions that are too critical and too cogent for the introducer to answer himself. He may say, for example, that he represents an organization that is much concerned about the suffering caused by the war and that he is proposing to visit the other side in the hope of facilitating arrangements regarding refugees, or an exchange of wounded prisoners. Would this be agreeable?

The diplomat will subsequently make a similar sort of statement to the leader, but at this stage he has to establish a personal acceptability as well as his institutional legitimacy. This will take some time, and until it is accomplished the offer of his services is likely to be neither accepted nor rejected. The leader will say, perhaps, that there is no harm in a visit to the other side so long as the private diplomat makes it quite clear that there has been no dilution of war aims, but he is likely to add that nothing much will be achieved because the enemy are criminals bent on destroying his people, and they have no interest in peace or justice, and care little about the suffering of their own people. The leader may, however, make a minor point, indicating a slight modification of a previous position, which could be conveyed to his enemies and have some significance for them.

The private diplomat should be satisfied with this sort of response, and proceed as best he can to visit the opposite camp. Here the procedure of seeking an introduction will be repeated, although, since he has something in the nature of a communication to impart, he may gain access more rapidly.

It is on his return visit to the first side, however, that real progress can be hoped for. If the private diplomat has been to the enemy, delivered the first leader's message, and returned with an answer, and throughout has displayed goodwill and not made partisan statements, he will have gone some way towards passing the test of reliability and usefulness.

Henceforth he will be able to speak more freely. He will have earned the right to say unpalatable things, which, coming from another person, would have been met with resentment and rejection. He will be able to criticize tactfully, to make suggestions, to discuss the conflict and its outcome – in short to act, for the first time, *as* a private diplomat.

I must stress at this point that I do not intend to discuss specific approaches to conflict resolution, that is to the process of bargaining, that he might adopt, since these are not intrinsic to private diplomacy. What is intrinsic to private diplomacy is its absolute separation from political interest and hence its potentiality to permit an open and relaxed relationship between human beings. Within that relationship the techniques employed for working towards a settlement will depend on the particular situation, and on the skills and insights of the individuals concerned, in precisely the same way as they would in official diplomacy, although in the latter case various additional pressures might be brought to bear.

The progression from suspicion to acceptance and trust may be relatively shorter or longer than I have suggested. An individual who is exceptionally compelling and convincing, or who has an original and cogent idea, or who is well known by repute, may move speedily into a fully operational role. Nor is it always necessary to deal with the top leadership to achieve results. But it seems probable that there will always be an initial testing period, long or short. In addition, the ultimate effectiveness of the private diplomat depends on his capacity to create a breathing-space of rationality during which the leader may be able to consider his problems and his enemies more objectively than when they were perceived through distorting lenses of distrust, fear, self-aggrandizement, and political pressure.

The besetting difficulty of the private diplomat is to maintain neutrality. Each side will be eager to convince him of its own goodness and of the wickedness of the other. Indeed, to nations in conflict the concept of moral neutrality is abhorrent: how can one be neutral about aggression, war crimes, treachery, etc.? He who is not completely with us is against us. But the private diplomat, if he is to work with both sides, must identify himself with neither side and yet act in a manner that is acceptable to both sides. And his difficulties in doing so are often compounded because he in fact feels more sympathetic to one side than to the other.

He maintains his impartiality not so much by carefully avoiding words that could suggest he had a preference, as by schooling himself. We are far too apt to view human affairs in terms of guilt or innocence, to ascribe blame for a situation to one side or the other. To do this we usually pick upon a particular point in time at which a train of events leading to a war or dispute was apparently started by an action attributable to one of the parties. But the point one picks, or at least one's interpretation of what then happened, is determined by one's sympathies. The impartial historian can usually go leap-frogging backward in history until events become so obscure as to be indecipherable, demonstrating a chain of interactions that led to the present crisis. It is rare indeed that, in the perspective of history, one nation can be shown to be more guilty than another. This does not mean, of course, that one side may not attract more sympathy than the other at the actual time of the conflict, but such sympathy is a useless and indeed destructive luxury to the private diplomat. Rather than believe that one of the participants is the aggressor and the other the victim, he should discipline himself to concentrate his sympathies on all those who are suffering as a result of the conflict: the soldiers and civilians who have been killed, wounded, or deprived; the statesmen faced by agonizing choices; the children who have lost their fathers; all the people whose lives are being made harder and less happy; the millions whose minds are being twisted by propaganda. From this standpoint it is irrelevant to think of who is right and who is wrong: it is war that is wrong as a means of settling human disputes.

A practical exercise in neutrality, which I have found useful in promoting these attitudes, is role-playing. My colleagues and I, when involved in particular projects of private diplomacy, have sharpened our wits by playing the parts of the leaders of the disputing states. This kind of exercise can help the private diplomat to withstand the assaults on his neutrality. People on each side will try to win him over, will explain why they are in the right, will tell him horror stories about the brutalities of their enemies. But if he is really neutral he will be able to express genuine sympathy and sorrow for suffering, misunderstanding, and agony of mind, without commitment to a partisan view. Eventually, when he has gained acceptance, his neutrality will be accepted along with everything else.

Once he has been accepted, the private diplomat will be of some importance to each side because he has access to the other. He can then begin to play his part fully. He will be used to convey messages and to bring back information, which, because he brings it, will be relatively more credible (in conditions of conflict everyone is highly suspicious of everyone else). His interpretations of what he has seen and heard will be carefully listened to. It is possible that, when he has visited the other side, he will bring back information, hitherto unknown or only partially known, that will be of value in the reaching of a settlement. Here a note of caution is necessary. The private diplomat may stumble on information that could affect military policy. This clearly should not be conveyed and it has in fact been my experience that there has been no expectation that he should pass on matters of tactical or strategic significance. He should concentrate on conveying information that might lead to a more realistic appraisal of the possibility of a settlement. In practice, however, it is not easy to discriminate between what is of military and what is of political importance. Take, for example, the matter of bombing policy. If the private diplomat is able to report that the people's will to resist is being hardened rather than weakened by the bombing of civilian targets, it may lead to a military reappraisal, but equally it may lead to moves that will facilitate a settlement. The private diplomat must make his own difficult decisions.

He will be able to explain and interpret. In particular, he will be able to point out that the people on the other side have a different point of view and see events quite differently. This is so obvious that it might seem unnecessary to state it. However, people on one side of a conflict tend to say in effect: 'We, of course, are in the right and stand for truth, justice, and peace. Our enemies are aggressors, cynical violators of international law and human decency, who cloak their evil intentions in hypocritical protestations. But we know, and they know, the real facts of the situation.' If the private diplomat can point out that people on both sides almost always say almost exactly the same thing about the other's wickedness and their own goodness – the well-known mirror-image – it may lead to greater realism.[11]

Here I should mention the controlled communication technique developed by John Burton (see Burton, 1969). He brings together social scientists and representatives of nations in conflict, in seminars designed to study the conflict objectively. These seminar discussions have shown that there are certain common elements in all conflict situations and that what each side had thought was unique about its position is in fact usual. As a result, perceptions change and so communication occurs. The advantage of this approach is that people are brought together and they develop new perceptions jointly. This is better than someone going back and forth between two countries attempting to change the perceptions of people separately. The disadvantage is that leaders cannot very well participate in Burton's seminars and so, if their subordinates come to see things differently, they face the tough and unpopular task of persuading their superiors at home that they were wrong. The comparable advantage of the approach I am describing is that it concerns the leaders themselves; for although leaders may have their minds changed by their subordinates, it is easier the other way round. But the approaches are not mutually exclusive.

A further advantage of the private diplomat is that he is not merely a catalyst, as are the social scientists in Burton's seminars. He can, for example, advise on the wording of messages and proposals so that they will neither inflame the opposition at home nor imply to the enemy that there is a weakening of purpose, but will, nevertheless, represent a step towards settlement. He can suggest ways of conveying hints, diplomatic smoke-signals, which, while saying nothing directly, indicate possible changes of attitude. He can help to devise formulae that might reconcile the divergent objectives of the two sides. I would not claim that his skill in these or any other tasks is greater than that of anyone else, but his intimacy with both sides should be an advantage and the acceptance he has won should mean that any ingenious proposals he makes are more seriously examined.

I mentioned that the private diplomacy described here and that practised by Burton and his colleagues are not mutually exclusive. Indeed, there should be a close relationship between private diplomats and others engaged in peacemaking. There are several reasons for this. In the first place, it is important to avoid conflicting or incompatible peace initiatives. Second, various sorts of collaboration may be possible. Third, there can be a valuable interchange of information. Wide contacts are particularly useful to a private diplomat; without them it may be very hard for him to keep adequately informed. In one effort of private diplomacy the range of contacts included, besides the two governments concerned, two other governments, the United Nations, two regional organizations, and at least two non-government organizations.

Close contact with diplomatic missions, with international agencies and the like, can go a considerable way towards reducing one of the private diplomat's inherent handicaps: lack of access to official sources of relevant knowledge. He is still likely, however, to suffer from two other major restraints: lack of services and lack of money. The private diplomat who has to make all his own travel plans, arrange his own appointments, and type his own letters and memoranda is less free to concentrate on the job than if he is assisted by a local office of the organization to which he is affiliated (if there is one). He is certainly much worse off than an official diplomat who has his own embassy to work through. Private diplomacy is not easy at the best of times; it is tense and difficult work, which demands complete attention. I would recommend that whenever possible private diplomatic missions should include an experienced secretary. Certainly, this type of mission should seldom be carried out by one person alone. The strain of waiting about, of awkward and sometimes dangerous journeys, of vital meetings; the periods of boredom coupled with uncertainty, doubt, and the heavy responsibility entailed – all this makes it vital that missions should include at least two persons who can think through their problems together, practise role-playing, and entertain and distract each other. I have no views on the optimum size, but I doubt whether a group of more than three, excluding the secretary, could gain the necessary personal closeness with key people.

The questions of size and secretarial help depend, of course, in part on the financing of the mission. Few potential private diplomats would be able to pay their own expenses and their sponsoring private agencies may also not be very affluent. But the private diplomat must be able to travel when he needs to, even if it means chartering a plane. He must be able to afford accommodation that will enable him to work properly, which often means that he must stay in an expensive hotel in a central position and have a suite in which meetings can be held. He must be able to hire a car and he should, preferably, be able to travel comfortably on long journeys, when his alertness on arrival may be a vital factor.

Of course it is also important that the money he uses should come from an acceptable source – private diplomacy would lose its particular qualities if it were funded by some public agency.

20 Bargaining

The case studies in Part I do not provide much material on bargaining, though there was some in the cases of the Firm and Thornley, and between the government of Ghana and the University of Ghana. Bargaining is, of course, a major element in international negotiations, but there is a considerable difference between bargaining in a relatively simple personal setting and bargaining in a highly complex and impersonal situation. In the case of the Firm, for example, there was a strong desire on both sides for a better relationship. In unpeaceful international relations, in contrast, there is little consideration for the other side. Each party would like, if possible, to get everything and to give nothing. It is only when it doubts its ability to achieve this that it begins to bargain.

Fear and Suspicion

International bargaining is dominated by mutual mistrust, fear of reaching an agreement that will be unpopular at home, fear of seeming to weaken, and determination to get the most while conceding the least, preferably to gain all and lose nothing (this is termed the zero-sum solution of conflict).

Distrustfulness can be illustrated by the parable of the prisoners' dilemma. Two men were suspected by a magistrate of having been accomplices in a crime. However, there was not enough evidence to secure a conviction. The magistrate therefore told each man that if he made a statement leading to the conviction of the other he himself would be let off with a one-year sentence on a much lesser charge while the other would receive the maximum sentence of ten years. If, however, both made statements about the other, each would receive five years. On the other hand, if neither made a statement, both would be convicted of a lesser

245

offence and imprisoned for two years. The dilemma of each prisoner was essentially one of trust. If he had faith that his colleague would not betray him and he therefore remained silent, he was in danger of the maximum sentence if his belief was misplaced, but if his colleague was loyal he would face no more than two years in jail. If he did not have any faith in his colleague and made what is the moral equivalent of a military pre-emptive strike, he might be imprisoned only for a year. But if both were equally mistrustful, both would be jailed for five years.

In the international sphere, mutual mistrust is usually strong enough to lead to agreements which are much less mutually satisfying than they might have been, the equivalent of the five-year sentence. But when two nations are actually engaged in hostilities, suspicion is so intense that agreement on the slightest point seems almost impossible. There cannot be a cease-fire because the enemy would have a chance to regroup; the Red Cross representative cannot fly in because the enemy would take advantage of the occasion to follow him with planes loaded with arms; the diplomat cannot meet one side's representatives in a neutral capital because the other side would make propaganda capital out of it. Let the other side make concessions: they, after all, need have no fear because we are honourable and they must know that we would not cheat.

The problem of trust is compounded by fear of showing weakness. If you mistrust someone sufficiently you mistrust his responses to any genuine overtures you may make. He will think that you are frightened, that he has got you on the run, and can therefore extort more favourable terms. So, instead of agreeing thankfully to your constructive proposal, he will stiffen his terms. Consequently, in order to show that you are not weakening, you will accompany each proposal or minor concession with a belligerent speech, a bombing raid, or intensified military action to show how unyielding you are. Unfortunately this tactic often cancels out the peace move and produces nothing but greater suspicion and more violent fighting. The possible catastrophic results of the fear of showing weakness are illustrated by the game of 'chicken', in which two youths hurtle towards each other in cars, the loser being he who swerves first. The danger is, of course, that neither will swerve. The Cuban missile crisis almost provided an appalling international example of 'chicken'. It will be recalled how President Kennedy's communication to Khrushchev provided the latter with an opportunity to back down which could be made to appear a political victory. By the same token some players of chicken have worked out signals to each other enabling them to swerve simultaneously, thus avoiding loss of face.

Mistrust will appear to be well founded if there is a sudden change in the agreed terms of settlement. If things are going well for one side and badly for the other, the losers may be prepared to settle for terms they would have rejected earlier; but if the tide turns again their demands will increase once more. The other side will view this fluctuation with righteous moral indignation: 'How can we deal with such deceitful and dishonest people?' they ask, forgetting that they would do exactly the same.

Suspicion of the other side often has the tragic consequence that genuine overtures are rejected without serious consideration. Thus if one party makes a slight concession in the hope that it may lead to the opening of peace talks, this is seldom greeted in the spirit in which it was made. On the contrary, since it was made by the untrustworthy enemy, it must be some sort of trick which only a fool would accept at its face value. The spontaneous response of the official spokesman is, consequently, to denounce it: it could have been made only to score propaganda points, to confuse the issue, or to whip up political support. In this way words lose much of their capacity to convey exact meanings. If one party to a quarrel really wishes to get its intentions across to its enemy, acts are more reliable. Graduated violence, as we learnt in the Vietnam war, has become a horrible code which can be fairly readily deciphered. Conversely, if a nation wishes to signify that it is genuinely ready to negotiate, a reduction of its violent activities is more convincing than anything else. It is convincing for the precise reason that it does involve a certain military risk and is likely, in addition, to arouse internal opposition from those who hold the conventional view that war solves problems.

Domestic affairs play a significant part in all bargaining. We must reach an agreement with our enemies which not only represents an equitable and advantageous solution to our problem but also will be viewed thus by the Cabinet, the electorate, the opposition, or whatever we are plagued with. In consequence we may press terms that are unrealistically harsh and so are rejected – but at least we shall remain in power.

These difficulties are so widespread that they might be thought of as inevitable natural hazards to peacemaking. They constitute enormous obstacles even to those who are genuinely seeking a compromise settlement. To those who appear to be negotiating, but are really stalling in the hope that more favourable conditions will arise, they may constitute a boon. Assuming, however, that both sides really want a settlement, if only because outright victory seems remote, the peacemaker's task is to find a route through the obstacles. He must also weave his way through some serious and common confusions of thought about the nature and purpose of conflict, namely that war is a means of solving problems and that violence can be adjusted to achieve particular results.

The Ineffectiveness of War
Most disputes that lead to violence tend to originate, Bailey suggests, in questions regarding territory or human rights (Bailey, 1969, pp. 18–19). Whether or not his tentative generalization is completely valid, it certainly covers a sufficient number of cases to serve as a basis of argument. In territorial quarrels either two sides claim the same piece of the world's surface or a nation or other group demands that the territory it occupies be independent of the controlling government. Human rights disputes are usually about minorities or other groups who in various ways, socially and politically as well as economically, are underprivileged. If nations or groups resort to violence to settle their disputes over these issues their military policy may, at a certain level, be rational. They wish to occupy or hold the disputed area; they hope to overthrow an oppressive government; they hope to capture the rebel leader; they intend to make a show of force which will discourage further aggression. If these objectives were speedily accomplished and did in fact bring the dispute to an end, there

would be little more to be said. But this is seldom the case, even if the policy is initially successful: the enemy tries to recapture the annexed territory; the fallen government's allies help to restore it to power; a new batch of rebel leaders emerges; aggression is countered by a stiffening will to resist. It then becomes clear or should become clear that the dispute will be ended only by a victory in which one side overwhelms the other (though this does not exclude an eventual second round), or through a settlement based on bargaining.

Assuming that neither side can really hope for absolute victory, military activity becomes important to each belligerent as a means of creating favourable conditions for negotiation. Thus the capture of a town or an airport, or the bombing of a factory or a bridge, is useful to the extent that it puts one party in a position to drive a harder bargain. Or this would be so if in warfare the other side did not immediately retaliate. Thus intensified military action or local successes by one side call for a response in kind by the other for the very reason that it does not want to be forced into negotiations from weakness. Moreover, the more ruthlessly one side presses its attacks the more the other fears and distrusts it and the less it is inclined to negotiate. Hence escalation becomes increasingly likely and a settlement more and more distant. Hence wars continue and widen, involving allies and supporters, some of whom are remote from the original dispute and have little idea of what it is all about except that, for political, economic, or ideological motives, they have somehow been sucked into its vortex.

Apart from the fact that military action aimed at bringing about a situation that will compel the other side to negotiate and seek a settlement frequently fails to achieve this end, violence develops its own momentum irrespective of any nominal or attempted influence on the process of bargaining. Wars appear to be governed by rules which have virtually nothing to do with the ultimate purpose of war, namely to change a particular relationship or to control a particular piece of territory. Thus we must 'meet force with force'; we must 'never let the enemy get away with anything'; we must go on bombing although we know it does no military damage and only toughens the enemy's will to resist; we must starve his civilians; we must demonstrate that his peace overtures have not deceived us by intensifying our attacks; we must publicly execute his guerrillas although we know, or should know, that this will only increase the determination of the survivors and encourage new recruits. Consequently, far from ending the war, military activity of this kind (to use the word policy would be to imply more purpose than usually exists) intensifies and prolongs it, making it messier, more destructive, and less conclusive. This is the trouble with war. It is undertaken, at times with apparent justification, in order to get some group or nation to change its behaviour, but the longer it persists, the more unattainable does that goal become. Acts of war are not conducive to a peaceful settlement, even when they bring an eventual end to fighting through the utter defeat of one side. The subsequent relationship between the former contestants is seldom peaceful, as we have defined the word. In short, the only way to restore peace is by ceasing to fight and beginning to negotiate. This statement would seem almost tautological but for the fantasy, believed by most people, that war solves problems. The first task of the negotiator who is moving from the stage of conciliation to that of bargaining is to convince everyone that it does not.

War is in fact an inefficient means of achieving the goals for which it was started. Even when the war is won in an outright military sense the aftermath is often bitter and destructive. Perhaps the most successful wars, in the sense of leading to desired ends, have been colonial wars of liberation in, for example, Indonesia, French Indo-China, and Algeria. But many more countries have obtained independence through almost bloodless political actions, and in the significant case of Kenya, although the colonial powers won the so-called Mau-Mau war, they lost the colony shortly afterwards. Outright military victory in civil wars is a peculiarly ineffective means of solving problems. These wars are waged, essentially, to prevent separatism or dissidence, and to promote unity and uniformity. The ultimate aim is a harmonious, united, and prosperous country. This is never achieved by killing, maiming, or starving the enemy into submission. The greater the force required to achieve victory, the greater the hatred, fear, and resentment; in fact the less will the war aims have been achieved.

But even when a leader is convinced of the futility of his war effort, it is hard for him to change his approach. His people still believe in the war mystique, and his opponents at home will overthrow him if he obviously abandons it. In addition, he has no reason to suppose that his enemy is of the same mind. The task of the third-party conciliator at this early stage of bargaining becomes clear. He has to devise and propose suitable first steps towards a settlement – this does not mean that he works out the terms of the settlement itself, but that he puts forward practical measures that may lead to negotiations out of which a settlement may develop. He has to suggest safeguards that will protect each side from abuse by the other in respect of any truce or deescalation that may be arranged, and he has to think of ways in which a move towards a settlement can be presented favourably to the domestic audience. Finally, as was mentioned in Chapter 19, he has to attempt to establish reliable communications between high officials of the two sides, if necessary acting as an intermediary.

Stages of Bargaining
A useful approach at the early stage of bargaining is to try to draw up a balance-sheet with the leaders of each side showing the advantages and disadvantages of different courses of action.[12] It can probably be demonstrated, for example, that an intensification of military action will lead to increased casualties which may heighten domestic dissatisfaction with the war; produce drastic counter-measures by the enemy; alienate some foreign supporters; make the enmey more suspicious of any past or future peace overtures; delay the solution to the problem which must, eventually, be sorted out jointly by both parties sitting around a conference table. Even if these consequences are acknowledged, they will probably be countered by the claim that it is necessary to attack in order to be able to bargain from a position of strength. This argument, as we have seen, is vulnerable to logic and experience. One part of the demonstration is to point out a frequently

forgotten fact that the enemy reacts as we do. If our determination is toughened by the bombing of civilians, so is his. If we wish to bargain from power, so does he. If we react violently to his violence, so does he to ours. If we are inhibited by mistrust, trapped by the need to appease our opposition, and deceived by the myth of war, so is he. If we both choose the armed solution we shall both be caught inextricably in the same upward spiral of anger, unreason, fear, suspicion, and hatred. If we are to escape from it, we must consider not only our own predicament, but also – and with understanding – that of the enemy. In this way we may be helped to see what he sees, and so to evaluate him somewhat differently.

The next part of the balance-sheet can list the probable effects of decreasing the level of violence. Fewer lives will be lost, and there will be less domestic discontent; the enemy may respond in kind; our peace-feelers may be more credible; world opinion will favour our restraint. The disadvantages are that the enemy may misread the signals, consider we are weakening, and try to push us further. Equally he may simply not be interested. In either case we may be forced to increase our efforts once more, but this is not disastrous. In any case, whatever its consequences, no move towards settlement can be made unless there is a reduction of violence by one side, and preferably by both sides together. Therefore if one side refuses to respond to any concession made by the other, it is abdicating its share of responsibility for achieving eventual peace. Although the logic of these arguments may have a strong appeal, it is likely, nevertheless, that each side will be still so obsessed with suspicion of the enemy that it will withdraw from the smallest risk – even the smallest risk of peace. If there is a hint of bilateral de-escalation, or of a temporary cease-fire, each side will – like the prisoners in the parable – be terrified that the other will cheat and thus put it at a disadvantage, with the result that the bilateral arrangement is likely to be postponed and diluted until it can serve very little purpose. It is ironical that such caution stems from a genuine concern to save lives. In effect it contributes to a prolongation of the war, and many more lives are ultimately likely to be lost than would be lost in a sharper battle consequent on betrayal. With a unilateral arrangement there is even greater fear that the enemy will take advantage of it. Consider American fears that a bombing halt in North Vietnam would enable the Vietcong to build up more powerful ground forces. Again it must be admitted that this caution is not unreasonable when the situation is appraised in terms of war, but the risk must be taken if the dispute is to move eventually from battlefield to conference table. (Fighting and negotiation can, of course, go on simultaneously, as in the Vietnam peace talks, but the talks would not have been begun without a bombing halt and they would not have dragged on so long if the level of violence had been still further decreased.)

The first moves towards de-escalation are the most difficult. Suspicion and distrust are then at their height. It is therefore essential that the initial step suggested should be one that both sides can agree to fairly readily, without fears for their security. It could be an exchange of seriously wounded prisoners, for example, carried out by a neutral power. More complex measures, such as a cease-fire or a control on arms imports, require more involved procedures of policing and surveillance. I do not intend to discuss these, since much of the literature on conflict research deals with these aspects of peacemaking: for example, attempts to reach arms-control agreements where the checks against cheating are of supreme importance, and the role of various United Nations peacekeeping forces.

At this early stage of bargaining, and indeed later if possible, it is advisable to move from issue to issue on which agreement can be reached (see Fisher, 1964, pp. 91–109). There are, however, likely to be divergences of opinion on this policy. The side that feels it has slightly the upper hand, but nevertheless wants a settlement, will usually be more apt to agree on minor questions in the hope that enmities will be lulled to a point where decisions on major issues can be stalled without excessive resentment. In this case, the somewhat weaker side must be shown that the trade-off for settling part of the dispute is sufficient to compensate for the postponement of the total settlement. Here the argument is that if total settlement and only total settlement is demanded now, nothing will in fact be achieved because the other side will not agree. On the other hand, nothing is lost by a small agreement; it does not preclude many other agreements in the future. (If the stronger side hope that the weaker will be appeased by the small concessions this is something purely in the minds of the stronger which need not affect the weaker.)

As more vital issues come up for discussion, bargaining becomes more intense. It is at this stage particularly that outside powers wishing for a settlement can contribute by adding attractions or deterrents to particular courses of action: favourable trade agreements established or withdrawn, mutual defence treaties renewed or cancelled, bases set up or dismantled, alliances offered or abrogated – all may serve as incentives in one direction or the other. The private peacemaker may perhaps play a less important part here than in conciliation. His position, however, helps him to offer credible analyses of the advantages and disadvantages of various bargaining postures and he may be able to make arrangements for some sorts of surveillance, for example the inspection of relief shipments to ensure that they do not include arms.

Throughout these processes, communication is of paramount importance. The private diplomat may be much involved in this, taking messages from one side to the other. But communication is more than a matter of passing information or proposals back and forth. In unfavourable circumstances these may constitute no more than a verbal continuation of the struggle. To reiterate obviously unacceptable proposals or to write angry or abusive letters only worsens the situation, emphasizing intransigence and unreasonableness. It is therefore desirable that part of the communication should be some form of demonstration of serious intent to seek a settlement. I have noted the fear that peace overtures may be thought to imply weakness, and the tendency for them to be accompanied, therefore, by some act of violence. But actions can be taken which have a symbolic significance: the return of war wounded, the release of political prisoners or civilian internees, a promise of amnesty for rebels. These may constitute a form of non-verbal communication which will promote negotiations. One advantage of such moves is that, while they offer to the enemy an earnest of good purpose, they need not inflame the hard-liners at home.

At this stage secrecy is vital. The cautious, tentative progression towards talks can be halted or reversed by the wrong sort of publicity. Damaging pressures can be brought to bear on both sides from internal sources and, in order to avoid opposition or even overthrow, the leaders may have to abandon or modify their plans. The secret assistance of the independent peacemaker who can move about without attracting much attention may be very useful.

This discussion has been carried out in the context of active hostilities because in these circumstances the problems of bargaining are most dramatically highlighted. But in many other international dealings the same elements exist. Mutual mistrust, and the fear that one country may cheat on an agreement to the other's detriment, are present in numerous issues, and the more vital the issue the greater the fear. Even in much less desperate or portentous relationships bargaining is affected by similar factors. I will therefore conclude this chapter by mentioning briefly a few aspects of bargaining as illustrated in some of the case studies.

Bargaining in Non-violent Situations
In the Firm, although the directors and the employees wished each other well, there was a considerable amount of mutual mistrust. The directors were afraid that if they gave the employees certain privileges they would be abused, and the Firm would suffer in consequence. The employees were afraid that if they asked for these privileges they would become unpopular with the directors and so lose their jobs and their homes. The task was to encourage the employees to prepare proposals that not only were reasonable in themselves but also were presented in a serious and convincing fashion. In the event this was achieved and the directors were sufficiently impressed by the common sense and responsibility demonstrated by the employees to yield with good grace.

At the University of Ghana there was bargaining of a different sort. The government repeatedly made demands to which the University could not have acceded without giving up the degree of autonomy without which an academic institution is lost. For example, if the faculty were to be hired or fired at the whim of a politician and students passed or failed according to their party loyalty, the University would have been destroyed. As it was, we (the University) tried to be accommodating on minor points and firm on major ones. When faculty (including the recent Commissioner of Education for Ghana) were dismissed on political grounds, I myself resigned. Nevertheless, the University survived several years of assault through its policy of combining flexibility on details with firmness on principle.

The universities of America have been the scene of much recent bargaining between students and faculty. This has been especially tense when the students have been black so that racial conflict has been added to the conflicts, already bitter in many places, of university life. A great deal of this bargaining has been foredoomed to failure: when 'non-negotiable demands' are presented in the glare of strident publicity, a mutually satisfying settlement is hard to achieve. But, then, those students whose aim is the destruction rather than the reform of the university probably do not wish to reach a settlement. Nevertheless, some bargaining has been carried out in a quiet and purposeful fashion and has led, by a process that was mutually enlightening, to a settlement acceptable to both sides. The main difficulties, as in the international field, are ignorance and lack of trust. The faculty do not really understand the students, and vice versa, and perhaps neither group understands itself. The students in particular often know little about how a university works, and make proposals based on ignorance. They will ask the Dean, for example, to let them appoint the professors, not realizing that the Dean does not do this himself and has no power to change the method of appointment; but his disclaimers are taken as prevarications. I have been impressed by the extent of the suspicion between the academic generations, and by the cynicism that has on occasion greeted apparently well-intentioned and liberal moves by the faculty. Bargaining that has been successful has generally followed the principles that are most likely to succeed in the international context: there has been an increasing realization of the position and difficulties of the other side; impossible demands have not been presented as non-negotiable; there has been no publicity; both sides have been patient and thoughtful; both sides have wanted a settlement which would be to the advantage of both; in a process of bargaining mutual trust has developed.

Repudiation of Settlements

It is perhaps wise to end on yet another note of caution, if not pessimism. The bargains struck by negotiators by no means always hold. The representative of one side may have gone too far in making concessions and the agreement he has reached will then be repudiated. Or the situation may change politically or militarily during the course of the bargaining, in which case what had been an acceptable arrangement becomes undesirable. Thus international negotiators have sometimes, in my experience, reached an accord which has been repudiated because of shifts in the balance of power within their governments that took place after the beginning of the discussions. Or again, the parties may have decided to negotiate because there was a military equilibrium, but if the stalemate is broken, it may well be that both sides will wish to reject the agreement reached by their negotiators: those who are doing well because they expect now to be able to press for more favourable terms; those who are doing badly because they fear that they might be forced under pressure to accept less favourable terms.

I have myself sat on a committee of faculty and students which was concerned with revising a part of the curriculum. The students regularly reported back to their constituents and eventually an agreement was reached which was pleasing to all. There was much mutual congratulation, for the issues had been both difficult and sensitive, and there was a dinner party, a published report, and comments in the press. But at the stage when the report had to be implemented the students claimed that their position had been falsified, that they had agreed to something quite different from what had appeared in the report, that they had been tricked.

Either the students were right, or they were wrong; in my opinion the latter. If I am right, what had probably happened was that the student members of the committee were thought to have become too friendly with the faculty members and to have been beguiled into signing a report that was insufficiently radical. In fact the report was extremely progressive, but the logic was that the professors, simply because they were professors, must have sold their souls to the establishment and so were incapable of radical thinking. Alternatively, there may have been a change in the student leadership – I heard rumours to this effect – and the new leaders, wishing to assert themselves, were perhaps unwilling to abide by agreements reached by their predecessors. Or perhaps the leaders were deposed *because* they were felt to have betrayed the student cause by signing the report. It is of the essence of such situations that one seldom can be quite certain.

Unfortunately there is very little that the peacemaker, whether conciliator or bargainer, can do to prevent changes in the home situation or on the battle-front from affecting a settlement.

21 Development

GENERAL CONSIDERATIONS

Development involves the restructuring of a relationship so that the conflict or alienation that had previously rendered it unpeaceful is eliminated and replaced by a collaboration that prevents it from recurring. Wise practitioners of politics and social reform have always attempted this task. Frequently they have failed because the relations between two groups are both complex and labile, depending on the relations between sub-systems within each of the two groups and on the relations between both groups and others. Thus relations between two nations are a function both of the social, political, and economic relations within each state, and of each nation's relations with third-party nations. Difficult or not, however, we must follow through to the phase of development. It must be attempted if precarious settlements brought about by conciliation and bargaining are not to break down. In almost all our case studies there is need for development; and later sections of this chapter refer specifically to the problems of Nigeria, the black Americans, and the poor countries in general. This first section outlines some general considerations concerning the stage of development.

The extent to which relations can be restructured or developed, and the means by which this is achieved, depend on the individual situation. In the case of the Firm, development took the form of a new constitution for the Amenities Committee and hence a new type of relationship between the directors and their employees. In Thornley it meant little more than the acceptance of a local government organization that was already in existence. In the villages of Pakistan, village development councils, which emerged spontaneously in many areas, dramatically symbolized the new

259

relations between the government and the people that the government was trying to build up. Development for the unfortunate Chakmas could be little more than an attempt to salvage something from the catastrophe that had befallen them.

With regard to the two wars discussed in Chapter 3, development of the relations between Biafra and Nigeria, and between Kashmir and India, would have to wait on a military solution to the war, as happened in the Nigerian case, or on successful bargaining over the principal points in dispute. Only then could the parties involved in each case attempt to rebuild their sadly unpeaceful relations with one another. We can hardly speculate on the future structure of these relations, but we may be fairly certain that hopes of more lasting peace can be founded only on closer association. If two hostile groups withdraw from each other there is little chance for enmity and prejudice to dissolve; and if their quarrel is exacerbated, violence may break out again. This in effect was the situation of France and Germany between the wars of 1870, 1914–18, and 1939–45. After World War II, however, they became closely associated through membership of the European Economic Community and other European organizations. In consequence it is widely felt that the chances of war between France and Germany in particular, and among the European countries in general, have considerably lessened. The road towards ever-closer association on a global scale is fraught with hazards. The logical conclusion, some form of world state, will almost certainly be bitterly opposed by many. The most powerful states, who have most to lose by some surrender of sovereignty, are likely to show the greatest hostility and the results could be disastrous. It would, moreover, be enormously difficult to maintain justice and equality in the super-state. But we must attempt to move in this direction, surmounting the dangers as we encounter them. If we do not do so, we shall meet the greater perils of a world divided into sovereign states of which a number have bitter feelings for each other and several possess nuclear weapons.

As we have seen, the post-colonial imperialism of economic and political exploitation is a serious obstacle to the development of the poor nations. By the same token, the pattern of inter-state relationship occasioned by this international class structure is inimical to equal association. The rich nations are in a position to use and manipulate the poor nations, and to a considerable extent they do so. Until they relinquish their hold on the poor nations and – even more – until they provide more substantial and impartial assistance, the world system will to some degree be blocked in its quest for closer and more balanced relations between its members. Many unpeaceful relationships will, therefore, continue both between the rich and the poor nations, and among the poor nations. The latter are at a disadvantage because to a considerable extent the economic stranglehold of the rich prevents them from forming adequate associations among themselves; too large a proportion of their resources goes to the rich nations, and both political and economic sanctions can be applied to prevent them from entering into arrangements which would enable them to be more self-sufficient. For these reasons, an essential step towards the development of a peaceful world will be the elimination of the modern form of covert imperialism.

Development can clearly take many forms, depending on material, political, geographical, and other factors. There is one principle, however, that I believe to be fundamental to the restructuring of relations in this developmental sense: this is the principle felicitously named 'autonomous interdependence'.[13] According to this principle, development signifies a relationship between groups – states, governments and communities, or groups within communities – in which each recognizes and respects the autonomy of the other, its right to organize itself according to its cultural and political preference; and at the same time each admits its dependence on the other for such matters as trade, communications, the sharing of scarce resources, the exchange of skilled persons, security, weather-forecasting, and so on. This principle is now much more widely accepted than it was immediately after World War II when the world seemed to be dividing itself into two great self-contained and dangerously hostile blocs. Now the political group known as the Third World has emerged, and the Western and the Eastern blocs are no longer so monolithic. In addition, innumerable small nation states have been established, several having fewer than a million inhabitants. There is widespread agreement that any group feeling strongly that it has a cultural and political identity has some right to develop that identity. This development may, of course, stop short of absolute political sovereignty – the Scots, for example, have not achieved complete separation from the United Kingdom. Nevertheless, there are many new independent nations, while many distinctive groups within nations (including the Scots) have acquired a greater control over their own affairs. Many of the new nations, as well as the intranational minority groups, are far from self-sufficient. Indeed, the structure of our world, with its great international agencies, its networks of communications, its complex economic interdependence, ensures that no nation is self-sufficient to the extent that was possible in the past. They all constitute parts of interlocking economic, political, communication, and strategic systems. This interdependence does not prejudice autonomy. The further it develops, however, and the more clearly it is recognized, the more likely it is that the rigid barriers of nationalism will be eroded. A nation may come to be regarded more as part of a system and less as an all-inclusive entity; at the same time its internal affairs, in so far as they do not interfere with the workings of the system, can be treated with tolerance and respect.[14]

These tendencies constitute grounds for hope, but as they become more clearly manifest they may be seriously opposed. Already, as we have seen, the rich nations have weakened the autonomy of the poor ones. In the future the principle of autonomous interdependence may demand sacrifices they are not prepared to make. In the meantime, however, we may take some encouragement from what has happened.

NIGERIA

Since I began to write this book, the civil war between federal Nigeria and the secessionist former Eastern Region, which called itself Biafra, has come to an end. This was a struggle in which the

Organization of African Unity, the Commonwealth Secretariat, and other groups attempted to play a conciliatory role and to assist in the early stages of bargaining. However, although both sides twice came together in full-scale peace talks, these efforts failed and the war was brought to a conclusion by an overwhelming military victory on the part of the federal troops. The peacemaking process, the re-establishment of harmonious relations between the former rebels, especially the Ibos, and the rest of the country, starts therefore with the phase of development.

The first steps were taken as soon as the fighting ended. Relief was brought to the devastated areas and medical teams began to tackle the immense problems created by malnutrition and undernourishment. More important was the spirit of reconciliation, the complete lack of vindictiveness, on the part of the victors. The Ibos were promised their old jobs back, their salaries increased by the increments they would have received had the war not taken place. Few wars have ended so gracefully.

But these are only the first steps in reconstructing the country in such a fashion that it will remain unified and peaceful. If I have been correct in my evaluation of the causes of the war, the process of development must have two main strands.

1. *Educational:* Communities that were closed to each other by fear, suspicion, ignorance, and prejudice must be brought to sympathetic understanding and acceptance of each other's idiosyncrasies. This is easily said. In fact if we knew properly how to do it, many of the world's ills would be over. It will require a tremendous effort on the part of the educational authorities to devise curricula that will help to engender a sense of both local and national identity, as well as to train the teachers who will teach them. And much more will be involved than the education of children. Community development and adult education workers, administrators, and those responsible for the mass media, will all have important parts to play, and these will have to be planned and executed with care. It will also be helpful to arrange occasions, work-camps, sporting events, conferences, and the like, at which representatives of the various groups in the country can

meet, with the aim of reaching a greater understanding of one another.

2. *Organizational:* The first step has already been taken to create a less dangerous national structure by replacing the previous arrangement of three powerful regions and one small one with twelve states. There may eventually be more states. The present system is provisional and will be reassessed, but, whatever the constitutional arrangement, the former inequalities remain and are likely to continue. The six states comprising the former Northern Region are still much poorer and less well educated than the six into which the former Eastern, Western, and Midwest Regions have been divided.

Herein lies a continuing danger for the stability of Nigeria. Whatever efforts are made to change people's attitudes will be wasted if those attitudes are seen to be justified by the facts. Although many of the attitudes that preceded the civil war were exaggerated beyond all bounds, there was a reasonable basis to most of them. It was vain to tell the Ibos, when thousands of them had been massacred, that their fears of the Northeners were groundless. It was equally pointless to tell the poor (the great majority) of the North that the Ibos were fellow-citizens who shared the same lot as the Northeners: they palpably did not. But now it is a question not only of relations between the Northeners and the Ibos, but of relations between the Northeners and Southerners as a whole. If economic inequality can be exploited as a political cause linking all the less well-endowed states, the future will be sorely troubled. For these reasons it cannot be doubted that the federal government, which has shown itself to be temperate and enlightened, will tackle inequality and social injustice as matters of the highest priority.

I would merely add that equality and justice constitute the essence of development everywhere (see the final section of this chapter). But it is only when we are shocked out of our inaction by a cataclysm (such as occurred in Nigeria) that we try to do what we should have been attempting – and in a purely technical sense it is very hard – all along.

THE BLACK AMERICANS

Having been a firm believer in integration, I have become convinced through personal experience of confrontation with black Americans that the only form of development that will lead eventually to a peaceful, because more equal, relationship between the races in the North American situation is the growth of Black Power. Integration essentially concealed the conflict by an appearance of equality; but few of the blacks became equal and those who did were integrated to white existence rather than the other way about – no white man was prepared to identify himself with the black community. And so, while men of goodwill hoped that everything was getting better, the conflict persisted and white racism was unabated.

Black Power is the opposite of integration. It demands not fusion, but separation. It is based on the dawning recognition that the black people of America form a distinctive cultural group which has long been denied the right to develop its culture and institutions, and the right to attain equality in the American community. First and foremost, then, Black Power is a movement aimed at creating conditions in which a minority group can build its identity more strongly; the political demands are secondary but inseparable. These have been expressed in a variety of ways. To some, Black Power is synonymous with complete control by the blacks of the USA. I take a less extreme view of what it would mean in practice, namely, that predominantly black communities should have the same control over their affairs as comparable white ones.

This interpretation of Black Power has been termed black racism, but this criticism is absurd.[15] Racial feelings exist and in many cases are greatly respected: who would expect the Irish to control B'Nai Brith or, more frivolously and even less probably, the Mafia? But there is a much more profound issue. In a strange way black Americans have been denied a sense of racial identity: they are in doubt as to who they are and whether they have any worth. Their mask is of an agonized non-person. They need to discover themselves and, like students, they cannot find out who and what they are unless they exercise authority, responsibility, and power. It is vital to understand that only when they have determined who they are will they be able to establish significant relations with those who are not them – the other, the white Americans. If I do not know who I am, I also do not know who you are.

It is hard to predict the eventual character of the relationship that may emerge. We can only hope that it will not be a destructive one, full of mutual hate; there is certainly much to be forgiven, and little likelihood that much will be forgotten. But no real relationship can exist if we continue to maintain that the black people will be integrated and everything will be fine. The blacks must first define who they are, and establish themselves in their own eyes and those of the whites; and then the deep differences between the races, their separateness, can be acknowledged – to deny neurosis is to ensure its continuance, to pretend that the mask is not there is to exclude forever the chance of removing it. Not until they have developed this identity will the blacks be able to talk as autonomous human beings, not creatures of mask and mirage, with the white community. And the white community will be able to respond only when they have faced themselves with the reality of blackness, of their own behaviour, and of the mask of white superiority and the mirage of Negro inferiority that have beguiled them for generations. Then there may be some coming together on a basis of mutual understanding and, in some respects at least, of equal power.

I am encouraged by certain post-colonial experiences. For some years the Kenyans (specifically the Kikuyu) and the British fought each other bitterly in the so-called Mau-Mau rebellion. Jomo Kenyatta, the Kikuyu leader, was imprisoned as the instigator of a monstrous rebellion against the kindly British rulers, and reviled as a sex fiend, drug addict, and alcoholic. But at length the fighting finished. There were constitutional changes, and at last Kenya became free. Kenyatta, released from jail, was elected President. Now that Kenya is independent, a sovereign nation exchanging diplomatic representatives with Britain, and holding as many votes at the United Nations as a former colonial power, there is at

266

length some equality of power and with that a new degree of tolerance and good faith. Kenyatta is a much respected elder statesman of the Commonwealth. What is more, he has an Englishman, and a Conservative at that, as one of his chief Cabinet members.

A redistribution of power can bring about a change of relationship. A degree of distance, based on a degree of autonomy, can lend perspective to one's connection with another group. Likewise, a heightened degree of identity in one group can enable it to have a more rational relationship with another political or cultural group. It may not be wholly admirable, but it may be workable. Fusion of identity and political role can lead only to destruction.

THE POOR COUNTRIES

The unpeaceful relations between the rich and the poor countries and within the poor ones are clearly linked. The rich countries exploit and manipulate the poor ones, giving at best insufficient aid, often with prejudicial strings attached. In order to obtain favourable political and economic terms, they support repressive régimes and promote development which is not in the interests of the mass of the people – and which in many cases does not conform to any accepted standard, including the most formal ones, of economic development. Thus in Liberia concessions to develop rubber and mineral resources were negotiated with members of the élite who derived great personal profit from the deal while wealth was drained out of the country, bringing advantage to no one but the foreign shareholders. The rich lands, moreover, impart a philosophy of development which promotes the conditions of unpeace I have described and sets up the Western system of gadget-ridden technology as a model of the good life, so tampering 'with desire mechanisms that have been delicately calibrated to match resource availability with demands of social integration' (Goulet, 1967, p. 2).

A different approach to development is needed if the whole range of international and intranational relationships is to be restructured into a peaceful mould. What is really needed on the part of the rich nations is a change of heart, leading them, first, to abandon the exploitative use they make of the poor nations, and, second, to give them assistance on a massive scale, substantial enough to enable them to overcome their most desperate problems of poverty. The requirements of the poor countries in this latter respect have been clearly defined, and indeed in general agreed on, at meetings of the United Nations Conference on Trade and Development. The rich countries should develop the will to accept some sacrifice for the sake of the poor ones, if only because they realize that the nations of the world form a single system (we are all either crew or passengers of space-ship earth, as Barbara Ward (1966) has recently reminded us) and that their fates are intimately connected. At present, aid programmes follow economic and geo-political interests, which are essentially short-term ones; until they are discarded and replaced by long-term global interests we can expect little major change. As an example of a constructive approach to problems of global development, I quote extensively from the recommendations of the Haselmere Declaration, whose signatories believe that rich countries should:

'1. Refrain from using their economic and political power to thwart the efforts of poor countries to gain a larger share of the benefits of trade and technology.

2. Refrain from economic retaliation and military intervention against poor countries which take political initiatives of which they disapprove.

3. Abolish all quotas and other special protective devices applied by developed countries to the manufactured exports of poor countries. No new ones should be introduced. Compensation for interests in rich countries damaged by the loss of such protection should be made by the government of the rich country concerned.

4. Abolish all subsidies to agricultural production in rich countries competing with production in poor countries. Compensation again should, if necessary, be made by the government of the rich country concerned.

5. Raise the income received from primary commodities sold to them by poor countries in the same way that rich countries subsidize their own agriculture. It should be acknowledged that the bargaining position of agricultural producers tends to be weak and that the prices of their produce are particularly susceptible to fluctuation and long-term decline. International agreements to stabilize the prices of the poor countries' main commodity exports should be concluded soon – especially for cocoa, sugar, and bananas.

6. Abolish or reduce tariffs affecting the exports of poor countries, with no exceptions to protect special interests.

7. In general, ensure that the international trading, financial and monetary system, rather than discriminating against poor countries, discriminates in favour of them. Rich countries should not, for instance, use their power to make poor countries observe "rules" which, in any case, they do not themselves observe.

8. Cancel all debts owed to them by the poor countries.

9. Commit themselves to a greatly increased long-term and automatic transfer of resources to poor countries. The latter will then be in a position to pursue their own economic and social policies. This will avoid the present situation in which aid has unacceptable political and economic strings.

More specifically we suggest the following lines of action:

a. All transfers of financial resources from rich countries to poor should go through an international institution. There should be a universal formula, decided in advance, on how these automatic transfers of aid should take place. We suggest that the criteria of size of population and degree of poverty are the ones that should determine how much each country should receive. The rich countries for their part would give in proportion to their wealth. The transfer of aid should be committed for periods of at least five years ahead at a time. Unlike most aid given today it should be in the form of grants, not loans. The developing countries have, given time to adjust, an unlimited capacity to absorb such aid. But as an approximate goal we suggest that rich countries should provide £3,000 million by 1970, £6,000 million by 1975, and £20,000 million by 1980. This compares with the £2,280 million the rich are giving at present.

b. The impending reforms in the international monetary system offer another channel of help to the developing countries. A new form of international liquidity besides gold and the reserve currencies of sterling and dollars is to be created. When this is allocated to the member countries of the IMF we suggest that it goes not mainly to the rich nations as presently planned, but only to the poor. Rich countries would then have to earn the new international money created by exporting to poor countries, rather than having it allocated free.

10. Collectively recognize that poor countries do not need to adopt the rich countries' way of life and may in fact be threatened by it. They should welcome and sympathize with attempts to create societies different from their own. Tanzania is an example of what we mean. The Arusha Declaration of February 1967, made by the governing party of Tanzania, charts a course of economic and social development that will attempt to build on traditional African society rather than try to propel traditional society unthinkingly into massive urbanization, industrialization, élitism, and dependency on foreign investment and aid' (Haselmere Declaration Group, 1968, pp. 10–11).

History will show whether the rich nations can discard the folly of blind self-interest soon enough to save them from catastrophe. In the meantime, however, although the poor countries are so dependent and so profoundly influenced (albeit often unconsciously and often by reaction) by the rich ones, it is possible (as in the case of Tanzania) for them to act independently, to forge their own philosophy of development and to apply it.

Before attempting to define a different approach to development, I should stress two points. First, I do not discount the importance and value of economics and economic planning in development. I am simply suggesting that economic development is not an end in itself, but a means to ends which must be defined in much wider cultural, social, political, and moral terms. Economic development may be vital in striving towards these ends; but some of the means by which it is achieved may, by creating various sorts of unpeaceful relationship, be prejudicial to them. Economic growth must be thought of as the servant of development, not as development itself.[16] Second, I should emphasize the variability of circumstances. I can perceive no general rule save that conditions vary so greatly that there can be no universal blue-print for development. I can only suggest general ways of thinking which can be applied to specific issues, and draw attention to situations which, in my opinion, are widespread.

Goulet describes development as 'the well-coordinated sequence of changes whereby a given population, and all sub-populations comprising it, move from a phase of life perceived as less human to one perceived as more human, as speedily as possible, at the lowest cost possible, and with maximum solidarity both within and among nations' (1967, p. 1). I would add that the achievement of development implies a move towards a form of society which provides certain conditions for human life. I call these conditions safety, sufficiency, satisfaction, and stimulus.

Safety implies a social order in which there is a low level of violence, in which the individual is safeguarded from abuse by landlords, employers, and the state, and in which – perhaps as a necessary condition for this – he has some part (which it is unnecessary to attempt to define) in the political process.

Sufficiency means the absence of want. It is, of course, a relative term: what would be penurious deprivation to the average American would be untold plenty to the average Indian. By sufficiency I intend to convey a condition that would be considered adequate within the society concerned. At the least it would require standards of nutrition, housing, clothing, and health provision that would ensure that no one was prevented from developing his personal potential through preventable ill health.

271

By satisfaction I mean that life should in general be pleasant. In particular, I mean that sufficiency should not be attained at an excessive psychic and cultural cost.

By including stimulus I emphasize the importance of growth and change and individual opportunity. It is not my intention to advocate a smug, static society. In fact no such society could meet the challenge of development. I refer to opportunity for the individual human being to grow to his full stature through education and comparable means; and, at another level, to the establishment of a social order that will permit and encourage him to take an appropriate place in it.

A nation intending to develop peacefully along these lines will have to set itself objectives in many spheres, of which the following constitute a few examples:

1. The involvement of the people responsibly, participantly, and appropriately in the development of the nation.

2. The development of an education system that, while academically sound and indeed universal in certain respects, prepares young people both to live creatively in the culture and to promote national development.

3. The restructuring of land, holdings, wealth, and privilege without injustice, waste, or lowering efficiency.

4. The involvement of particularist groups, and especially of their leaders, in national development without impairing their cultural autonomy.

5. The development of industry without creating slums and alienation.

6. The development of industry without impoverishing the rural areas.

7. The development of an administration that is honest and efficient without being oppressive.

Conclusion:
Peaceful Relationships

It would be comforting to believe that peaceful relationships, once established, were permanent; that when peoples had passed through the stages of miserably passive subjection, angry revolt, and tense negotiation, and had ultimately reached mutual accommodation and development, their troubles were over. We might then expect that eventually, in however distant a future, mankind would achieve harmony. But I can view no such hopeful horizon. We blunder, it seems to me, from one situation only to find that another, equally dangerous, has come into existence.

If international accord is reached, we may find ourselves faced with domestic conflict. If domestic conflict is resolved, we may find ourselves beset by agonizing personal dilemmas. The skein of human life is woven of great happenings and small. Every enormous event – a war, an alliance, an international crisis – is made up of a mosaic of smaller ones involving myriad groups and individuals. At the moment when we are congratulating ourselves that the big issue has been brought under control, one of its component parts may be quietly growing and changing, cancer-like, to create disaster for the next generation. There is a constant interaction between what goes on within man and what occurs between men; between communal action and what occurs between members of the community. What makes it additionally hard to predict the human future, and hence to stabilize human relationships, is that any individual, or group, or nation, may be involved at one and the same time in countless relations of all types, both peaceful and unpeaceful. These interact. The tension of unpeacefulness may spill over into a peaceful relationship to disrupt it. In the same way, large-scale relations may affect small-scale ones, and vice versa.

Other influences, too, militate against peace. First, if we follow Lorenz and Ardrey, there are the territorial and aggressive instincts. I have not discussed these, for they would not – if indeed there was general agreement about them – alter the shape of the problems we have considered, though they would certainly add to the difficulties of resolution. Second, it must be remembered that in perhaps the majority of unpeaceful relationships there is a stronger party who gains at the expense of the weaker. Thus he has good reason for not wanting to change the structure of the relationship, as well as the power to prevent it from being changed.

In short, peace is not easily attained and is at best only partial (if we consider the gamut of relationships concerned in any single situation) and relative. Even so, it is not a condition that just happens. It must be striven for, and, when attained at any level, cherished and protected with strength and skill.

And so I conclude on a sombre note.

The very complexities I have just mentioned contain, however, a germ of hope. Even the great conflicts are not monolithic; and of the innumerable relationships that make up the fabric of our lives, and of the societies we belong to and influence in some measure, though many are unpeaceful, *certainly many are peaceful.* It is within the capacity of everyone to increase the number of peaceful relationships in which he is involved, and to decrease the number of unpeaceful ones. If our concepts of peace and unpeacefulness, and consequently our objectives, are clear, there are several spheres of life in which we can take action and in so doing possibly have an effect (though often too indirect and obscure for recognition) upon a larger sphere.

I have long believed that much of life's sadness and futility stems from our failure first to understand ourselves, and next to match the talents we discover within to the tasks that lie without. We are overshadowed, made to feel puny and impotent, by the enormity of the world's disasters, and conclude that there is nothing we can do except 'opt out' and cultivate our souls until the holocaust. But I hope that the diversity of the case studies presented here, and the variety of the approaches to the alleviation of unpeaceful relations, will suggest that we are never completely powerless. There is something each of us can do, and in doing it we may (as Maslow would maintain) reach the next stage in our psychological development, becoming human beings more free because less fearful and constrained, more altruistic because we see a purpose in our altruism. In this context, as frequently in religious or philosophical writing, the implicit themes of freedom, love, and peace are interwoven – the triad upon which our happiness and our survival depend.

But I call upon St Francis of Assisi for a supreme expression of the peacemaker's purpose:

'Lord, make me an instrument of Thy peace. Where there is hatred, let me sow love; where there is injury, pardon; where there is doubt, faith; where there is despair, hope; where there is sadness, joy; where there is darkness, light.'

1. This process is outlined schematically by Dencik (1969).
2. As I write there is a split in the ranks of peace researchers between those who follow the line that might rather unfairly be characterized as 'peace at any price' and those who are prepared to countenance disturbances, amounting if necessary to physical violence, to change what Galtung calls structural violence (see Note 1, p. 27). I prefer to think in terms of applying the right peacemaking technique at the appropriate stage of the conflict. The works of Schmid (1968 and especially 1970) and Dencik (1969) are particularly relevant.
3. As outlined in *Proposals for a New Educational Policy* (Ministry of Education and Scientific Research, Government of Pakistan, 1969). The policy for Tanzanian education, derived from *The Arusha Declaration* (1967), is described in Resnick (1968), especially by Nyerere (ibid., pp. 48–70). The approach in Cuba is described by Jolly (1964).
4. W. B. Yeats, 'The Great Day'.
5. See also Davidson (1969, p. 37).
6. Quoted (and translated) by O'Brien (1970, p. 57).
7. In relation to Norway and Denmark see Skovodin (1969) and Bennett (1969).
8. See also Sharp (in press).
9. Throughout this book a number of intellectual strands, quite apart from particular topics, are interwoven. Since, in this section, I attempt an outline of psychological factors affecting conciliation (and indeed other aspects of peacemaking), it is perhaps appropriate here to refer to some of the influences that have affected my thinking about these problems.

   I learnt much from my association with the Tavistock Institute of Human Relations and such men as Ben Morris, A. T. M. Wilson (see Wilson, 1946, 1947), and E. L. Trist (see Curle, 1947, and Trist and Bamforth, 1951) in the years immediately after World War II. What was known as the 'Tavistock approach' owed its intellectual impetus to a combination of psychoanalysis (particularly the work of Klein, 1948) and the topological psychology of Kurt Lewin (1935, 1947), as applied to work with groups. Essentially, the Institute's concern was to understand both what happened within the individual's psyche and what happened 'outside' him in society. The object-relations approach of Klein revealed the pantheon of persons interacting within the individual and so determining his behaviour. The topological approach of Lewin provided a means of describing the behaviour of individuals interacting in society. Through attempts to relate these two levels of understanding and to provide a continuous description of individual and group behaviour, a few simple yet powerful ideas emerged. One was that the more individuals are inwardly divided, the more will they be divided from others; thus the more it is possible to break down barriers in one dimension, the more individuals (or groups) should be able to establish connections with others. A related concept was that authoritarian behaviour and compulsion tend to erect barriers, reducing flexible and responsible participation; the converse of this stressed the value of participation and in so doing linked psychological, social, and political levels (as in the contemporary concept of participatory democracy). In this connection see Adorno et al. (1950), Lewin (1947), Lippett and White (1947), and Trist and Bamforth (1951).

A further theme is that human beings commonly act below their potential and are capable of greater things, intellectually and creatively, than is generally thought. I originally owed this view to the oriental philosophies, in which – largely as a result of my travels – I became interested as a young man. More recently, psychologists such as Maslow and Chiang (Maslow, 1968; Chiang and Maslow, 1969) have expressed a similarly positive – though very different – view of human potentiality. Among the orientals, or rather those influenced by them, I was particularly struck by Ouspensky (1954). Interestingly, his teachings were not at some levels entirely incompatible with object-relations theory, in the sense that he held malfunctioning to be the consequence of inner disunity. The concept of awareness or self-consciousness (there are many terms) is also common to both Eastern psycho-philosophical systems (such as Zen – see Suzuki, 1960) and Western psychotherapy; though they differ greatly, of course, as to the possible consequences of awareness.

My ideas on identity, which I link to awareness, owe much to Erikson (1959, 1968). Frank's analysis of psychological factors in conflict (1968) I found helpful throughout. I owe a debt, hard to identify exactly, to Brown (1966) and to Laing (1960, 1967).

My own expression of ideas derived from these influences is to be found in Curle (1947, 1949, 1955a).

10. There are interesting discussions of the role of the leader by Grinspoon (1964, pp. 238–47) and Frank (1968, pp. 170–82).

11. This situation is well described by Warren (1964).

12. The use of balance-sheets of this type is described by Fisher (1969, especially pp. 100–5).

13. This phrase was coined by my friend Merrill Jackson.

14. This theme is developed in Burton (1968).

15. The ineffectiveness of integration as a policy for solving American racial

problems and the desirability of what is in effect Black Power are argued in two papers by Ferry (1967 and 1968). He deals firmly with the criticism that Black Power is simply white racism in reverse.

16. Thus Furtado writes 'economic development is, in the strictest sense, a means' (1962, p. 2).

ABERLE, KATHLEEN (1967a). Western Imperialism and Black Africa. Social Change Project, Detroit, Michigan. (Mimeo.)

——(1967b). World Revolution and the Science of Man. In T. Roszak (ed.) (1967). (This paper appears under the name of Kathleen Gough in the 1969 edition of Roszak.)

ACHEBE, CHINUA (1959). *Things Fall Apart.* New York: Obolensky & Astor.

——(1961). *No Longer at Ease.* New York: Obolensky & Astor.

ADORNO, THEODORE, et al. (1950). *The Authoritarian Personality.* New York: Harper & Row.

Arusha Declaration, The, and Tanu's Policy on Socialism and Self-reliance (1967). Dar-es-Salaam, Publicity Section, Tanu.

BAILEY, SIDNEY D. (1969). *Instrumentalities and Procedures for Settlement of Disputes.* United Nations Institute for Training and Research, New York, 24 January.

BENNETT, JEREMY (1969). The Resistance against the German Occupation of Denmark 1940–5. Pp. 182–203 in A. Roberts (ed.) (1969).

BLACK, C. E. (1966). *The Dynamics of Modernization.* New York: Harper & Row.

BLACKBURN, ROBIN (1967). The Unequal Society. In R. Blackburn and A. Cockburn (1967).

—— and COCKBURN, ALEXANDER (1967). *The Incompatibles: Trade Union Militancy and the Consensus.* Harmondsworth: Penguin Books.

BOULDING, KENNETH (1962). *Conflict and Defense: A General Theory.* New York: Harper & Row.

BRINTON, CRANE (1957). *Anatomy of Revolution.* New York: Vintage Books.

BROCH, TOM, and GALTUNG, JOHAN (1966). Belligerence among Primitives. *Journal of Peace Research,* No. 1.

BROWN, NORMAN O. (1966). *Love's Body.* New York: Random House.

BURTON, J. W. (1968). *Systems, States, Diplomacy and Rules.* Cambridge: Cambridge University Press.

—— (1969). *Conflict and Communication.* London: Macmillan.

CABRAL, AMILCAR (1969). *Revolution in Guinea: An African People's Struggle.* London: Stage 1.

CAMUS, ALBERT (1951). *L'Homme révolté*. Paris: Gallimard.

—— (1950). *Les Justes*. Paris: Gallimard.

CARMICHAEL, STOKELEY, and HAMILTON, CHARLES V. (1967). *Black Power: The Politics of Liberation in America*. New York: Random House.

CHIANG, HUNG-MIN, and MASLOW, ABRAHAM H. (eds.) (1969). *The Healthy Personality*. Princeton, N.J.: Van Nostrand.

CHOWDHURY, G. W. (1968). *Pakistan's Relations with India, 1947-1966*. London: Pall Mall Press.

CLARK, KENNETH B. (1965). *Dark Ghetto: Dilemmas of Social Power*. New York: Harper & Row.

CLARKE, MICHAEL (1966). *Industrial Relations: Notes for Managers*, No. 11. London: The Industrial Society.

CLEAVER, ELDRIDGE (1968). *Soul on Ice*. New York: Dell.

COHN-BENDIT, D. *et al.* (1968). *The French Student Revolt*. New York: Hill & Wang.

COLEMAN, JAMES S. (1958). *Nigeria: Background to Nationalism*. Berkeley: University of California Press.

College of the Potomac: Principles and Practices (November 1968). (Mimeo.)

COMMISSION ON INTERNATIONAL DEVELOPMENT (1969). *Partners in Development* (The Pearson Report). New York: Praeger.

Comparative Education Review (1966). Special issue on Student Politics (Vol. 10, No. 2).

COX COMMISSION (1968). *Crisis at Columbia*. New York: Random House.

CURLE, ADAM (1947). Transitional Communities and Social Reconnection, Parts I and II. *Human Relations* **1** (1) and (with E. L. Trist) **1** (2).

—— (1949). Incentives to Work: An Anthropological Appraisal. *Human Relations* **2** (1).

—— (1952). What Happened to Three Villages. *The Listener*, Vol. 48, No. 1242.

—— (1954–5). Some Psychological Factors in Rural Sociology. *Tribus* **4/5**.

—— (1955a). The Psychological Theory of Group Work. In P. Kuenstler (ed.), *Social Group Work in Great Britain*. London: Faber.

—— (1955b). From Student to Teacher Status. *The New Era in Home and School* **36** (2).

—— (1960). Tradition, Development and Planning. *Sociological Review* **8** (2).

—— (1962). African Nationalism and Higher Education in Ghana. *Universities Quarterly* **16** (3).

—— (1963). *Educational Strategy for Developing Societies*. London: Tavistock; second edition (paperback), 1970.

—— (1966). *Planning for Education in Pakistan*. Cambridge, Mass.: Harvard University Press; London: Tavistock.

—— (1968). Educational Planning: The Adviser's Role. *Fundamentals of Educational Planning Series, No. 8*. Paris: Unesco, International Institute for Educational Planning.

Daedalus (Fall, 1968). The Conscience of the City, especially Part IV.

Daedalus (Winter, 1968). Students and Politics.

DAHL, ROBERT A. (1963). *Modern Political Analysis*. Englewood Cliffs, N.J.: Prentice-Hall.

DAVIDSON, BASIL (1969). *The Liberation of Guinea*. Harmondsworth: Penguin Books.

DENCIK, LARS (1969). Peace Research: Pacification or Revolution. Notes on Intra-Peace-Research Conflict. Paper delivered at the Third General Conference of the International Peace Research Association, Karlovy Vary, September.

DEUTSCH, KARL W. (1967). *Arms Control and the Atlantic Alliance*. New York: Wiley.

—— (1968). *The Analysis of International Relations*. Englewood Cliffs, N.J.: Prentice-Hall.

DUMONT, RENÉ (1966). *False Start in Africa*. London: Sphere Books.

DURKHEIM, ÉMILE (1930). *Le Suicide: étude de sociologie*. Paris: Alcan.

Economist, The. Still No Property-owning Democracy. 15 January 1966.

Economist, The. 27 August 1966.

EDUCATION AND WORLD AFFAIRS (1966). *Nigerian Human Resource Development and Utilization*. New York.

ELLUL, JACQUES (1969). *Violence*. New York: The Seabury Press.

EMERSON, RUPERT (1960). *From Empire to Nation*. Cambridge, Mass.: Harvard University Press.

ERIKSON, ERIK H. (1959). *Identity and the Life Cycle*. New York: International Universities Press.

—— (1968). *Identity, Youth and Crisis*. New York: Norton.

ETZIONI, A. (1967). Sociological Perspectives in Strategy. In *Transactions of the Sixth World Congress of Sociology*, Vol. 2.

FANON, FRANTZ (1965). *The Wretched of the Earth*. New York: Grove Press.

—— (1967). *Towards the African Revolution.* (Political Essays.) New York: Monthly Review Press.

FARBER, JERRY (1969). *The Student as Nigger.* N.Y.: Contact Books.

FERRY, W. H. (1967). Farewell to Integration. Century 21 Lecture, Stanford University, 8 November. (Mimeo.)

—— (1968). Hail to Co-existence. Center for the Study of Democratic Institutions, April. (Mimeo.)

FISHER, ROGER (ed.) (1964). *International Conflict and Behavioral Science.* New York: Basic Books. See specifically Fisher's chapter on 'Fractionating Conflict'.

—— (1969). *International Conflict for Beginners.* N.Y.: Harper & Row.

FRANK, JEROME D. (1968). *Sanity and Survival: Psychological Aspects of War and Peace.* New York: Random House.

FRIERE, PAULO (1970). *Pedagogy of the Oppressed.* N.Y.: Herder & Herder.

FULBRIGHT, J. WILLIAM (1970). *The Arrogance of Power.* Harmondsworth: Penguin Books.

FURTADO, CELSO (1962). Nordeste: Novos Depoimentos no. 11 Ciclo de Estudios. *O Estado de Sâo Paolo,* 26 January.

GALBRAITH, J. KENNETH (1961). A Positive Approach to Foreign Aid. *Foreign Affairs* **39** (3).

—— (1967). *The New Industrial State.* Boston: Signet Books.

GALTUNG, JOHAN (1969a). Peace, Peace-Theory, and an International Peace Academy. International Peace Research Institute, Oslo, International Peace Research Association, Groningen, and Gandhian Institute of Studies, Varanasi. PRIO Publications No. 23–8, Varanasi, February. (Mimeo.)

—— (1969b). Feudalism, Structural Violence, and the Structural Theory of Violence. Paper prepared for the Third General Conference of the International Peace Research Association, Karlovy Vary, September. (Mimeo.)

GEIGER, THEODORE (1967). *The Conflicted Relationship: The West and the Transformation of Asia, Africa and Latin America.* New York: McGraw-Hill.

GILBERT, RICHARD V. (1963). The Works Program in East Pakistan. Talk delivered at a conference on Labour Productivity, Geneva, December. (Mimeo.)

GOLDTHORPE, JOHN H. (1966). Attitudes and Behaviour of Car Assembly Workers. *British Journal of Sociology* **17** (3).

GOODMAN, PAUL (1962). *The Community of Scholars.* New York: Random House.

GOULET, DENIS (1967). Ethical Issues in Development. Paper delivered at a conference on The University: Development, Justice and Peace, University of Notre Dame, 1–3 September.

GOVERNMENT OF PAKISTAN PLANNING BOARD (1956). *The First Five Year Plan, 1955–1960.* Karachi. Chapters on 'Social Welfare' and 'The Special Areas and other Tribal Territories' are relevant.

GREEN, REGINALD H., and SEIDMAN, ANN (1968). *Unity or Poverty: The Economics of Pan-Africanism.* Harmondsworth: Penguin Books.

GRIER, W., and COBBS, P. M. (1968). *Black Rage.* New York: Bantam Books.

GRINSPOON, LESTER (1964). International Constraints and the Decision Maker. In R. Fisher (ed.) (1964).

GUTTMAN, E., and THOMAS, E. L. (1946). The Adjustment in Civil Life of Soldiers Discharged from the Army on account of Neuroses. *Ministry of Health Report No. 93.* London: HMSO.

HASELMERE DECLARATION GROUP (1968). *The Haselmere Declaration.*

HUNTINGTON, SAMUEL P. (1965). Political Development and Political Decay. *World Politics* **18** (3).

JAQUES, ELLIOTT (1948). Interpretive Group Discussion as a Method of Facilitating Social Change. *Human Relations* **1** (4).

JALÉE, PIERRE (1968). *The Pillage of the Third World.* New York: Monthly Review Press.

JOLLY, RICHARD (1964). Education. Pp. 161–282 in D. Seers (ed.), *Cuba: Revolution, Economic and Social.* Chapel Hill, N.C.: University of North Carolina Press.

KAMARCK, ANDREW M. (1967). *The Economics of African Development.* New York: Praeger.

KELMAN, HERBERT C. (ed.) (1965). *International Behavior: A Social-Psychological Analysis.* New York: Holt, Rinehart & Winston.

KENISTON, KENNETH (1968). *Young Radicals: Notes on Committed Youth.* New York: Harcourt, Brace & World.

KENYATTA, JOMO (1938). *Facing Mount Kenya: Tribal Life of the Kikuyu.* London: Secker & Warburg.

KLEIN, MELANIE (1948). *Contributions to Psychoanalysis, 1921–1945.* London: Hogarth.

LAING, R. D. (1960). *The Divided Self.* London: Tavistock.

—— (1967). *The Politics of Experience.* Harmondsworth: Penguin Books.

LAKEY, GEORGE (1969). Strategy for Non-Violent Revolution. *Peace News*, 12 December.

—— and PARKMAN, PAT (1969). El Salvador 1943–44: They didn't Call it Non-violence, but –. *Peace News*, 14 November.

LAKHANPAL, P. L. (1965). *Essential Documents and Notes on the Kashmir Dispute, 1947–1966.* Delhi-6: International Books.

LAMB, ALASTAIR (1966). *Crisis in Kashmir, 1947–1966.* London: Routledge & Kegan Paul.

LEWIN, KURT (1935). *A Dynamic Theory of Personality: Selected Papers.* New York: McGraw-Hill.

—— (1947). Frontiers in Group Dynamics, II. *Human Relations* **1** (2).

LEWIN, JULIUS (1963). *Politics and Law in South Africa: Essays on Race Relations.* London: Merlin Press.

LEWIN, T. H. (1869). *The Hill Tracks of Chittagong and the Dwellers therein: With a Comparative Vocabulary of the Hill Dialects.* Calcutta: Bengal Printing Co.

LIDDELL HART, B. H. (1969). Lessons from the Resistance Movement – Guerrilla and Non-Violent. In A. Roberts (ed.) (1969).

LIPPETT, R., and WHITE, R. K. (1947). An Experimental Study of Leadership and Group Life. In T. M. Newcomb and E. L. Hartley (eds.), *Readings in Social Psychology.* New York: Holt, Rinehart & Winston.

LIPSET, S. M., and WOLIN, S. S. (1965). *The Berkeley Student Revolt: Facts and Interpretation.* New York: Doubleday.

MAHMOOD, SEYED (1895). *A History of English Education in India, 1781–1893.* Aligarh.

MALCOLM X, and HALEY, A. (1965). *Autobiography of Malcolm X.* New York: Grove Press; London: Hutchinson, 1966.

MANNONI, DOMINIQUE O. (1964). *Prospero and Caliban: The Psychology of Colonialism.* New York: Praeger.

MARCUSE, HERBERT (1964). *One-dimensional Man: The Ideology of Industrial Society.* London: Routledge.

MASIHUZZAMAN (1964). Cultural Segregation in Pakistan. (Mimeo.)

MASLOW, ABRAHAM H. (1968). *Towards a Psychology of Being.* Second edition. Princeton, N.J.: Van Nostrand.

MAYER, ALBERT, *et al.* (1958). *Pilot Project, India.* Berkeley: University of California Press.

MEZIROW, JACK D. (1963). *Dynamics of Community Development.* New York: Scarecrow Press.

MILLER, WILLIAM ROBERT (1965). *Non-Violence: A Christian Interpretation.* London: Allen & Unwin.

MINISTRY OF EDUCATION AND SCIENTIFIC RESEARCH, Government of Pakistan (1969). *Proposals for a New Educational Policy.* Islamabad: Government Printer.

MITCHELL, G. DUNCAN (1950). Social Disintegration in a Rural Community. *Human Relations* **3** (3).

MURRAY, ROGER (1956). Militarism in Africa. *New Left Review* **38** (July–August).

MYRDAL, GUNNAR (1944). *An American Dilemma.* New York and London: Harper.

—— (1957). *Economic Theory and the Under-developed Regions.* London: Duckworth.

NATIONAL ADVISORY COMMISSION ON CIVIL DISORDERS (1968). *Report.* New York: Bantam Books.

NICHOLSON, J. L. (1964). Redistribution of Income in the United Kingdom. *Income and Wealth*, pp. 121–85.

NKRUMAH, KWAME (1965). *Neo-colonialism: The Last Stage of Imperialism.* London: Nelson.

NYERERE, JULIUS K. (1968a). *Ujamaa: Essays on Socialism.* Dar es Salaam: Oxford University Press (Eastern Africa).

—— (1968b). Education for Self-reliance. Pp. 48–70 in I. Resnick (ed.) (1968).

O'BRIEN, CONOR CRUISE (1970). *Camus.* London: Fontana/Collins.

OUSPENSKY, P. D. (1954). *Psychology of Man's Possible Evolution.* New York: Knopf.

RAPOPORT, A. (1966). Models of Conflict: Cataclysmic and Strategic. In A. de Reuck (ed.), *Conflict in Society.* Boston, Mass.: Little, Brown; London: Churchill.

REDFIELD, ROBERT (1941). *The Folk Culture of Yucatan.* Chicago: University of Chicago Press.

RESNICK, IDRIAN N. (ed.) (1968). *Tanzania: Revolution by Education.* Arusha: Longmans of Tanzania.

ROBERTS, ADAM (ed.) (1969). *Civilian Resistance as National Defence.* Harmondsworth: Penguin Books. (First published under the title *The Strategy of Civilian Defence,* London: Faber, 1967.)

ROBERTSON, SIR GEORGE (1898). *Chitral: The Story of a Minor Siege.* London: Methuen.

ROSS, N. S. (1969). *Constructive Conflict: An Essay on Employer–Employee Relations in Contemporary Britain.* Edinburgh: Oliver & Boyd.

ROSZAK, THEODORE (ed.) (1967). *The Dissenting Academy.* New York: Random House; Harmondsworth: Penguin Books, 1969.

SCHELLING, THOMAS C. (1960). *The Strategy of Conflict.* Cambridge, Mass.: Harvard University Press; London: Oxford University Press.

—— (1966). *Arms and Influence.* New Haven, Conn.: Yale University Press. New edition, 1967.

—— (1969). Some Questions on Civilian Defence. In A. Roberts (ed.) (1969).

SCHMID, HERMAN (1968). Politics and Peace Research. *Journal of Peace Research,* No. 3, pp. 217–31.

—— (1970). Peace Research as a Technology for Pacification. In *Proceedings of the International Peace Research Association, Third General Conference.* Assen.

SCHOMBERG, R. C. F. (1938). *Kafirs and Glaciers.* London: Martin Hopkinson.

SCHWARZ, F. A. O. (1965). *Nigeria: The Tribes, the Nation or the Race: The Politics of Independence.* Cambridge, Mass.: MIT Press.

SHARP, GENE (1969). The Technique of Non-Violent Action. In A. Roberts (ed.) (1969).

—— (in press). *The Politics of Non-Violent Action.* Philadelphia and Boston: Pilgrim Press.

SKOLNICK, JEROME H. (1969). *The Politics of Violence.* New York: Ballantine Books.

SKOVODIN, MAGNE (1969). Norwegian Non-Violent Resistance during the German Occupation. Pp. 162–81 in A. Roberts (ed.) (1969).

SUZUKI, D. T. (1960). *Manual of Zen Buddhism.* New York: Grove Press.

TITMUSS, R. M. (1962). *Income Distribution and Social Change.* London: Allen & Unwin.

TOCQUEVILLE, ALEXIS DE (1850). *L'Ancien régime et la révolution.* (Many editions.)

TRIST, E. L., and BAMFORTH, K. W. (1951). Some Social and Psychological Consequences of the Longwall Method of Coal-getting. *Human Relations* **4** (1).

TURNBULL, COLIN (1962). *The Lonely African.* New York: Simon & Schuster.

US DEPARTMENT OF HEALTH, EDUCATION AND WELFARE (1969). *Towards a Social Report.* Washington: US Government Printing Office.

VAN DEN BERGHE, PIERRE L. (1965). *South Africa: A Study in Conflict.* Middletown, Connecticut: Wesleyan University Press.

WARD, BARBARA (1966). *Space Ship Earth*. London: Hamish Hamilton.

WARREN, ROLAND L. (1964). The Conflict Intersystem and the Change Agent. *Conflict Resolution* **8** (3).

WILLIAMSON, JEFFREY G. (1965). Regional Inequality and the Process of National Development: A Description of the Patterns. *Economic Development and Cultural Change* **13** (4), Part II.

WILSON, A. T. M. (1946). The Serviceman Comes Home. *Pilot Papers*, No. 1.

——, DOYLE, M., and KELNAR, J. (1947). Group Techniques in a Transitional Community. *The Lancet*.

WOODROW, H. (1962). *Macaulay's Minutes on Education in India written in the years 1835, 1836 and 1837*. Calcutta.

WORSLEY, PETER (1967). *The Third World*. London: Weidenfeld & Nicolson.

WRIGHT, BERIC (1966). The Sick Society. *Director*, October.

YOUNG, ORAN R. (1967). *The Intermediaries*. Princeton, N.J.: Princeton University Press.

Indexes

Name Index

Subject Index